Beyond War

Beyond War

The Human Potential for Peace

Douglas P. Fry

OXFORD
UNIVERSITY PRESS

2007

OXFORD
UNIVERSITY PRESS

Oxford University Press, Inc., publishes works that
further Oxford University's objective of excellence
in research, scholarship, and education.

Oxford New York
Auckland   Cape Town   Dar es Salaam   Hong Kong   Karachi
Kuala Lumpur   Madrid   Melbourne   Mexico City   Nairobi
New Delhi   Shanghai   Taipei   Toronto

With offices in
Argentina   Austria   Brazil   Chile   Czech Republic   France   Greece
Guatemala   Hungary   Italy   Japan   Poland   Portugal   Singapore
South Korea   Switzerland   Thailand   Turkey   Ukraine   Vietnam

Copyright © 2007 by Douglas P. Fry

Published by Oxford University Press, Inc.
198 Madison Avenue, New York, NY 10016
www.oup.com

Oxford is a registered trademark of Oxford University Press

Library of Congress Cataloging-in-Publication Data
Fry, Douglas P., 1953–
    Beyond war : the human potential for peace / By Douglas P. Fry.
      p. cm.
    Includes bibliographical references and index.
    ISBN 978–0–19–530948–5
1. War.   2. Warfare, Prehistoric.   3. Peace—Social aspects.   4.
Ethnology.   5. Conflict management—Social aspects.   I. Title.
    U21.2.F79   2007
    303.6′6—dc22
                                                      2006023638

Printing number: 9 8 7 6 5 4 3 2 1
Printed in the United States of America
on acid-free paper

To Hanna, Heather, Jeremy, Geoffrey, Caroline, Tyler, Zachary, Kayla, and other members of the next generations

Contents

Foreword

People often get a bit nutty when considering ideas about the "inevitability" of human behavior. Such notions come in many forms. For example, there's the idea that it is preordained that females will be inferior to males at math. Or that certain genes determine certain behaviors. Or that it is inevitable that a guy will take a hostile view toward his dad having a penis.

Some of the time, these conclusions arise from confusing correlation with causality, or problems with discerning statistical relationships, or failing to understand the idea of biological vulnerability and interaction with the environment. And some of the time, they are just plain weird, complete with fin-de-siècle Viennese froth.

I've fallen for this myself. I've studied baboons in East Africa for decades. In the process, I've gotten to know my nearest neighbors, nomadic pastoralist Masai tribespeople. Until I had kids of my own, the only ones on earth I'd been repeatedly exposed to were Masai kids, and my own peers, growing up in Brooklyn. And based on that data set, here is something that I firmly believe is an inevitable human behavior: Once a boy discovers that if you inflate a balloon and let the air out, it will make a noise, it becomes universal and inevitable that he will do this by the butt of one of his friends, claim that said friend has gas, and get the giggles.

So, as I said, people get a little nutty.

One of the truly well-entrenched realms of It-Is-Inevitable-That is that it is inevitable that humans will be violent and that human societies will wage warfare. Sometimes a view like this comes with a pretty foul agenda. Consider Konrad Lorenz, co-founder of ethology, expert on bird behavior, and Nobel laureate. In the 1960s, in his hugely influential book *On Aggression*, Lorenz proclaimed that human aggression is universal and inevitable. The stance he took makes considerable sense—Lorenz was a venomous racist, a man who used his academic pulpit in Germany to write Nazi propaganda poisonous enough to turn one's stomach, a man who went to his death insisting that he spent the thousand-year Reich communing with the little birdies that he studied. Don't blame people if they're violent—they're just following their inevitable biological orders.

But you don't have to be Lorenz to believe in the inevitability of human violence. Anyone noticing the blood-drenched world we live in would have to take that idea seriously. And academics of various stripes have as well.

Students of primatology and human evolution sure thought this. The 1960s saw the rise of the Robert Ardrey/man-the-territorial-hunter/big-cojones school of human evolution. Drawing upon the social system of the savanna baboon as a surrogate for our formative history in the savanna, the conclusion was that we are by nature a violent, stratified, male-dominated species. Jane Goodall's work with chimps seemed to confirm this further, demonstrating murder, cannibalism, organized group violence, and something resembling genocide among our closest relatives.

The game theorists were awash in the inevitability of violence and noncooperation as well. The heart of game theory, the Prisoner's Dilemma game, repeatedly showed that good guys finish last, that the first individual who spontaneously starts cooperating in the game is competitively screwed for the rest of time, as the noncooperators snort derisively at the naiveté. Neuroendocrinologists weighed in also. Testosterone increases aggression, as it increases the excitability of parts of the brain relevant to aggression; girls inadvertently exposed to testosterone prenatally become more aggressive.

And, naturally, none of this is true.

Even those violent chimps and baboons can reconcile after fights, have cooperative, altruistic relationships, can even establish and transmit cultures of low aggression. Then there are the bonobo chimps, a separate species that is as genetically related to us as are chimps, a species that is female-dominated, has remarkably low rates of aggression, and solves every conceivable social problem with every conceivable type of sex. The game theorists, meanwhile, have spent recent years revealing the numerous circumstances that select for cooperation rather than competition even in competitive games drenched in realpolitik. And normal levels of testosterone turn out not to cause aggression as much as exaggerate preexisting social tendencies toward aggression; without the latter, testosterone doesn't remotely translate into inevitable aggression.

In this superb book, Douglas Fry gives lie to the inevitability of violence by surveying another set of disciplines, namely, cultural anthropology, archaeology, and human paleontology. He trashes the urban myth of inevitable aggression in numerous ways. These include documenting the varied human cultures with minimal or no intra- or intergroup violence, exploring the social systems and ecosystems that predispose toward cultures without warfare and their social mechanisms for sidestepping group violence, revealing the mistakes in classifications that have given rise to erroneous labeling of certain societies as warlike. The book also reveals other mistakes that infest this literature: A virtuosic chapter analyzes the fatal flaws in a famed, canonical study that seemingly displays the reproductive, evolutionary benefits of murder in an indigenous society.

All this is done in a way that is encyclopedic and authoritative. And well-written, and often moving, and surprisingly often—given such an intrinsically dour subject—funny. It seems inevitable at this point in a foreword to list the sorts of people who should read this book—jurists, legislators, parents, butchers, bakers . . . Instead, I will avoid another supposed inevitability and simply say this book should be read. It is important.

Robert M. Sapolsky

Preface

When I first began studying anthropology, one aspect of the discipline that appealed to me was its breadth. Where do we come from? What is our nature? What does it mean to be human? Why do we behave the way we do? What are the prospects for our future? Anthropology addresses big questions. Literally the "study of humankind," anthropology lends itself to a *macroscopic perspective*. It focuses not just on the present, but also on the past. It seeks to understand specific cultures as well as recurring patterns that span societies. Anthropology simultaneously embraces the biosocial diversity and uniformity of humanity.

There is a natural tendency to think in terms of the here and now of everyday life. But as we enter the twenty-first century, many of the challenges facing humanity demand a broader context. The macroscopic perspective of anthropology, with its expansive time frame and culturally comparative orientation, can provide unique insights into the nature of war and the potential for peace. A cross-cultural perspective shows, for instance, that humans everywhere seek justice—although the paths to justice vary. Some entail violence but others do not. Much violence, in fact, stems from people defending their rights or attempting to correct injustices. Anthropological and historical cases show that it is possible to replace violent means of justice seeking with nonviolent approaches. Herein lies a broader lesson for creating and maintaining peace.

A macroscopic anthropological view suggests that it would be possible to replace the institution of war with more effective, less brutal ways of seeking security, defending rights, and providing justice for the people of this planet. In an era of nuclear missiles and other weapons of mass destruction, trying to achieve security through the threat or use of military force is like trying to perform heart surgery with a chain saw. For the good of us all, we must replace the war system with viable institutions for creating peace, delivering justice, and guaranteeing security.

In adopting a view that spans millennia and crosses cultural space, I draw on data from many anthropological fields: archaeology, hunter-gatherer research, ethnographic descriptions of particular societies, comparative cross-cultural studies, research on cultural belief systems, and applied anthropology (a field that focuses on real-world problem solving). The book also includes theory and data from fields beyond anthropology, for example, behavioral ecology, game theory, animal behavior, and evolutionary biology. The goal is to attain a view of the human capacities for violence and peace that is as complete and integrated as possible.

In my experience, some people, accustomed to the international war system, assume that it simply is not possible to find better ways to resolve differences and to assure security. However, the wealth of anthropological data considered in this book suggests otherwise. Humans have a tremendous capacity for resolving conflicts without violence. In today's world, we need to apply these skills in new ways and on a grander scale. We need to think in new, bolder ways about creating realistic alternatives to war. Too often, short-term, shallow security analyses prevail over more comprehensive planning for a secure future. Rather than focusing exclusively on narrow issues, such as how many fighter jets to order this year or what to do about the local "hot spots" most likely to erupt into violence this month, we need to address a set of broader, critically important questions that are centrally relevant to providing genuine, long-term safety and security for the people of the planet. How can we improve the quality of life for all humanity, reduce the social and economic inequalities that foment hostility, hatred, and terrorism, and create new procedures and institutions for providing justice and resolving differences without war? In short, at the global level, how can we replace the law of force with the force of law?

A central goal of this book is to thoroughly explore how anthropology contributes to understanding war and peace. I hope to challenge existing ways of thinking about war, peace, security, and justice. These are topics that concern each and every one of us on this interdependent planet where we all breathe the same air and would perish together in the same nuclear winter. By questioning traditional thinking, I hope that the book will promote reflection, discussion, and action for a safer world.

Helsinki, Finland
June 8, 2006

Acknowledgments

As I've worked on this book and its predecessor, *The Human Potential for Peace*, many friends and colleagues graciously have engaged in discussions on relevant topics, provided bibliographic information or other forms of help, supplied photographs, or read and commented on draft chapters. I warmly thank John Archer, Roger Archer, Ofer Bar-Yosef, Jan Beatty, Megan Biesele, Kaj Björkqvist, Chris Boehm, Bruce Bonta, James Côté, Mark Davis, Frans de Waal, Bob Dentan, Carol Ember, Mel Ember, Kirk Endicott, R. Brian Ferguson, Tim Finan, C. Brooks Fry, Kathy Fry, Sirpa Fry, Agustin Fuentes, Peter Gardner, Tom Gregor, Jonathan Haas, Marvin Harris, Robert Hinde, Bob Hitchcock, Paul L. Jamison, Allen Johnson, Terttu Kaivola, Talia Krohn, Ray Kelly, Sue Kent, Hanna Korpela, Mari Laaksonen, Catherine Lutz, Katie MacKinnon, Joyce Marcus, Peter Meylan, Carolyn Nordstrom, Carl O'Nell, Karin Österman, John Paddock, Fred Rawski, Carole Robarchek, Clay Robarchek, Nancy Ries, Maria Rodriguez, Heikki Sarmaja, Cliff Sather, Kenneth Smail, Peter K. Smith, Les Sponsel, Jukka-Pekka Takala, Cybele Tom, Bob Tonkinson, Jim Welch, and Camilla Westermark.

I very much appreciate the guidance of the editorial team at Oxford University Press. I thank Jan Beatty for recommending the proposal to her colleagues, Elda Rotor for helping to shape the project into its current form, and especially Cybele Tom for providing truly excellent suggestions. I gratefully acknowledge

Cybele's critical role in shaping the content and presentation, fine tuning the arguments, and enhancing the readability of the book. I also thank Lelia Mander for so capably overseeing production and Sue Warga for splendid copyediting.

Material in this book was collected during research projects supported by the United States Institute of Peace (grant number 023-99F), the National Science Foundation (grant numbers 81-17478, 97-10071, and 03-13670), the Wenner-Gren Foundation for Anthropological Research (grant number 4117), and an Indiana University Skomp Fellowship (number 26-235-77). I am very grateful to these institutions for supporting my research on human aggression and conflict resolution over the years. It should also be clear that the opinions expressed in this book do not necessarily reflect the views of these granting agencies.

I owe warm thanks to my wife, Sirpa Fry, and my father, Brooks Fry, for their unfaltering support during the entire writing project. Sirpa has heard—repeatedly, I'm afraid—about the trials and tribulations of working on a project of this nature. She always has offered sound, supportive advice and honest, helpful reactions to my prose, for which I remain most grateful.

Beyond War

1

Charting a New Direction

Many ideas in science seemed crazy at one time but are now regarded as being settled, either having been laid to rest (as in the case of cold fusion) or firmly established (as in the case of plate tectonics, which grew out of an earlier "crazy" theory of continental drift). . . . But, even the weirdest theories of science must pass one rigorous test or be discarded: their predictions must be in agreement with phenomena observed in the physical world.

—ROBERT EHRLICH, *NINE CRAZY IDEAS IN SCIENCE*

This book takes the road less traveled. It examines how cultural beliefs about war bias scientific interpretations, affect perceptions of human nature, and may even close our minds to the possibility of developing alternatives to armed conflict. The book reexamines existing interpretations against the actual evidence in an attempt to untangle fact from fantasy. As we will discover, there is a lot of fantasy floating around out there. A thorough review of the evidence leads, first, to a critique of the status quo picture of war and human nature—here dubbed the "man the warrior" perspective —and, second, to the construction of a new interpretation of human aggression. The book argues that warfare is not inevitable and that humans have a substantial capacity for dealing with conflicts nonviolently. There are ways to move beyond war.

A sleuthing analogy may help to clarify what this book is all about. Imagine that Holmes and Watson don't know the sex of a person who has just moved into their neighborhood, but they have heard that the new neighbor lives alone. Walking by the house on Saturday afternoon, they observe the following clues. The name on the mailbox is Tyler Geoffrey. The pickup truck parked in front of the house has a somewhat sexist bumper sticker that, in advertising Carol's Pizzeria, attempts to humorously equate women with pizza. Glancing in the side window of the truck, Holmes astutely observes that the driver's seat is adjusted far back from the steering wheel. Based on these facts, the obvious conclusion is that the new neighbor is a man. It seems crazy to argue that a tall, pickup-driving, sexist person named Tyler might be a woman.

According to the "man the warrior" view, humans (especially males) are warlike by nature. Advocates of this perspective forge a tight evolutionary link between chimpanzee and human violence, emphasize sex differences in aggression, and recite a litany of barbarity, atrocity, and brutality to support this portrait of humanity. The validity of this "man the warrior" view may seem rather obvious; after all, we all know that humans make war and that wars always seem to be raging somewhere. However, a different—but *not* polar opposite—perspective will be suggested in this book. According to this new view, clearly humans are capable of creating great mayhem, but they also have a remarkable capacity for working out conflicts without resorting to violence. Specifically, a careful reexamination of the actual evidence will lead us to the conclusion that humans are not warlike by nature.

If this sounds improbable to some readers, I must beg for indulgence and ask that we suspend judgment until we examine the evidence and arguments. Data from a vast array of archaeological and ethnographic research will give us a comprehensive picture that leads to new interpretations. This view is broader, by far, than merely looking at current political events or using data from a single academic field, culture, or time period.

To express the challenge in terms of our sleuthing analogy, how solid is the seemingly obvious conclusion that Holmes and Watson's new neighbor is a man? Bear in mind that our sleuths haven't actually seen the person. We can begin to question assumptions. What if Tyler Geoffrey was the previous resident's name? What if Tyler in this case actually is the name of a woman? What if the pickup truck belongs to someone else? Or, assuming that the truck in fact does belong to the new neighbor, aren't some women tall? And don't some women drive pickup trucks? It is even possible, although perhaps not probable, that a woman could own a truck displaying a bumper sticker that most women would shun. What if she borrowed the truck from a male friend for moving? The main point is that the initial "obvious" conclusion rests on a set of assumptions and may be absolutely wrong.

Similarly, I propose that the evidence supporting the "man the warrior" view of humanity is in fact very limited. And, as unlikely as it might sound at first, most of the assumptions of this neo-Hobbesian view are simply flawed. The way to evaluate this issue is to look carefully at the evidence and the arguments.

Holmes and Watson realize that if they really want to be sure that their new neighbor is a man, they should look for more clues. Watson proposes that they knock on the door to say, "Welcome to the neighborhood." Unfortunately, no one responds, but while they are waiting, Holmes surveys the interior of the house through an adjacent front window. Watson knocks a second time and looks displeased, noticing that Holmes is not so subtly peering through the window.

Holmes has noticed a small table near the front door and partly under the front window. Holmes also can see across the living room to a bar-height kitchen counter. On the table near the front door Holmes notes a hairbrush with long dark hairs, a makeup kit, and a key ring containing five keys and a small plastic figure of Snoopy. Scattered on the living room sofa, which faces the window, Holmes spies a violet sweater, the unread daily newspaper, a cookbook, and two magazines—*Better Homes and Gardens* and an issue of *Glamour* with model Heather Graham on the cover. The room has various cardboard moving boxes, some open, some sealed. A signed photograph of actor Jeremy Irons protrudes from one of them. Looking across the living room, Holmes scans a miscellaneous assortment of small items on the kitchen counter. One item in particular catches Holmes' attention, a plastic bottle brightly labeled "Multivitamins plus Iron."

In light of this more extensive investigation, Holmes and Watson are ready to modify their initial conclusion. They still have not been able to gather all of the information they hoped for— meeting the new neighbor face-to-face—but they have been able to collect many new clues by looking in the window. Moreover, they have weighed the importance of different types of information in their minds to arrive at a comprehensive judgment. Watson remarks to Holmes as they continue their walk, "I've seen more women driving pickup trucks than single men's homes with stuff like that." Holmes replies, "Precisely, Watson. And also consider what paraphernalia were *not* there."

A careful reevaluation of the evidence will lead our thinking in a new direction. It will reveal how the human potential for conflict resolution tends to be underappreciated, whereas warfare and other forms of violence tend to be emphasized, exaggerated, and naturalized. Exposing this bias has real-world significance. Naturalizing war creates an unfortunate self-fulfilling prophecy: If war is natural, then there is little point in trying to prevent, reduce, or abolish it. After all, if we can't help being warlike, why should we even bother resisting such tendencies? The danger of assuming that humans are fundamentally warlike is that this presumption may help justify "doing what comes naturally." It also may contribute to an exaggerated fear that naturally warlike "others" are eager to attack us. Harboring such assumptions also can stifle the search for viable alternatives to war: Why attempt the "impossible"?

This book presents a novel slant. It brings some largely neglected yet highly relevant anthropological findings to center stage. It offers a new perspective. A wealth of cross-cultural information exists on conflict management from around the world. This book draws on this bounty of anthropological material, for instance, to illustrate how conflict resolution occurs in cultures everywhere, to document that numerous nonwarring societies exist, to unearth archaeological evidence on the very recent beginning of war, and to explore the nature of peace and aggression among nomadic hunter-gatherers. A consideration of nomadic hunter-gatherer bands will form the centerpiece of a new evolutionary perspective on aggression. We will travel to the Arctic, Australia, Africa, and beyond to examine the nomadic hunter-gatherer adaptation close up. The resulting fresh perspective will rest soundly on anthropological data, much of which previously has been ignored or dismissed.

A macroscopic view suggests that humans have the *capacity* to replace the institution of war with international conflict resolution procedures to ensure justice, human rights, and security for the people of the world—social features that are sorely underdeveloped in the current international war system. This conclusion, as we will see, stems from a comprehensive review of the anthropological data on war, social organization, conflict management, and human evolution. Such a macroscopic anthropological perspective, spanning evolutionary time and cross-cultural space, is considerably broader than most current-day political perspectives. It can provide novel insights about the possibilities of achieving and maintaining peace.

The "man the warrior" perspective is well entrenched in Western thinking. This is not surprising because the belief that war is part and parcel of human nature has a long history. Thomas Hobbes philosophized in *Leviathan*, published in 1651, on the natural state of war; renowned psychologist William James saw humans as naturally bellicose; Sigmund Freud devised a death instinct to account for some forms of human destructiveness.[1] But it is an often ignored fact that scientists and scholars, as human beings, are members of a culture too. Like everyone else, they are exposed to cultural traditions and worldviews that influence their thinking and perceptions. When the learned and shared beliefs of a culture hold that humans are innately pugnacious, inevitably violent, instinctively warlike, and so on, the people socialized in such settings, whether scientists or nonscientists, tend to accept such views without much question.

One example of how cultural beliefs about the naturalness of war are reflected in scholarship involves the landmark treatise *A Study of War*, by judicial scholar Quincy Wright.[2] Wright observed that some societies in his large cross-cultural sample were nonwarring but, nonetheless, he classified the whole sample within four categories of war. Consequently, the nonwarring societies were labeled as engaging in war because there simply were no alternatives such as "peaceful" or "nonwarring" in the classificatory scheme. This creates a false impression that all societies make war. Wright's war classification is merely one example of research that reflects a belief bias in Western culture that war is natural.

Another example that we will consider in this book involves the inordinate amount of attention given to one anthropological article on the South American Yanomamö. At the same time, published critiques of the article are swept under the rug.[3] The article purports to show that men who have participated in killing someone have more children than men who have not killed anyone. This particular finding has achieved celebrity status, being reiterated over and over again. The implication is that this finding tells us something extremely important about evolution and human nature: Evolution may well have favored killers and warriors over their less violent peers. If so, then "man the warrior" tendencies have evolved as part of human nature.

Similarly, another finding that has been played up as having the utmost relevance for understanding the origin of human warfare is that chimpanzees at Gombe Reserve in Tanzania killed off members of a neighboring group one by one. Similar behavior may have occurred among other chimpanzees also. In any case, why should this type of behavior among *chimpanzees* be repeatedly touted as so important for understanding *humans?* And why do writers taking this approach simultaneously brush over unaggressive bonobos—a species that is just as closely related to humans as are chimpanzees—and instead link humans to so-called killer chimps?

Again we see a "man the warrior" bias in models that continue to favor chimpanzees over bonobos for drawing inferences about human nature. Primatologist Frans de Waal points out that "reconstructions of human evolution [if based on bonobos instead of chimps] might have emphasized sexual relations, equality between males and females, and the origin of the family, instead of war, hunting, tool technology, and other masculine fortes."[4]

In researching this book, I have encountered example after example of how primatological, archaeological, and cultural findings are interpreted so as to bring them into line with prevailing cultural beliefs about the warlike nature of humanity. Quite frankly, I did not anticipate encountering such a pervasive bias.

Proposing an alternative to the well-established "man the warrior" view will undoubtedly generate controversy and resistance. Controversies tend to become polarized. Shades of gray are forcefully relabeled as either black or white. The middle ground evaporates and recondenses at the poles, representing the most extreme views. But as physicist Robert Ehrlich points out, "The nice thing about ideas in the sciences is that they can be supported or refuted by data."[5] I propose that a fresh, comprehensive consideration of the facts will reveal that a new perspective on war and peace makes a lot of sense *because it corresponds closely with the actual evidence*.

A common pitfall involves conceptually muddling war and other types of aggression. We will see several examples of the confusion that this creates. So let me make it very clear that when I express the conclusion that warfare was a rare anomaly through most of prehistory, I am *not* denying the existence of other forms of violence—fights, murders, executions—over evolutionary time. Similarly, when I argue that warfare is not an evolutionary adaptation, I am in fact talking about warfare, not all forms of human aggression. When I suggest that humanity could abolish the institution of warfare, my conclusion is based on a study of the anthropological material, not a blind faith that humans are angels. On the world stage, there will always be a need for police and jails, laws and courts, and arbitrators and mediators. Abolishing war will not mean an end to conflict. It will mean that conflicts are handled in less destructive ways.

Toward the end of the book, we will consider practical applications of a macroscopic anthropological perspective for understanding, preventing, and diminishing war. By drawing comprehensively on anthropological material, I will argue that potentially war could be replaced by international conflict management procedures and institutions to effectively handle disputes in the twenty-first century and beyond. Rather than jumping immediately into the exploration of real-world applications such as these, we must build a necessary foundation and consider the anthropological findings on war and peace from diverse cultural settings and across millennia. To start out, let's turn our attention to the powerful sway that cultural beliefs hold over each and every one of us and how this affects our views of human nature.

2

Do Nonwarring Societies Actually Exist?

During the time men live without a common power to keep them all in awe, they are in that condition which is called war; and such a war, as is of every man, against every man. . . . No arts; no letters; no society; and which is worst of all, continual fear, and danger of violent death; and life of man, solitary, poor, nasty, brutish and short.
—THOMAS HOBBES, *LEVIATHAN*

A batch of recent books from archaeology, primatology, and psychology echo a Hobbesian theme: Humans are warlike by nature. *The Dark Side of Man* melodramatically asserts: "We live in a world in which cheaters, robbers, rapists, murderers, and warmongers lurk in every human landscape." An evolutionary psychology textbook explains that "human recorded history, including hundreds of ethnographies of tribal cultures around the globe, reveals male coalitional warfare to be pervasive across cultures worldwide." *Demonic Males* argues that human warfare has ancient evolutionary roots: "Chimpanzee-like violence preceded and paved the way for human war, making modern humans the dazed survivors of a continuous, 5-million-year habit of lethal aggression."[1]

With some variation from author to author, this portrayal of humanity claims that warfare is ubiquitous or nearly so. Humanity is warlike. Nonwarring societies are dismissed as virtually or totally nonexistent. Some authors propose that even the simplest and oldest type of society, the nomadic hunting-and-gathering (foraging) band, is warlike. Lawrence Keeley writes, for example, "There is nothing inherently peaceful about hunting-gathering or band society." Other researchers assert that "no truly peaceful foraging people has ever been found or described in detail." As a theme spanning such arguments, not only is warfare viewed as pervasive across cultures, but it also is assumed to be an extremely ancient practice. Additionally, some authors propose that warring, assaulting, raping, and murdering have an instinctual basis—that evolutionary processes have favored warfare and other forms of violence.[2]

Some years ago, biologist Edward O. Wilson posed and then answered this question: "Are human beings innately aggressive? . . . The answer to it is yes. Throughout history, warfare, representing only the most organized technique of aggression, has been endemic to every form of society, from hunter-gatherer bands to industrial states." Many people concur. College students from Connecticut and Florida filled out attitude surveys designed to assess beliefs about war and human nature. Respondents were asked if they agreed that "war is an intrinsic part of human nature" and that "human beings have an instinct for war." Approximately half the students linked war to human nature and instincts. It is not difficult to find expression of such views. *Time* magazine published a letter from a reader that stated: "Modern psychology tells us it is the genetically determined, typical male aggression, the 'dark side of man,' that helps men climb the corporate ladder." I once chatted with a man who had lived through World War II as well as the Korean, Vietnam, and Gulf Wars. He stated with absolute certainty: "There always has been war and there always will be war."[3]

One possibility is that this view of humanity represents an accurate reflection of reality. On the other hand, such interpretations may merely reflect a commonly shared cultural belief in Western society that war is natural and inevitable. Cultural belief systems contain "notions of the nature and attributes of humanity. They decide whether we are good, evil, or neutral." As learned and shared phenomena, "belief systems tend for the most part to reside at the level of assumptions and presuppositions."[4] They usually are at work on a subconscious level. Certain beliefs may diverge sharply from hard observation and evidence, but nonetheless people tend not to question the validity of such beliefs. Indeed, it may not occur to them to question their beliefs because they have already adopted them as part of their cultural heritage. The statement that "there always has been war and there always will be war" may well be a reflection of a shared belief whose veracity is assumed and widely accepted without systematic testing. For many people, the supposed truth of the statement is patently obvious, and having lived through several wars only entrenches that sentiment.

Beliefs about human nature and war also are implicitly reflected in many Western writings about war, including those by scientists and scholars as notable as Thomas Hobbes, Jonathan Swift, Thomas Huxley, William James, Sigmund Freud, and Francis Crick, who like other people tend to accept their culture's belief system without question.[5] People in Semai society tend not to question the existence of supernatural spirits called *mara'*; they simply know that they exist. Zapotecs tend not to question that a sudden fright can cause a disease called *susto*. So it is with cultural beliefs. They are simply accepted by cultural insiders most of the time.[6]

Do all societies really engage in war? Is there evidence of war going far back over the course of human evolution? If the answer to these questions is yes, then the view that war is ancient, natural, and inevitable gains support. If the answer is no, this view is undermined. We don't have to vote on the question, for, to repeat physicist Robert Ehrlich's comment, "the nice thing about ideas in the sciences is that they can be supported or refuted by data."[7] In the remainder of this chapter, we will examine whether warfare occurs in all cultures or not. In future chapters, we will consider data on the antiquity of war.

Warfare and Feuding from a Cross-Cultural Perspective

In a cross-cultural study of warfare, Carol and Melvin Ember presented their findings on the frequency of war in 186 societies from around the world in two ways: first, for all the societies in the sample, and second, for only the societies not pacified by a colonial or national government. For the whole sample, which is called the Standard Cross-Cultural Sample (SCCS), warfare was reported as "absent or rare" in 28 percent of the societies ("absent" meant absent and "rare" meant less than once in ten years). For nonpacified societies only, the Embers found warfare to be "absent or rare" in 9 percent of the sample.[8]

Drawing conclusions about warfare frequency from this research turns out to have a wrinkle or two. The Embers defined war so broadly as to encompass feuding and revenge killings when undertaken by more than one person: "a warfare event could involve the ambush of a single person of an 'enemy' group."[9] The inclusion of feuding and revenge killings in the Embers' tally of war is an absolutely crucial point to consider if one wants a meaningful assessment of the ubiquity of war.

Including under "warfare events" feuding and revenge homicides if conducted by two or more persons both increases the number of societies that are reported to practice war and raises estimates as to how often warfare presumably occurs within these societies. For example, this practice leads the Embers to report, not surprisingly, that the Andaman Islanders warred "every year." By contrast, Alfred Radcliffe-Brown, who conducted fieldwork among the Andamanese, writes that "fighting on a large scale seems to have been unknown amongst the Andamanese." Other experts conclude that the Andaman Islanders had feuds but that "war between whole tribes does not seem to have occurred" and that "true warfare did not exist, and there was not even much fighting or feuding."[10]

Try this thought experiment: When you read that a given culture makes war every year, what mental image do you form about what is going on? I'll wager my paycheck that the words "makes war" immediately bring to mind substantially more carnage than the ambushing of a single person.

The overall conclusion based on the Ember and Ember study can be stated as follows: Even when *war* is defined so broadly as to include individual instances of blood revenge and feuding, it is still "absent or rare" in 9 percent to 28 percent of the societies in a large cross-cultural representative sample of societies, depending on whether one includes only unpacified societies or all the societies in the sample.

Keith Otterbein has been studying war, feuding, and other forms of violence since the 1960s.[11] He defines *feuding* as blood revenge that follows a homicide and distinguishes it from *warfare*, defined as "armed combat between political communities."[12] Based on ethnographic data for fifty cultures from around the world, Otterbein found that four societies (8 percent of the sample) never engaged in war.[13] Clearly, the vast majority of Otterbein's sample practiced warfare, but not all. Taking a comprehensive overview of

North American cultures, Harold Driver concluded that whereas feuding sometimes existed, "most of the peoples of the Arctic, Great Basin, Northeast Mexico, and probably Baja California lacked true warfare before European contact."[14]

Turning for a moment to feuding, cross-cultural studies show that rates of feuding vary from one society to the next, and that feuding, like warfare, is not present in all societies. Keith and Charlotte Otterbein found blood feuding to be absent in 56 percent of a sample of fifty societies from around the world and infrequent in another 28 percent of the sample. Psychologists Karen Ericksen and Heather Horton investigated blood feuding using the 186 SCCS societies, the same cross-cultural sample used by the Embers in their study of warfare. They found that the classic blood feud—when both the malefactor and his relatives are considered to be appropriate targets of vengeance—exists in 34.5 percent of the societies. Overall, some form of kin group vengeance was considered legitimate in 54 percent of the cross-cultural sample and not legitimate in the remaining 46 percent of the societies. Even in societies where kin group vengeance was socially permitted, by no means was it always carried out.[15]

Viewing these two cross-cultural studies of feuding in tandem shows that approximately half of the societies in the samples allow blood feuding and half do not, and even when it is socially permitted, other approaches for dealing with grievances are often adopted in place of seeking vengeance. As we will explore in Chapter 7, feuding can be seen as a judicial mechanism—a way that aggrieved parties seek their own justice.

It is important to define terms such as *war* and *feud* clearly to avoid confusion. A biologist commented that "war—lethal conflict—is older than humanity itself."[16] By such a general conception of war as lethal conflict, the killing of even one individual by another, even within the same society, could be counted as an act of war. Is this really in accordance with a popularly shared concept of war? Is it war when an Englishwoman poisons her husband? Is it war when South American bandits rob and kill their victims on a deserted highway? Is it war when an Australian Aborigine hunter, accompanied by his brother, gives chase to the man who ran off with his wife, catches up with the lovers, and spears his rival? With poetic license, we might employ martial vocabulary and imagery to such acts of lethal conflict. However, these lethal conflicts are clearly homicides, not war as generally conceived. Defining war so broadly as to encompass a plethora of individual and group conflict behavior—murder, robbery-homicide, revenge killings, and feud, which stem from diverse motivations and are often in-group events —can facilitate making the claim for the universality of war. But clearly such word games distort the concept of war. When examined more closely, much of the aggressive behavior subsumed under sweeping definitions of war, such as "lethal conflict," do not correspond with a general impression of what actually constitutes war.

A definition of *warfare* that is in correspondence with the common usage of the word and that captures important features of war, as different from homicide, revenge killings, and feud, is:

> A group activity, carried on by members of one community against members of another community, in which it is the primary purpose to inflict serious injury or death on multiple nonspecified members of that other community, or in which the primary purpose makes it highly likely that serious injury or death will be inflicted on multiple nonspecified members of that community in the accomplishment of that primary purpose.[17]

This definition highlights that war is a group activity, occurs between communities, and is not focused against a particular individual or that person's kin group (as occurs in feuding), but rather is directed against nonspecified members of another community. This definition is useful because it clearly excludes individual homicides and feuding and, consequently, clarifies that *war entails relatively impersonal lethal aggression between communities*. Finally, this definition is more detailed than Keith Otterbein's "armed combat between political communities," but nonetheless these definitions are in rough correspondence.[18]

Nonwarring Societies

While researching this book, I compiled a list of cultures that were nonwarring according to the foregoing definition of war (see Appendix 2).[19] I looked for direct ethnographic statements to the effect that a culture lacks war, that a people do not engage in warfare, or that the members of a society respond to threats from other groups by moving elsewhere rather than fighting, and so on. The Semai of Malaysia are a good example (Figure 2.1). Nonviolence characterizes daily life. They do not war and they do not feud. Even when confronted with slave-raiders, "the Semai response was always a disorganized and headlong flight into the forest."[20]

I was able to locate over seventy nonwarring cultures (see Figure 2.2). The list is far from exhaustive. Although not included on the list, certain religious "enclave societies"—groups existing within larger societies—such as the Amish, Hutterites, and Quakers have pacifist belief systems and consistently have forsaken warfare. Certain nations also have not been involved in warfare

Figure 2.1 A Semai woman prepares food. The Semai strongly value social harmony and use a type of mediation-arbitration assembly called the *becharaa'* to resolve disputes nonviolently. Traditionally, Semai have fled from, rather than fought with, outsiders. Will the Semai be able to retain their nonviolent approach to life in the face of an increasing onslaught of outside influences and social disruptions? (See Appendix 1.) (Photo courtesy of Mari Laaksonen.)

for very long periods of time. Sweden has not been to war in over 170 years; Switzerland, known for its neutrality and aided by natural mountain barriers, has not engaged in war for almost two hundred years; and Iceland has been at peace for over seven hundred years. In recent history, twenty countries have experienced periods without war that have lasted at least a hundred years. Costa Rica abolished its military after World War II—a very concrete statement of the country's intention not to engage in war. Former Costa Rican president Oscar Arias notes, "The stability

"There is no ethnographic evidence to suggest the existence of long-standing intergroup animosity akin to feud [among the Mardu]. There is no word for either feud or warfare in the language of the desert people. Their accounts of conflicts are phrased in kinship terms and on an interpersonal or interfamily rather than intergroup level."

"Warfare in the sense of organized intertribal struggle is unknown [among the Arunta]. What fighting there is, is better understood as an aspect of juridical procedure than as war."

"All informants denied that any major conflict had occurred 'as long as could be remembered.' Admirable relations existed between the Sanpoil and all of their immediate neighbors."

"These people [the Saulteaux] have never engaged in war with the whites or with other Indian tribes."

"There is no warfare in their [Machiguenga] region, no villages or superordinate political structures, no lineages or other named social groupings beyond the household, and a very loose 'kindred.'"

"Warfare, either actual or traditional, is absent [among the Hanunóo]."

"There are no [Hanunóo] classes, no servants, no officials, and no warfare."

"Relations with Subanun of the same or other groups are invariably devoid of warfare and class distinctions. . . . Social relationships, unmarred by warfare, extend outward along ties of proximity and bilateral kinship."

"[The Veddahs] live so peacefully together that one seldom hears of quarrels among them and never of war."

"I can report a complete absence of feuding within Paliyan society and a corresponding total lack of warfare."

"There is no evidence of Semang warring with one another or with non-Semang."

"The Jahai are known for their shyness toward outsiders, their non-violent, non-competitive attitude, and their strong focus on sharing. . . . In times of conflict, the Jahai withdraw rather than fight."

"Among the Andamanese quarrels between groups sometimes lead to bloodshed, and thus to feuds, which might continue for months or even years. . . . War between whole tribes does not seem to have occurred."

"The stability of Costa Rican democracy stems primarily from the fact that it possesses no military institution. . . . The Constitution of 1949 expressly prohibited the subsequent creation of an army. Both the Constitution and the underlying spirit of peace live on to this day."[21]

Figure 2.2   A sampling of ethnographic statements on nonwarring societies

of Costa Rican democracy stems primarily from the fact that it possesses no military institutions."[22]

We began this chapter by noting that many people espouse beliefs as to the naturalness and universality of war. I raised the possibility that such views, rather than being based on an objective evaluation of the data, instead might be part of a cultural belief system that includes a warlike image of humanity and a corresponding assumption that war occurs in all cultures.

The cross-cultural studies by the Embers and Otterbein correspond with the list containing over seventy nonwarring cultures by pointing to the same conclusion: *Many nonwarring cultures do in fact exist.*[23] *Not all societies make war.* Thus nonwarring societies are not merely figments of the imagination. A substantial number of cultures engage in warfare, but some do not. Thus the belief that war is a universal feature of societies everywhere, as expressed by numerous persons including some eminent thinkers, is nonetheless false. It would seem that the presupposed "truth" of this belief about war and human nature, as an aspect of a broader cultural belief system, is simply accepted as self-evident by many people. Actively checking the validity of this belief against the available anthropological evidence, if such an endeavor ever comes to mind in the first place, might seem superfluous. Edwin Burrows offers a conclusion that is apropos: "We generally assume that we know, from . . . observation, what is universally human. But a little scrutiny will show that such conclusions are based only on experience with one culture, our own. We assume that what is familiar, unless obviously shaped by special conditions, is universal."[24] To gain a broader perspective, it may prove beneficial to take a look at some societies that are less warlike than our own.

3

Overlooked and Underappreciated: The Human Potential for Peace

In the Waurá view, self-control over violent aggressive impulses, compassion for children, and acceptance of the responsibility to share material wealth are all basic attributes of human beings.

—EMILIENNE IRELAND, "CEREBRAL SAVAGE"

Although war and other types of violence may be very noticeable, a close examination of cross-cultural data reveals that people usually deal with conflict without violence. Humans have a solid capacity for getting along with each other peacefully, preventing physical aggression, limiting the scope and spread of violence, and restoring peace following aggression.[1] In this chapter we will consider a couple of ethnographic cases that illustrate this human potential for peace—the nonwarring, nonfeuding Siriono and Paliyan.

The suggestion that peacefulness and the nonviolent handling of conflict predominate in human affairs might seem to be contradicted by daily observations, especially to people who have become accustomed to Hollywood films and daily newscasts stuffed with images of murders, rapes, riots, and wars. A study of over two thousand television programs aired between 1973 and 1993 on major networks in the United States found that more than 60 percent featured violence and over 50 percent of the leading characters in these shows were involved in violence.[2] However, as professors of criminal justice Bahram Haghighi and Jon Sorensen write, "the media tend to distort the types of criminal victimization occurring and exaggerate true accounts of criminal victimization in the community."[3] In other words, violence-saturated programming can contribute to a false, unrealistically violent picture of the world.

In actuality, the vast majority of people on the planet awake on a typical morning and live through a violence-free day—and this experience generally continues day after day. The overwhelming majority of humanity spends an average day without inflicting any physical aggression on anyone, without being the victim of physical aggression, and, in all likelihood, without even witnessing any physical aggression with their own eyes among the hundreds or thousands of people they encounter. Perhaps surprisingly, this generalization holds in even the most violent cultures on earth. Clayton and Carole Robarchek conducted fieldwork among a culture, the Waorani of Ecuador, where over 60 percent of the deaths in the last several generations were violent ones. Yet the Robarcheks report that "even during this period when the raiding was comparatively intense, years passed between raids." And whereas the rate of spearings had markedly decreased by the time the Robarcheks did fieldwork, they never actually saw the Waorani kill anyone. Furthermore, they note that Waorani "child socialization is indulgent and non-punitive, both husbands and wives care for children, and children's relations with both parents are warm and affectionate." They also report that "we saw no violence between spouses. . . . The only overt violence that we saw during both of our field trips was one instance of a child attacking his brother." Daily life is tranquil.[4]

Another illustration comes from my research in a Mexican Zapotec community that I refer to as San Andrés. Interspersed between periodic acts of physical aggression such as fistfights, wife beatings, and the physical punishment of children, most typical daily scenes are peaceful.[5] The point is that even though violence undeniably does occur at times, it is not as prevalent as people sometimes assume, even in so-called violent cultures. At times, discussion of crime and crime statistics exaggerate violence. In order to "see" the daily violence, more often than not, one relies on images relayed by the news crews scouring the planet in search of mayhem from war zones, riots, terrorist attacks, or sensational crime scenes.

In actuality, one can travel from continent to continent and personally observe hundreds of thousands of humans interacting nonviolently. Even if searching for conflict, an observer may find people talking over their differences, ridiculing a rival, persuading and coaxing someone, and perhaps arguing. An observer also may find people negotiating solutions to their disputes, agreeing to provide compensation for damages, reaching compromises, while perhaps also reconciling and forgiving one another, all without violence, within families and among friends, neighbors, associates, acquaintances, and strangers. In contrast to violence, such pervasive human activities rarely make the news. Peace is the norm, violence the shocking exception. Additionally, time and again, individuals from various cultures simply walk away from conflict—and such widespread avoidance and toleration tend to be both invisible and considered not newsworthy.

Terms such as *aggression* and *conflict* have multiple meanings and applications in daily speech. The word *aggression*, for instance, can suitably apply to a schoolyard fight, the unrelenting persistence of a telephone solicitor, spouse abuse, or Hitler's invasion of Poland. The term *conflict*, likewise, can refer to phenomena as disparate as psychic turmoil and warfare.

Conflict is defined as "a perceived divergence of interests—where interests are broadly conceptualized to include values, needs, goals, and wishes—between two or more parties, often accompanied by feelings of anger or hostility."[6] *Aggression* means the infliction of harm, pain, or injury on other individuals. Sometimes aggression is subdivided into verbal and physical aggression. A central point is that conflict need not involve any aggression whatsoever. *Aggression* and *conflict* are not synonymous.

In this book, the term *violence* is reserved for severe forms of physical aggression, including war and feud. Thus, simply shouting angrily at someone without any physical contact is neither physical aggression nor violence. Shouting is verbal aggression. If the verbal tirade escalates to slapping or pushing, this mild physical aggression generally would not be considered serious enough to warrant calling it violence. Violence entails forceful attacks, usually with weapons, that can result in serious injury or death.

Dealing with interpersonal and intergroup conflict is an important part of daily human existence. Conflict will arise in any social group with a membership greater than one. But again, most conflict does not entail violence. We are all very familiar with the massacres, wars, and genocide reported from around the globe. Let's now consider two hunter-and-gatherer band societies, the Siriono and the Paliyan, which—in stark contrast to the types of events that make the news—deal with almost all conflicts nonviolently. In these ethnographic descriptions, you no doubt will find both similarities and differences to your own society.

Siriono of Bolivia

Numbering about two thousand people at the time they were studied, the semi-nomadic Siriono inhabit a tropical area in Bolivia.[7] They have few material possessions. Whereas good hunters have slightly higher status than average, Siriono society is basically egalitarian. Allan Holmberg reports that "a form of chieftainship does exist, but the prerogatives of this office are few." *Best hunter* might be a better term than *chief*, for "little attention is paid to what is said by a chief" and the so-called chief lacks the power to demand compliance with his wishes. One mark of the chief's position is the tendency, in contrast to other men, to have more than one wife. This puts a further burden on his hunting skills.

Women have about the same privileges as men, and both sexes engage in about the same amount of work. Women take part in drinking feasts and ceremonies. Both women and men enjoy active sex lives. "While lying naked in their hammocks, husband and wife are frequently observed fondling each other, and if desire mounts to a sufficient pitch (if, for instance, a man begins to feel an erection), the couple may retire to the bush for immediate sexual intercourse."[8]

In terms of conflict, verbal quarreling is common, especially between spouses, but physical aggression is not. Of seventy-five disputes among various people, forty-four involved food, nineteen were related to sex, and twelve resulted from other causes. Congruent with his weak authority, the chief tends not to get involved in the disputes of others. Holmberg states that "the handling of one's affairs is thus largely an individual matter; everyone is expected to stand up for his own rights and to fulfill his own obligations." Consequently, the participants usually settle quarrels themselves. Avoidance is also employed when people get angry. A typical male response is to go hunting: "If they shoot any game their anger disappears; even if they do not kill anything they return home too tired to be angry."[9]

The Siriono do not engage in war. "We find neither the organization, the numbers, nor the weapons with which to wage war, aggressive or defense. Moreover, war does not seem to be glorified in any way by the culture." When foreigners such as rubber tappers began to encroach on areas occupied by Siriono and to kill them early in the twentieth century, the Siriono reciprocated on several occasions by killing intruders. Overall, the Siriono strategy has been to avoid warlike peoples such as the Yanaigua and the Baure: "Both tribes are equated by the Siriono under one term, *kurúkwa*, a kind of monster, and are carefully avoided by them whenever possible."[10]

Siriono bands interact peacefully. They do not claim exclusive territories. If hunters from one band come across signs that another band is occupying a given area, the hunters abstain from hunting in the vicinity, thus respecting the rights of the first band to any game in the area. Within Siriono society, murder is almost unknown, as is sorcery, rape, and theft of nonfood items. Holmberg heard of only two killings, one in which a man killed his wife at a drinking feast and the other in which a man, in an odd-sounding incident, killed his sister, perhaps accidentally, when he threw a club at her while perched in a tree. As is typical among nomadic hunter-gatherers, if conflict becomes intense between individuals or families within a band, one party simply joins another group. Most conflicts are resolved without the band splitting up, however.[11]

As in many societies, adultery is common among the Siriono. If adulterers are discreet, their affairs may be ignored. However, too-frequent extramarital flings that arouse public attention can lead to jealousy.

> The Siriono say of a person in whom sexual desire is aroused that he is *ecimbasi*. To be *ecimbasi* is all right when sexual activity is confined to intercourse with one's real spouse, and occasionally with one's potential spouses, but one who takes flagrant advantage of his sex rights over potential spouses to the neglect of his real spouses is accused of being *ecimbasi* in the sense of being promiscuous. Such accusations not infrequently lead to fights and quarrels.[12]

Another interesting aspect of Siriono sexuality involves how women and men at times engage in reciprocal exchanges. Acíba-eóko had several times tried to seduce one of his potential wives— that is, a socially legitimate extramarital sex partner. This woman had refused because she did not want to provoke a quarrel with her husband. One day the woman saw Acíba-eóko returning from the hunt with a fat peccary (a South American pig-like beast). She was eager to get some of the meat.

> She waited until Acíba-eóko was alone—his wives had gone for palm cabbage and water—and approached him with the following request: *"ma nde sóri tai etíma; sediákwa"* ("Give me a peccary leg; I am hungry"). He replied, *"éno, cúki cúki airáne"*

("O.K., but first sexual intercourse"). She replied, "*ti, manédi gadi*" ("No, afterward, no less"). He said, "*ti, námo gadí*" ("No, now, no less"). She replied, "*eno, maNgíti?*" ("O.K., where?"). He answered, "*aiñti*" ("There"), pointing in the direction of the river. Both of them set out, by different routes, for the river, and returned, also by different routes, the woman carrying firewood, about half an hour later.[13]

Notice how both parties acted discreetly to prevent conflict with their spouses. Asymmetry exists in how jealous Siriono men and women deal with adultery. A husband tends to express anger toward his wife; a wife tends to express anger at her female rival. On occasion, women attack rivals with their digging sticks. As mentioned, angry men may "go hunting" to cool off. Male-male disputes may be settled through wrestling matches at periodic drinking feasts. The wrestling matches have rules that limit aggression, and generally participants use self-restraint and adhere to the rules. If not, others intervene. Holmberg explains that "aggression at drinking feasts is limited to wrestling matches; any other type of fighting is frowned upon and is usually stopped by non-participant men and women. On one occasion Eantándu, when drunk, struck an opponent with his fists. Everyone began to clamor that he was fighting unfairly, 'like a white man.' He stopped immediately."[14]

Paliyan of India

The Paliyan of southern India have a population of over three thousand. Some Paliyan now live in settled communities, but others remain in mobile foraging bands, usually between fifteen and thirty individuals in size. To focus on the nomadic bands that move camp every few days, "the membership of a Paliyan band is always in flux."[15] Peter Gardner reports that nomadic Paliyan subsist totally on the foods they forage, which consist of over one hundred species of plants and animals, with wild yams being the staple. About three times a year, hunters cooperatively kill a wild pig, less often an elk-sized sambar deer, and more often a variety of smaller prey. Members of both sexes gather yams, hunt, fish, collect honey, and prepare food. Food is not a scarce resource. Gardner explains that people spend only three to four hours a day in the pursuit of food and show "no anxiety whatsoever about its supply."[16]

Paliyan prefer to live in a band with their primary relatives. Gardner discovered that virtually equal numbers of people were living with maternal kin as with paternal kin. Additionally, "if a husband and wife come from different groups they may move back and forth irregularly." Most marriages are monogamous, and interestingly, the age difference between husband and wife averages 14.3 years; husbands were older than their wives in 69 percent of the marriages.[17]

The Paliyan place great value on individual autonomy, equality, and respect. To Paliyan thinking, anyone who interferes with the freedom of another person is acting disrespectfully. The value of equality comes into play because "everyone merits equal respect by virtue of being a human being." Gardner specifically illustrates gender equality by noting, "If a woman decides to bring her lover into the household as a second husband, and if her original partner elects to go along with the change (instead of moving out), her polyandry is her own concern."[18] As this instance reflects, the broader principle is that neither a wife nor a husband has the right to give orders to the other.

Another reflection of Paliyan autonomy and equality involves hunting groups. As in social relations generally, no one dominates the decision making; the members of the hunting group operate via discussion and consensus. At the end of the hunt, the game is meticulously apportioned into equivalent piles. Not only are the shares of meat equal, but also each contains identical types of meat. "When all have agreed that the piles are of equal size, each hunter takes one, whatever his role in the hunt."[19]

Figure 3.1 After three Paliyan families from southern India went fishing together, a man and his young son make an initial division of the catch into three equal-sized piles. The high level of personal autonomy and sexual egalitarianism apparent in Paliyan society is typical of nomadic hunter-gatherer societies generally. In accordance with their belief system, which emphasizes nonviolence and respect for other people, the Paliyan do not engage in feuds or make war. (Photo courtesy of Peter Gardner.)

The Paliyan live in accordance with a nonviolent ethos. In daily life, Paliyan avoid competition, shy away from interpersonal comparisons, and shun the seeking of prestige. Moreover, there are no real leaders, and the Paliyan usually deal with conflicts through avoidance rather than confrontation. Aggression is incompatible with the values of respect, equality, and autonomy. For the most part, the Paliyan use effective nonviolent techniques to deal with interpersonal conflict. First, individuals employ self-restraint, as reflected in this ideal: "If one strikes, the struck man keeps still. It is our main motto." Second, Paliyan avoid drinking alcohol, which is sometimes available when they encounter outsiders. Third, people remove themselves from conflict situations. Avoidance is relatively easy in this individually autonomous, nomadic society. Fourth, a third party may assist in relieving tension: "A self-appointed conciliator distracts with wit or soothes with diplomacy, this is done in a respectful way, never at the expense of the principals."[20]

Gardner recorded only twenty episodes of disrespect, including those in which children were involved, over a four-and-a-half-month period in a largely foraging band. Most instances of disrespect were rather mild, as when adults lightly slapped children or when someone whose feelings had been hurt simply left the band in total silence.[21]

Even the most serious cases, such as those involving marital jealousy, were very mild from a culturally comparative perspective. The vast majority of the disrespect cases involved no physical contact whatsoever, and sometimes no verbal exchange either, such as when one party responded by leaving. Overall, the rate of disrespect cases came out to just under one case per person per year. Can you imagine living in such a peaceful society with these types of values? Gardner reports that the Paliyan have strong beliefs against murder, and he failed to uncover any actual homicides. The Paliyan do not engage in feuds or war and respond to threats of violence from outsiders by moving away.[22]

The point is not that we should seek peace by returning to a nomadic life in the forest. That certainly wouldn't work. Rather, the nonviolent, nonwarring Siriono and Paliyan provide a poignant illustration of the human capacity for living in peace and at the same time argue strongly against the belief that war is a natural attribute of humanity. In the next two chapters, we will employ a macroscopic time perspective to examine the prehistoric origin of war. We will also consider how current-day assumptions about the naturalness of war and other forms of violence often have biased interpretations of the past.

4

Killer Apes, Cannibals, and Coprolites: Projecting Mayhem onto the Past

At the heart of science is an essential balance between two seemingly contradictory attitudes—an openness to new ideas, no matter how bizarre or counterintuitive, and the most ruthlessly skeptical scrutiny of all ideas, old and new.

—CARL SAGAN, *THE FINE ART OF BALONEY DETECTION*

In my youth, I heard my father tell a story that my grandfather had related to him about the leading nineteenth-century pathologist Rudolf Virchow. I later discovered that my grandfather had written the story down:

> [Robert] Koch wanted to demonstrate the tubercle bacillus to Virchow and invited him to his laboratory. When Virchow refused to go, [Julius] Cohnheim urged him to do so, telling him it was his duty to see the demonstration. Finally, he succeeded in gaining Virchow's consent. Consent it was, too, for Virchow felt it was real condescension on his part to honor one of whose work he did not approve, one whom in derision he called "the boy from the country."

He took to Koch's laboratory the microscope he had used so successfully in examining pathological tissues, and asked Koch to show the bacillus on it. Koch explained that the bacillus was so small that it required special staining and a high-powered microscope to show it. Whereupon Virchow, pointing to his low-power microscope, said: *"What that microscope does not show does not exist."*

We are apt to think that a scientist always welcomes truth, but at times, he, too, may close his mind and obstruct progress.[1]

People who presume that war is a "natural" attribute of humankind also tend to assume that it is an extremely ancient practice. War is seen as "older than humanity itself."[2] However, such presumptions are not in accordance with the worldwide archaeological record. With the story about Rudolf Virchow in mind, let us begin an exploration of the antiquity of war with a tale about how preexisting beliefs can affect one's interpretation of the past.

Killer Apes and Cannibals

In 1925 a young anatomy professor, Raymond Dart, reported the discovery of an extraordinary fossil skull from a South African limestone quarry at Taung.[3] The specimen was clearly a primate juvenile. The face and most of the lower jaw were intact, and in an extraordinary stroke of good fortune minerals had entered the brain case during fossilization and hardened to form a cast of the brain. Dart realized that the "Taung child" fossil showed both apelike and humanlike features, gave it the scientific name *Australopithecus africanus*, literally "southern ape of Africa," and argued that this creature may have been an ancient ancestor to humanity.

However, at the time, most experts dismissed Dart's conclusions largely because the "Taung child" did not fit their preconceived ideas about humanity's past.[4] The Taung specimen lacked the large brain that many experts were certain must have developed very early in human evolution. Additionally, expert opinion at that time held that Asia, not Africa, was the continent where humanity had its roots, due in part to the earlier discovery of *Homo erectus* fossils in Java. Influenced by such erroneous assumptions, many leaders in the field dismissed Dart's important find as merely a fossil ape with minimal relevance to the understanding of human origins.

Eventually, the physical evidence of the Taung skull itself, in conjunction with the discovery of additional australopithecine specimens and a more general shift in paleontological thinking, won out over erroneous preconceptions. Again, preconceived beliefs sometimes cloud an objective evaluation of the evidence. This lesson foreshadows our main story about Raymond Dart.

Following the Taung discovery, first Robert Bloom and later Dart himself searched for and found additional australopithecine fossils. Some specimens were classified as belonging to the same species as the Taung child, *Australopithecus africanus*, and other fossils eventually were given the species name *Australopithecus robustus*— or robust southern ape. These australopithecine fossils from South Africa are roughly two million to three million years old. Subsequently, australopithecine remains that are even older have been found in other parts of Africa.

Whereas Dart had been absolutely correct in his assessment of the importance of the Taung child to an understanding of human evolution, his reconstructions of australopithecine behavior revealed that he had an active imagination but lacked an understanding of fossilization processes. Joseph Birdsell recounts how he once asked Dart what percentage of the australopithecines he thought had been murdered. "Why, all of them, of course," Dart replied. Perhaps Dart's answer should not be taken absolutely literally; nonetheless, in his writings Dart argued that specimen after specimen showed evidence of having met a violent end.[5]

Dart interpreted fractured fossil skulls and shattered bones as indisputable evidence that humanity's earliest ancestors were killers of both animal prey and of each other, proving humanity's "carnivorous, and cannibalistic origin." Dart noted that 80 percent of the ancient baboon skulls found with the australopithecine specimens from three sites appeared to have had their heads bashed-in. Many of the baboons and some of the australopithecines showed a particular type of fractured skull consisting of paired depressions or holes. Dart interpreted the puncture holes in one australopithecine skull as a deliberate mutilation of a victim for ritualistic purposes.[6]

Dart argued that the paired depression damage on baboon and australopithecine skulls resulted from the australopithecine hunter-murderers' preference for using particular large-animal leg bones as bludgeons, because this type of bone happens to have two bony projections that might make paired indentations if wielded just right. Dart wrote murder into his descriptions of broken bones, concluding that one hominid succumbed to "a severing transverse blow with [a] bludgeon on the vertex and tearing apart of the front and back halves of the broken skull." Another australopithecine, according to Dart, supposedly died from a "vertical blow in the left parietal region [the side of the head] with a rock." Dart also thought that the Taung child had succumbed to a blow to the head. Thus in Dart's view, at least some species of australopithecines were chronic head bashers of baboons and of each other, or in Dart's imaginative prose, "confirmed killers: carnivorous creatures, that seized living quarries by violence, battered them to death, tore apart their broken bodies, dismembered them limb for limb, slaking their ravenous thirst with the hot blood of victims and greedily devouring livid writhing flesh."[7]

Writer Robert Ardrey enthusiastically publicized the killer ape interpretation of humanity's predecessors.[8] And the opening scenes of Kubrick's 1968 blockbuster film, 2001: A Space Odyssey, portray an ancestral ape wreaking havoc with a bone-turned-weapon. Later in the movie, a group of these human ancestors brandish bone bludgeons in an attack on their unarmed rivals, beat the opposing group's leader to death, and drive the rest away from a waterhole. How many people have had their own images of humanity's past shaped by viewing such vivid, dramatic, fictional portrayals of prehistoric violence?

Dart's reconstruction of human ancestors as violent killer apes may have seemed plausible to Ardrey, Kubrick, and many other people, but his interpretations of damaged skulls as indicating widespread murder and cannibalism were questioned by physical anthropologists such as Sherry Washburn and Carlton Coon.[9] Some of the shattering of the bones and skulls resulted from natural geological processes that occurred during fossilization as piles of rock and dirt compressed the specimens over many millennia. As for the various baboon skulls and occasional australopithecine specimens with paired depression fractures or holes, C. K. Brain examined the collections of animal bones more extensively than Dart had done and arrived at a more plausible explanation for much of this damage: large predators. Brain demonstrated that an extinct leopard species, whose remains were found at the same geological layer as the australopithecines, had projecting canine teeth that corresponded with the paired puncture holes on skulls

Figure 4.1 This reconstruction of the past illustrates how the paired puncture holes on the skull of an australopithecine specimen were likely made by the protruding lower canine teeth of an extinct leopard. Fossil remains of both species were found at the site. (Redrawn with permission from C. K. Brain, "New finds at the Swartkrans australopithecine site," *Nature* 225 (1970), 1112–199.)

(see Figure 4.1).[10] Thus the evidence suggests that predators were eating the ancient baboons and the australopithecines alike. The forces of geology then continued the destructive processes; consequently, most of the australopithecine skeletal remains found two million to three million years later showed major damage. The murderous, cannibalistic killer apes that Dart so vividly portrayed in fact turned out to have been merely lunch for leopards. Dart's gruesome reconstructions were a fantasy.

What we read into the past depends in part on our culturally based beliefs about human nature. Dart, as a member of Western culture, apparently shared with many other people a set of beliefs about the natural aggressiveness of humans. Dart wrote:

> The blood-bespattered, slaughter-gutted archives of human history from the earliest Egyptian and Sumerian records to the most recent atrocities of the Second World War accord with early universal cannibalism, with animal and human sacrificial practices or their substitutes in formalized religions and with the world-wide scalping, head-hunting, body-mutilating and necrophilic practices of mankind in proclaiming this common bloodlust differentiator, this predaceous habit, this mark of Cain that separates man dietetically from his anthropoidal relatives [for example, chimpanzees, bonobos, and gorillas] and allies him rather with the deadliest Carnivora.[11]

Such beliefs, I suggest, played a significant role in Dart's casting the australopithecines as cannibalistic murderers. Archaeologist Robert Foley warns: "The danger has always been that the prehistoric world will simply be a reflection of the world in which we ourselves live."[12] Are current-day beliefs about the ubiquity and antiquity of war being projected back into the past?

Unlike Virchow, Dart *was* willing to look through the high-powered microscope. After weighing the evidence presented in Brain's careful study, Dart changed his mind and conceded that Brain's conclusions were sounder than his own.[13] Recall that Dart himself had experienced the closed-mindedness of leading scientists who for decades had dismissed his Taung skull as unimportant because it did not match their opinions about human evolution. Could it be that Dart had become keenly aware of the power of preconceptions to bias one's own interpretations? Perhaps such insights helped him, years later, to change his own mind about australopithecine bloodlust.

Whereas Dart's cannibalistic, killer ape portrayal of the australopithecines cannot be substantiated by the evidence, there is much indisputable archaeological evidence of violence, including warfare, in the very recent past. For instance, Maria Ostendorf Smith reports on violence apparent in seven archaeological sites in western Tennessee mostly dating between about 2,750 and 4,500 years ago. Ten out of 439 skeletons show uncontestable evidence of lethal violence, including projectile points within the skeletons, cut marks indicative of scalping or dismemberment, and stab wounds. All ten victims were male.

The question remains whether these men were the victims of homicide, feud, or war. Relating to part of the Northwest Coast of North America, Herbert Maschner notes changes in the archaeological record over recent millennia. About 5,000 years ago, primarily nonlethal injuries, such as those from club blows, appeared on some skeletal remains. Then, by 1,500 to 1,800 years ago, evidence of warfare became clearly apparent. By this time, there were defensive sites, larger villages built in defensible locations, and a decline in population.[14]

Lawrence Keeley argues that evidence of warfare has sometimes been overlooked. For example, archaeological indications of warfare among the Classic Maya—fortifications and countless depictions of war captives and armed soldiers—were dismissed as "unrepresentative, ambiguous, or insignificant."[15]

Another example illustrating Keeley's point comes to mind from my experience in the Mexican highlands of Oaxaca. At the awe-inspiring mountaintop archaeological site called Monte Albán—the center of the ancient Zapotec civilization—huge stones with carved depictions of human figures can be found amidst the temples of the central plaza. These stylized human portraits at first were referred to by the festive name "dancers" (*danzantes*). However, in line with Keeley's point, the obvious facts that many so-called dancers have closed eyes (as in death), are naked, and have had their genitals mutilated combine to suggest that these are the images of the militarily vanquished (Figure 4.2).[16]

Whereas Keeley is undoubtedly correct in his assertion that archaeologists in some instances literally and figuratively

Figure 4.2   As is typical of states, the ancient Zapotec civilization engaged in warfare. A collection of human figures carved on large stones and originally mounted in rows on the side of a temple at Monte Albán appear to depict the corpses of vanquished enemies. Note the closed eyes and denigrating elements (such as nudity and genital removal or mutilation), which are typical features of these misnamed *danzantes*. (D. P. Fry photo collection.)

have turned war captives into dancers, there also are many cases, and probably more numerous instances, where the reverse has occurred. In addition to the Dart case just considered, excavators have regularly "seen" violence where none in fact existed. The first interpretations of the *Homo erectus* fossils from a site called Zhoukoudian in China held that these human predecessors hunted and consumed each other. This interpretation was widely accepted for several decades. However, subsequent careful analysis by Lewis Binford and Chuan Ho revealed absolutely no support for cannibalism at Zhoukoudian. Benefiting from new analytical methods, Binford and Ho demonstrated that the type of bone breakage and other observations that previously were assumed to have resulted from cannibalism were actually attributable to natural fossilization processes.[17]

The next tale began somewhat over 50,000 years ago in Europe. When a skull of a male Neanderthal was discovered in 1939 in a cave south of Rome at Monte Circeo, lying in a circle of stones in the presence of no other bones, its right side smashed, and its foramen magnum (the big hole at the base of the skull through which the spinal cord connects to the brain) artificially enlarged, excavator Alberto Carlo Blanc interpreted the findings as a clear case of human sacrifice, the man having been killed by a skull-shattering blow. Paul Bahn comments, "Many popular works on prehistory have accepted this view unquestioningly."[18]

However, two recent reanalyses of the facts, by Mary Stiner and by Tim White and Nicholas Toth, show this interpretation to be based more on speculation than on precise observations of the site and skull itself. An investigation of the cave geology shows that the circle of rocks is consistent with patterns formed by landslides. In fact, the so-called circle of stones forms an irregular cluster, not a circle, giving no indication of human arrangement. Whereas

Blanc apparently had viewed evidence of carnivores in the cave as irrelevant information, the new investigators noted the presence of hundreds of bones, many gnawed, and fossilized hyena feces. Stiner concludes, based on a detailed study of the great number of animal bones in the cave, that the so-called Neanderthal ritual chamber appears in fact to be a spotted hyena den. The edges of the enlarged foramen magnum lack any stone tool cut marks or scraping marks that would be apparent had hominids actually removed the brain for cannibalistic purposes. On the other hand, White and Toth note that "the damage to the cranium is consistent with damage caused by carnivore chewing." In short, there is absolutely no evidence for murder or cannibalism related to the Monte Circeo skull.[19]

William Ury summarizes the outcome of comprehensive work by White and Toth: "In specimen after specimen for which the claim of violence had been made, they reviewed the evidence and found alternative explanations equally or more persuasive." In one case, for example, previous researchers had interpreted marks on a Neanderthal skull, referred to as Engis 2, as showing that the person had been scalped. White and Toth present a set of super-enlarged photographs that show how the marks resulted from repairing, making casts of the skull, and otherwise working with the cranium in the laboratory. Their conclusion: "None of the marks have anything to do with prehistoric behavior."[20]

A Story of Gastronomic Proportion

Some years ago, a student stopped by my office and announced that he would like to write his research paper on coprolites. It wasn't long before he was back again and, looking a bit sheepish, told me that he would like to change his paper topic. Coprolites had not turned out to be what he had thought they were. This student is not alone, for as coprolite specialist Karl Reinhard observes, "analysts generally don't last long in this specialty."[21] Coprolites— ancient feces that have been preserved by drying or mineralization —offer excellent evidence about the diet of prehistoric populations. Reinhard takes a small specimen from a coprolite, rehydrates it, and uses microscopic techniques to study the remains of someone's prehistoric meal.

In recent decades, Reinhard has studied coprolites from the southwestern United States in the region occupied by the Anasazi—or the Ancestral Pueblo culture—from about 1200 BC onward. They ate a mixed hunter-gatherer and agricultural diet that was primarily herbivorous. Wild plants were well represented, as were protein residues from animals such as rabbits, pronghorn, and bighorn sheep. Insects, lizards, and snakes apparently were favorite snacks. Such findings, while interesting, tend not to make the news. Even the remarkable finding of a deer vertebra, one inch in diameter, within an Ancestral Pueblo coprolite didn't make the *New York Times*.

Reinhard recalls how in 1997 a specimen, resembling a tan cylinder of dirt, arrived in his lab: "The coprolite was unremarkable —it was actually a little disappointing." This particular coprolite, from a site called Cowboy Wash, was disappointing because it contained none of the foods typically eaten by the Ancestral Pueblo people, as reflected across hundreds of coprolites from some half-dozen sites. Instead, this fecal sample reflected a meat-only meal—something unheard of, notes Reinhard, in the context of Ancestral Pueblo coprolite analysis. Clearly a scientist enthralled with his work, Reinhard comments, "I have analyzed hundreds of

Ancestral and pre-Ancestral Pueblo coprolites that were more interesting." Where were the tiny seeds to be identified species by species? Where were the fibrous vegetable residues? Where were the itsy-bitsy bone fragments from small rodents, lizards, or birds? Reinhard concluded that this boring, atypical coprolite probably was not of Ancestral Pueblo origin at all: "The complete lack of plant matter in the Cowboy Wash coprolite tells me that it was not from an individual who observed the Ancestral Pueblo dietary tradition."[22]

The coprolite then made its way to a different university, where some of Reinhard's colleagues, using a new biochemical technique, discovered that it contained the remains of digested human flesh. Their scientific report appeared in the journal *Nature* and was followed by articles in *Discover, The New Yorker*, and *Smithsonian* magazines, among many others. Reinhard called it "a media feeding frenzy."[23] Cannibalism—even very old cannibalism—was big news. The press ate it up. Reinhard observes, apparently with some frustration, that some journalists opted for the sensationalistic slant that a people once thought to be relatively peaceful were revealed actually to have been cannibals. Hobbes was right all along!

The scientific record shows hundreds of coprolites from a prehistoric society that display no evidence of cannibalism—and one that does. Does proclaiming the Ancestral Pueblo people to have been cannibals on the basis of one piece of evidence make sense? Such a conclusion is akin to calling Wisconsin residents cannibals on the basis of what was found in Jeffrey Dahmer's freezer. A likely possibility is that the coprolite from Cowboy Wash, lying at the edge of this society's domain, contains the remains of Ancestral Pueblo people massacred and eaten by cultural outsiders.

Most journalists were uninterested in publishing Reinhard's experience-based assessment that the coprolite was not of Ancestral Pueblo origin. Reinhard concludes: "I have looked at more Ancestral Pueblo feces than any other human being, and I do have an opinion: The Ancestral Pueblo were not cannibalistic."[24]

Assumptions Come Tumbling Down

> Now Jericho was shut up inside and out because of the Israelites; no one came out and no one went in. . . . As soon as the people heard the sound of the trumpets, they raised a great shout, and the wall fell down flat; so the people charged straight ahead into the city and captured it. Then they devoted to destruction by the edge of the sword all in the city, both men and women, young and old, oxen, sheep, and donkeys. (Joshua 6:1, 20–21)

The famous walls of Jericho have been generally accepted as the first clear evidence of warfare, dating from 9,000 to 9,500 years ago. However, accepting this apparently obvious interpretation may be jumping the gun. Marilyn Roper provides a thorough consideration of the famous walls, and by the end of her discussion she has, like a good defense attorney, cast a shadow of doubt on their supposed military function. Her central observation is that absolutely no other indications of war are present besides three so-called fortifications: the walls themselves, a so-called moat, and a tower. There are no indications of war injuries among the skeletal remains. There is no evidence of major fires having destroyed the village. There is no evidence of a rapid change of artifacts reflecting an invasion of the village. Furthermore, five other sites in the region dating from the same time period have no walls around them. This observation raises a question: If there had been a threat of warfare in the region, why would only Jericho have fortifications? Moreover, there is no archaeological evidence of the existence of a plausible enemy having been in the region at the time when the walls were constructed. Roper also points out that the so-called moat didn't actually surround the site.[25] Why construct a partial moat? The walls themselves also may not have gone the full circumference of the site, but the subsequent construction of a road on one side of the village obscures the definitive answer to this question.

C. Richards challenges Roper for even questioning the accepted military explanation of Jericho's walls: "It seems to me that the burden of proof should be on those who think there was NO early warfare, rather than the reverse. . . . All this contradicts the principle of parsimony. Why strain and resort to complex explanations when there is a simpler one—warfare?"[26]

Two ideas come to mind. First, we have just considered how several simple, or "obvious," explanations have tumbled in the face of more sophisticated analyses of the evidence. Thus the *simple* explanation for the walls of Jericho, warfare, may not be the *correct* explanation. Second, in light of our consideration of how implicit assumptions about the nature of humanity may affect interpretations of the past—remember Dart—another comment by Richards hints at a similar connection: "Man has fought for so many varied reasons that it is highly risky to overlook or reject outright the possibility of some built-in tendency toward war in man's genes or in some universal characteristic of human life such as long dependency, the frustrations of social living, and so on."[27]

Such beliefs may predispose Richards toward seeing evidence of war in the walls of Jericho.

If we open our minds to the possibility that the large, solid walls at Jericho might not be fortifications, then we are left with a critical question: Why were they built? Ofer Bar-Yosef asked exactly this question and came up with what at first sounds like a truly crazy idea.[28] Remembering, however, that the now accepted idea of continental drift also seemed totally bizarre when it was first suggested, let's humor Bar-Yosef for the moment. Bar-Yosef turned his eye to the physical geography and climatology of the famous site. He observed that other archeological sites in the region, when located near streambeds called *wadis*, were partially or entirely covered with accumulated debris from flooding, mudflows, or sheetwash. So was Jericho.

Wadis are similar to the arroyos of the southwestern United States. They are dry most of the time but can flash-flood during downpours in the rainy season, moving tons of sand, rock, and silt to downstream locations. Bar-Yosef observed that Jericho is located on a sloping plain, and that Wadi el-Mafjar descends from the hills into a drainage basin close to the Jericho site. Climatological indicators suggest the seventh millennium BC was wetter than today, and additionally, Bar-Yosef writes, "that the wadis of the region once carried more water than they do today seems obvious from the erosion reported by Kenyon [an excavator of Jericho in the 1950s] on the northern edge of the [Jericho] mound."[29]

Bar-Yosef points out that if one supposes the walls to have been built as fortifications, then several nagging, unanswered questions present themselves. As debris gradually accumulated both inside and outside the Jericho walls while the site was inhabited—thus making the walls easily scalable by supposed enemies—why didn't the inhabitants immediately build the walls higher or remove the debris from outside the wall to keep the defenses effective against possible foes? If there was a threat of attack, then why were no other sites in the region fortified until a couple of millennia after the Jericho walls were built? In other words, why would Jericho be the only settlement in the region fearful of enemy attack? Why would a tower be constructed *inside* the wall in such a way as to preclude using it to protect the wall from attackers, rather than as part of the wall's fortifications? On the other hand, once the assumption that the walls served a military purpose is lifted, answers to the foregoing questions become clear.

"Given all the available data," concludes Bar-Yosef, "it seems that a plausible alternative interpretation for the Neolithic walls of Jericho is that they were built in stages as a defense system against floods and mudflows. . . . [The response of the inhabitants] was to build a wall and then, when necessary, dig a ditch."[30] While the jury is still out, the flood control explanation seems to account for the data more thoroughly than the fortification explanation. In light of Roper's questioning and Bar-Yosef's reevaluation of the facts, the fortification explanation may be yet another example of how the past has been "violencified," rather than "pacified," by interpretations that rest more on assumption and speculation than a careful analysis of the data. We next will question the assumption that warfare is extremely ancient—that "there always has been war"—not only by looking carefully at the earliest evidence of warfare, but also by reviewing several archaeological sequences that show how war has originated in particular locations.

5

The Earliest Evidence of War

"For what a man more likes to be true, he more readily believes," wrote Francis Bacon (1561–1626). We researchers resist this natural tendency; we do not try to "discover" or "scientifically prove" preconceived notions, to find what we like to be true. . . . We seek evidence, hard evidence.

—LYNN MARGULIS, "SCIENCE: THE REBEL EDUCATOR"

In *Demonic Males*, Richard Wrangham and Dale Peterson attempt to convince their readers that human and chimpanzee violence stem directly from an ancestral ape common to both species. They propose that human males are violent by temperament and that modern humans are "the dazed survivors of a continuous, 5-million-year habit of lethal aggression." Later they suggest, "This notion of the violent male seems reasonable to anyone familiar with crime statistics, and explains why we can't find paradise on earth." Wrangham and Peterson are linking two propositions. The first proposition, that human males engage in severe physical aggression on the average more than do human females, is supported by much evidence, including crime statistics from diverse countries. However, Wrangham and Peterson's second proposition regarding the absence of "paradise," or, more precisely, that "neither in history nor around the globe today is there evidence of a truly peaceful society," *is simply false.*[1]

This second proposition is contradicted, as we have seen, by the existence of numerous nonwarring societies (see Appendix 2) and also by internally peaceful societies such as the Paliyan.[2] Additionally, there are problems of logic here—as becomes apparent if we consider an analogy involving female and male height. The evidence showing that within given societies males are taller on the average than females cannot be used as an argument that societies with relatively short people do not exist. That is, evidence of sex differences *within* societies (for example, height or crime rates) does not in and of itself speak to the amount of variability (in height or crime rates) that exists *among* societies. Sex differences in male and female height no more demonstrate that Efe pygmies do not exist than sex differences in male and female crime rates demonstrate that peaceful societies do not exist. This point is illustrated visually in Figure 5.1.

Exaggerating War

Wrangham and Peterson are aware that the existence of nonwarring and nonviolent societies contradict their assertions about five million years of lethal aggression, a violent male temperament, and the "ubiquity of warfare and violence across time and space." Their solution to this mismatch between the anthropological evidence and their views is to deny the data. As Johan van der Dennen writes, "Peaceable preindustrial people constitute a nuisance to most theories of warfare, and they are thus either 'explained away,' denied, or negated."[3]

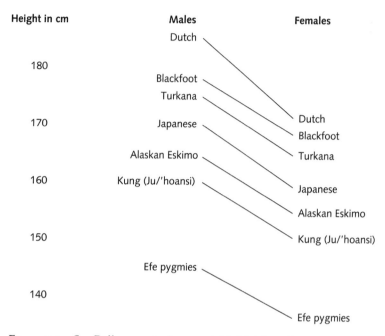

Figure 5.1   Sex Differences in Average Adult Height in Representative Populations

Adult height is affected by a number of interacting variables, including genetics, hormones, disease, and diet. Across many societies, a recurring pattern is evident: the male average height is greater than the female average height. This does not mean, of course, that every woman in a given population is shorter than every man. The figure shows that average height differences also occur from one population to the next for both males and females. The figure illustrates visually that it is illogical to conclude on the basis of sex differences in average stature that recur across populations that relatively short-statured populations, such as the Efe pygmies, do not exist. Likewise, it is illogical to conclude that populations with extremely low homicide rates, such as the Semai or Norwegians, do not exist based on sex differences in committing homicide.

Sources: Paul Jamison, "Anthropometric variation," in P. Jamison, S. Zegura, and F. Milan (eds.), *Eskimos of Northwestern Alaska: A Biological Perspective* (Stroudsburg, Penn.: Dowden, Hutchinson, and Ross, 1978), 40–78, Table 4.1; Sara Stinson, "Growth variation: Biological and cultural factors," in S. Stinson, B. Bogin, R. Huss-Ashmore, and D. O'Rourke (eds.), *Human Biology: An Evolutionary and Biocultural Perspective* (New York: Wiley-Liss, 2000), 425–64, Figure 12.1.

What is the oldest archaeological evidence of war? Wrangham and Peterson are unable to cite any archaeological evidence to substantiate their belief that warfare is millions of years old. If we turn to the facts, worldwide the archaeological site with the earliest indications of *possible* war or feuding is a cemetery dated at 12,000–14,000 years ago. Excavations of this ancient burial site, Jebel Sahaba in Sudanese Nubia near the Nile, revealed that twenty-four out of fifty-nine skeletons showed evidence of violence. This is a very high percentage of violent deaths in a skeletal population, and some scholars attribute it to warfare or feuding, while others caution that homicides and executions also could account for the violent deaths. Thus the evidence of war from this site is ambiguous. Clearly, all the deaths did not occur on a single occasion. The next earliest indications of warfare, including the ambiguous walls of Jericho, are more recent than 10,000 years ago.[4]

After reviewing the archaeological evidence on prehistoric homicides and warfare, Lawrence Keeley reaches the conclusion "that homicide has been practiced since the appearance of modern humankind and that warfare is documented in the archaeological record of the past 10,000 years in every well-studied region." I would not be surprised if occasional homicides occurred long before the emergence of modern humans. In fact, Marilyn Roper's review of published sources suggests that homicides did occur even before modern humans arrived on the scene some 40,000 to 50,000 years ago.[5]

Our current focus, however, is on the antiquity of *warfare*, not the antiquity of murder. Keith Otterbein points out that Keeley, under the heading "Prehistoric War," includes archaeological instances of homicide and "violent death" (a rather ambiguous term) along with the evidence for warfare. In other words, many of the examples Keeley mentions under the label "Prehistoric War" actually do not pertain to war at all. Otterbein criticizes Keeley for surreptitiously shifting concepts: "I object to sliding from 'violent death' in the Paleolithic to 'warfare' in the Late Paleolithic without comment upon his changing use of terminology." Furthermore, pertaining to the same section of Keeley's book, Raymond Kelly questions Keeley's assertion that certain European mass burials were probably the result of war. "In winter there is no inducement to prompt burial, especially during a time of general illness and famine. . . . Multiple burials should not be interpreted as evidence of war unless skeletal indications of trauma or proximate projectile points support this."[6]

In sum, Keeley intermingles archaeological examples of individual homicides, sometimes ambiguous cases of "violent death," and perhaps even nonviolent deaths due to starvation and disease with the archaeological examples of warfare, all under the heading "Prehistoric War." This creates an impression that there is more and older evidence for warfare than actually exists. However, despite this unfortunate exaggeration of warfare—and this is really the crucial point—Keeley finds no solid evidence of warfare, anywhere in the world, older than about 10,000 years before the present (BP in archaeological lingo).

The archaeological record yields additional important data related to the first evidence of warfare, namely, insights about the development of social systems. Simple hunter-gatherer band societies are nomadic and egalitarian; they lack ranked social hierarchies and well-defined position of leadership or authority. By contrast, complex hunter-gatherers have partially or totally given up the nomadic lifestyle and "may exhibit elaborate economic and political status-differentiation systems, including rank distinctions and chiefs."[7]

Evidence suggests that the simple tends to precede the complex, and archaeologically speaking, complexity is very recent. Bruce Knauft explains: "Complex hunter-gatherers were most common after 12,500 BP, usually transitional between simple hunter-gathering and agricultural systems." This observation is of central importance as we consider the origin of war, for it makes little sense to talk about war divorced from social organization.[8] As we will see in the next chapter, warfare is rare among simple egalitarian hunter-gatherers and pervasive among complex hunter-gatherer societies.[9]

So, broadly speaking, the archaeological record shows a recurrent pattern. The nomadic hunter-gatherer band was *the* form of human social organization until just before the agricultural revolution.[10] However, agriculture didn't just appear overnight and then spread instantly to all corners of the globe. Whereas the development of agriculture is correctly heralded as a landmark in world prehistory, bringing innumerable changes to the human species, the pre-agricultural revolution, the emergence of complex hunter-gathering societies in some places, also was a monumental transformation in human existence.[11] Donald Henry comments on the magnitude of the change from a simple nomadic existence to a settled pattern of complex hunting and gathering:

> The replacement of simple hunting-gathering societies composed of small, highly mobile, materially impoverished, egalitarian groups by a society that was characterized by large, sedentary, materially rich and socially stratified communities represented a dramatic shift from an adaptive system that had enjoyed several million years of success.[12]

The shift thus involved many interrelated changes in the way people lived. The typical archaeological signs of social complexity include higher population density than among simple hunter-gatherers, larger settlement size, and the presence of permanent shelters and ceremonial areas. Variability in burial features indicates that a social hierarchy existed, as high-status individuals were entombed in more elaborate ways than commoners.[13]

No War, Some War, Lots of War

Maschner reports an archaeological time sequence for the Northwest Coast of North America. Starting at about 5,000 years ago and continuing for at least a couple of millennia, the skeletal evidence of aggression consists almost exclusively of nonlethal injuries—and there are not many of these. Given the lack of archaeological signs of warfare and the nonlethality and rarity of the injuries themselves, an apt interpretation is that some interpersonal aggression, perhaps in the form of contests, was occurring. Warfare clearly appears later in this particular prehistoric sequence, corresponding with certain social changes toward complexity, and large-scale war is evident only in the last 1,800–1,500 years before the present. "The first large villages appear, status differences become apparent, a heavy emphasis on marine subsistence develops, and warfare becomes visible in the archaeological record."[14]

Another prehistoric sequence speaks with the same tongue. In the Near East, between 12,000 and 10,000 BP hunting-and-gathering subsistence patterns gave way to a new economy based on plant and animal domestication. The archaeological record shows no evidence of war at 12,000 BP and then evidence for sparse war by about 9500 BP, followed by evidence of spreading and intensifying warfare in more recent times. Different sets of clues —the nature of living sites, human skeletal remains, and cultural sequence data—show this development of warfare over several millennia in this region.[15]

At the early stages, for instance, occupation sites were out in the open and defensive structures were lacking. This suggests the absence of war. At the intermediate stages, an increasing number of sites show walls and ditches, some of which certainly related to defense. At later stages, ending about 7,000 years ago, the presence of defensive structures at certain sites along a major trade route is indisputable.[16] The skeletal remains show a corresponding sequence over these millennia, beginning with a few isolated instances of skeletal damage and ending with clear evidence of village massacres. Many kinds of archaeological evidence indubitably show warfare after 7000 BP. For example, a military garrison indicates the presence of professional warriors, a feature associated with a well-developed sociopolitical hierarchy. In subsequent millennia, warfare in the Near East became all the more prevalent, and fortifications became "the rule rather than the exception."[17]

Environmental Stress and the Birth of Anasazi War

The Anasazi, or Ancestral Pueblo, were the prehistoric ancestors of the current Pueblo people of the American Southwest. Jonathan Haas explains that "the chronological, palaeo-environmental and archaeological records from the south-west provide a level of detail that allows us to see both the presence and absence of prehistoric warfare, and to examine closely the causes, nature and evolution of warfare on local and regional levels."[18] The transition from nomadic foraging to settled farming took place gradually. The archaeological evidence between AD 700 and about AD 1200 shows absolutely no signs of warfare.[19] Beginning about AD 1150, the climate in this area began to change and the environment deteriorated. By AD 1260, the evidence of warfare is unmistakable. Arrowheads pierce skeletons, skeletons lack skulls, and skulls lack skeletons. Some villages have been destroyed, others have constructed protective palisades, and still others have moved to highly defensible locations.

> Anasazi co-existed peacefully with culturally different groups around their borders for more than a thousand years, and within the Anasazi culture area, ethnically distinct groups lived side by side for centuries, generation after generation, with absolutely no signs of organized conflict or war. The violence markers of raiding, killing, and burning appear only very late in Anasazi culture, as a complex response to changing demographic patterns and a prolonged period of severe environmental stress.[20]

Ancient Oaxaca: From Nomadic Foraging to Warring State

Kent Flannery and Joyce Marcus report no evidence for group conflict among the small nomadic bands that foraged in the Valley of Oaxaca in southern Mexico between 10,000 and 4000 BP. Toward the end of this period, the transition from hunting and gathering to sedentary villages was under way. By 2800 to 2450 BP, three rival chiefly centers existed in the Valley of Oaxaca, buffered from each other by unoccupied zones. Near the end of this period, one center, San José Mogote, was attacked and its main temple burned. The survivors relocated to the mountaintop called Monte Albán (Figure 5.2) and began constructing defensive walls, some 3 kilometers in length. Monte Albán was to become the capital of the Zapotec state. This state waged war with a professional army and by about 1700 BP had expanded its domain some 150 kilometers beyond the Valley of Oaxaca.[21]

Figure 5.2   By the time of Christ, Zapotec civilization was already flourishing in the Oaxacan highlands of Mexico. The capital of the ancient state, Monte Albán, was built in an easily defensible location on a string of three mountaintops that command spectacular views in all directions. Monte Albán's main plaza includes many temples, a large ball court, subterranean passageways, and a distinct arrow-shaped building, shown here, which may have had important astronomical purposes. (D. P. Fry photo collection.)

The foregoing archaeological time sequences illustrate how warfare may originate in particular areas and increase along with the development of sociopolitical complexity. These sequences show a recurring pattern. First, among simple nomadic foragers there is no archaeological evidence for warfare. Then, as some hunter-gatherer societies make changes toward increasing complexity, sometimes, but not always, warfare makes an appearance in the archaeological record.[22] With the development of states, the archaeological record often shows increases in the frequency and intensification of war, a phenomenon that may be exacerbated by population pressures or environmental change.

Specialists who have evaluated the archaeological evidence regarding warfare have reached similar conclusions. Recall that Keeley, who is emphasizing warfare, pins down the time frame for warfare as within the last 10,000 years.[23] Haas concurs: "Archaeologically, there is negligible evidence for any kind of warfare anywhere in the world before about 10,000 years ago."[24]

In Figure 5.3, the oldest evidence for warfare is put in time perspective. Clearly, war is a very recent development. The archeological record documents that war becomes more frequent and intensifies with the development of the state level of sociopolitical organization, beginning a mere 5,000 to 6,000 years ago.

Regarding the lack of any indications of warfare in the archaeological record much beyond the 10,000-year mark, it has sometimes been said that the absence of evidence is not evidence of absence. However, as archaeological data have accumulated from many corners of the world, it is now clear that warfare does leave definite marks.[25] Brian Ferguson observes: "Where a cultural tradition is known from many sites and skeletons, absence of any

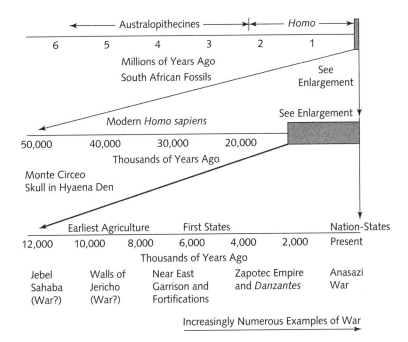

Figure 5.3   War and the Evolutionary Timeline

Lawrence Keeley is correct when he points out that some war existed before civilization, that is, before the development of states. However, when viewed in the time frame of human evolution, civilization is an extremely recent development (dating from only 6,000 years ago at the earliest). Human precursors within the genus *Australopithecus* are 5 million to 6 million years old. With relatively small brains, the australopithecines walked erect on two legs. The genus *Homo* is about 2 million years old and shows an increased brain-size-to-body-size ratio over time, the first evidence of stone tool manufacture, and the first controlled use of fire. The species *Homo erectus* preceded *Homo sapiens* in time. Archaic *Homo sapiens* dates from at least 200,000 years ago, while anatomically modern *Homo sapiens* (modern humans) appears in the archaeological record only in the last 40,000 to 50,000 years. Agriculture was developed during the last 10,000 years, the period corresponding with the first archaeological indications of warfare. The first states, early civilizations, appeared about 5000 to 6000 BP (3000 to 4000 BC). From this period onward, there are ample examples of warfare in the archaeological record. The rest of the story, literally, is history—and thus archaeologically very recent.

sort of evidence suggesting war can indeed be taken as reasonable evidence of war's absence."[26] Furthermore, as we have just considered, many areas show the clear sequential development of war over time. Unambiguous fortifications around settlements, specialized weapons such as clubs and daggers not used for hunting, depictions of martial scenes in artwork, a substantial number of burials with projectile points either embedded in the bones or else lying within the frames of skeletons, evidence of massive fires followed by a change in cultural artifacts, a reduced number of male remains buried in cemeteries (suggesting significant male death elsewhere), and repetition of such findings across the archaeological sites of an area—these and other indicators show the presence of warfare. And when multiple lines of evidence point in the same direction, we can be fairly certain that warfare was occurring.

Knowing that warfare leaves an archaeological trail means that when we have an archaeological record with no indicators of warfare, this information tells us something meaningful as well. Ferguson points out, "If we were talking about anything less ideologically weighted than war, such as the origin of agriculture or settled village living, no one would take seriously a claim that such *might* have existed in distant millennia. The time of origin would be simply, uncontroversially fixed at the point of the earliest evidence."[27]

Aside from what the archaeological record tells us, there also is a series of compelling, logical reasons to explain why warfare was a rare anomaly during all but the last tiny fraction of human prehistory. For one thing, the social organization of simple nomadic hunter-gatherers, the only form of social organization for the vast majority of human prehistory, is simply not conducive to making war. As we will consider in the next chapter, an association between warfare and the complexity of social organization has been replicated in many cross-cultural studies.[28] We also have just seen how prehistoric archaeological sequences from around the world show that war and social complexity go hand in hand. In coming chapters, we will explore in greater detail why the paucity of warfare prior to the agricultural revolution should be no surprise based on what we know about nomadic hunter-gatherer social organization and lifestyle.

The archaeological sequences that we have just considered show that *beliefs* about warfare being very ancient are not linked very closely to the observable *evidence*. Cultural belief systems include presuppositions about human nature. Consequently, beliefs that war is an intrinsic part of human nature, that humans are naturally aggressive or have instincts for war, and the like tend to be accepted as part of a cultural belief system. However, turning to facts, a careful examination of cross-cultural data in Chapters 2 and 3 showed that warfare, while common in recent centuries, is not a cultural universal. In actuality, many nonwarring cultures exist (Appendix 2). Similarly, the belief that "there always has been war" does not correspond with the archaeological facts of the matter. The earliest unambiguous evidence of warfare dates from less than 10,000 years ago, and war becomes more common with the rise of the state several millennia later. After reviewing the archaeological record, Leslie Sponsel reaches the conclusion that "during the hunter-gatherer stage of cultural evolution, which dominated 99 percent of human existence on the planet . . . lack of archaeological evidence for warfare suggests that it was *rare or absent for most of human prehistory.*"[29] Keeley might see Sponsel as attempting to pacify the past, but on the other hand, recall that Keeley exaggerated the evidence for warfare by including, along with prehistoric war, cases of homicide and some other questionable examples. When it comes down to the actual archaeological evidence, however, Keeley acknowledges the very recent time frame for warfare.[30] Sponsel's conclusion about the rarity or absence of warfare for most of prehistory, while perhaps contradicting popular beliefs as to the great antiquity of war, nonetheless is in accordance with the archaeological facts.

6

War and Social Organization: From Nomadic Bands to Modern States

The Batek abhor interpersonal violence and have generally fled from their enemies rather than fighting back. I once asked a Batek man why their ancestors had not shot the Malay slave-raiders, who plagued them until the 1920s . . . with poisoned blowpipe darts. His shocked answer was: "Because it would kill them!"

—KIRK ENDICOTT, "PROPERTY, POWER AND CONFLICT AMONG THE BATEK OF MALAYSIA"

In the midst of World War II, Quincy Wright published a magnum opus called *The Study of War*. The two-volume work, totaling well over a thousand pages, draws on information from fields as diverse as psychology, sociology, anthropology, history, and political science, as well as Wright's own discipline, international law. In considering anthropological data, Wright and his team of assistants used a large cross-cultural, worldwide sample.[1]

Wright was able to rate the vast majority of the societies, 590 in all, regarding warfare.[2] Thirty societies (5 percent of the total) were found to lack warfare: The literature revealed no evidence of warfare, no military organization, and no special weapons. Another 346 societies (59 percent of the sample) were rated "to be unwarlike or to engage only in mild warfare," provided that "no indication was found of fighting for definite economic or political purposes in the more specialized literature."[3] Combining these two groups leads to the observation that nearly two-thirds of this large worldwide sample (64 percent) are nonwarring or mild-warring. This is no trivial observation. According to Wright, the rest of the societies engage in war for economic or political purposes (29 percent and 7 percent, respectively).

It is also important that a substantial number of the unwarlike groups engaged in nothing more than feuding. If we conceptually untangle feuding from warring—as I've argued we should—then the societies that Wright coded as unwarlike based solely on descriptions of feuding should more appropriately be thought of as nonwarring. But putting this issue aside for the time being, Wright's findings make a very important point: *War is either lacking or mild in the majority of cultures. The cross-cultural picture is not nearly as Hobbesian as is often assumed.*

And there is more to this story. The classification scheme that Wright devised incorporates the term *war* into all possible categories. Thus the societies determined by Wright to have no war are referred to by the label "defensive war." The societies defined as unwarlike or having only mild warfare (which amounts, again, to nothing more than feuding in some cases) are classified under the label "social war." The "social war" category is a mixed bag of small-scale night raids, blood-revenge expeditions, headhunting parties, individual duels or contests, and pitched battles. In other words, "social war" clearly catches feuds as well as war and perhaps also encompasses revenge homicides and juridical contests, the latter being, in reality, a mechanism for resolving conflict. The meanings of Wright's remaining two categories of war are more straightforward: "Economic war" entails economic objectives, military training, and mass tactics, and "political war" has political aims, usually sought through the use of standing armies. The main point is that Wright's labeling scheme manages to include all 590 societies under the war umbrella. Readers must study the fine print, so to speak, in a footnote to get a detailed description of what the categories of warfare actually entail.[4]

How does Wright justify putting the label "defensive war" on societies that are described as lacking warfare and feuding? Wright writes, "These people have no military organization or military weapons and do not fight unless actually attacked, in which case they make spontaneous use of available tools and hunting weapons to defend themselves but regard this necessity as a misfortune."[5] At first, this reasoning may sound plausible, but Wright presents no actual evidence of defensive fighting having occurred in any of the nonwarring societies on his list. Wright seems to have overlooked the possibility that a group might flee or move away if attacked, rather than fight back.

Could Wright's "defensive war" category stem more from an assumption about what nonwarring peoples might do if attacked than from what the evidence shows nonwarring peoples to typically do? If we turn to ethnographic reports on the societies to which Wright applies the defensive war classification, such as the Semang, Jakun, Kubu, Batua (Batwa), and "Sakai" societies (such as the Semai), the typical pattern is one of avoidance and retreat, not defensive fighting.[6] The Greenland Inuit bands, another group classified by Wright as engaging in defensive war, lived within a nonwarring social system and had no need to defend themselves or to flee.[7] Additionally, avoidance and retreat have been reported for many other societies, most of them bands or tribes, including the Aweikoma, Buid, Chewong, Dorobo, Guayaki, Jahai, Northeastern Dene societies (such as the Hare, Dogrib, Yellowknife, Chipewyan, and Slavey), Panare, Shoshone, Siriono, and Wáiwai, among others.[8]

In Western thinking, it may be cowardly to flee from danger, but not all peoples think like Westerners. Fleeing is often seen as simply sensible.[9] Belief systems differ regarding the value placed on fighting or fleeing and also regarding the acceptability of violence. Recall the words of a Batek hunter quoted in the chapter epigraph —he was shocked at the question as to why poisoned blowpipe darts had not been used against slave raiders (see Figure 6.1). Additionally, whereas Westerners come from an agricultural tradition associated with defending particular pieces of land, many other societies do not. Moving away may involve a consciously chosen and sensible alternative to fighting. My point is not that non-warring groups *never* defend themselves if attacked, but rather that Wright greatly overemphasized this aggressive response, probably based on his own Western assumptions, when he created the category "defensive war" and then put all nonwarring societies into the category.[10] An examination of the ethnographic record does not support the viability of this assumption.

To recap, despite Wright's use of labels that imply some kind of warfare in all 590 societies, a closer look at the categories reveals that by Wright's own definitions, 64 percent of the cross-cultural sample are nonwarring or unwarlike. *Wright's findings show the cross-cultural spectrum of human societies to be much less warlike than typically assumed.* This important observation has hardly received any attention, perhaps in part because it was immediately obscured by Wright's labeling of *all* societies as practicing war.

Figure 6.1   The fluctuating nature of forager band composition applies to the Batek of Malaysia. The photo shows a family building a raft in 1981. The Batek use blowpipes and poison darts to hunt, but do not use these weapons against people. (Photo courtesy of Kirk Endicott.)

Social Organization

Social organization must be taken into consideration by anyone who is interested in the origin of war, the pursuit of human justice, or conflict management. From one society to the next, types of violence and approaches to conflict management vary in relation to social organization. The range of human social organization can be divided into four basic types: bands, tribes, chiefdoms, and states.[11]

Bands are small in size, generally with about twenty-five to fifty members; they are politically egalitarian, lack clear leadership, are nomadic or semi-nomadic, and engage in hunting and gathering as a way of making their living. The Siriono and the Paliyan, described in Chapter 3, are band societies. Individuals shift readily among different bands. Consequently, anthropologists refer to band composition as flexible and in flux. Additionally, band society lacks ranked statuses or classes and tends not to be subdivided into subgroups—social segments—on the basis of kinship or other distinctions. As we shall soon see, this last point, although often ignored, is of critical importance in understanding patterns of human aggressive behavior, including warfare. Nomadic, egalitarian hunter-gatherer band society is the oldest and simplest form of human social organization, extending back over humanity's evolutionary past. Anthropologists often note that members of the human line have spent over 99 percent of their existence on the planet living in nomadic bands. Before assuming that the evolutionary past was rife with warfare, it would be logical to first take a look at conflict patterns in band society.

Tribes tend to be sedentary and typically engage in horticulture or herding. Tribal settlements may contain a hundred or more people. Although headmen, big men, and other leadership roles tend to emerge in tribal societies, the leadership is weak. Tribal leaders attempt to exert their will through the art of persuasion and by leading through example, since they lack, for the most part, other forms of coercive power. Christopher Boehm uses the term *acephalous* (literally "headless") to reflect the lack of authority among tribal leaders. Headmen among the South American Yanomamö, for example, typify this pattern of weak leadership. The absence of positions of strong authority really means that tribal social organization remains largely egalitarian. Unlike bands, however, tribes tend to be segmented politically into lineages (societal subgroups with membership based on descent from a common ancestor), clans, or other such kinship distinctions. Evolutionarily, sedentary horticultural tribes represent a recent form of social organization compared to nomadic hunter-gatherer bands.

Chiefdoms exhibit considerable variability, although the existence of a social hierarchy is a distinguishing feature. Some chiefdoms vest minor authority in the chiefs, whereas in other cases chiefs wield considerable power. Chiefs are entitled to special privileges. Commoners pay tribute to chiefs, some of which the chiefs then redistribute back to their subjects. The economies of chiefdoms often are based on farming or fishing.

Complex sedentary hunter-gatherers are socially ranked societies with rulers and commoners, and sometimes slaves as well. They are chiefdoms. It is absolutely critical not to confuse complex sedentary hunter-gatherers with nomadic hunter-gatherer bands. These types of societies are as different as night and day. Complex hunter-gatherers exploit rich natural resources such as the salmon runs of the North American Northwest Coast. Population densities tend to be higher than in nomadic hunter-gatherer societies. Ethnographically, complex hunter-gatherers are very rare. Archaeological evidence shows the development of complex sedentary hunter-gatherer social organization to be recent, arising in particular places only within the last 25,000 years, yet most typically within the last 13,000 years or so.[12]

As recently as 5,000 to 6,000 years ago some early chiefdoms underwent further organizational transformations, and the world's first states were born. In the evolutionary history of the human species, this development of civilizations occurred only "yesterday."

The economy of states rests on agriculture. Typically, the rulers wield even more coercive power than do chiefs. Economic specialization, social class distinctions, centralized political and military organization, the use of writing and mathematics, urbanization, large-scale irrigation of crops, and the development of bureaucracy characterize states, ancient and modern. Boehm notes that "modern democracies may temper individual power with checks and balances, but centralized power still exists and is backed by coercive force supplied by professional policemen and soldiers."[13]

To summarize, in bands and tribes, leadership and political power are weak and dispersed, or uncentralized. By contrast, in chiefdoms and especially in states, political power is centralized at the top of a social hierarchy. Social relations in bands and tribes are relatively egalitarian compared to those within chiefdoms and states that are structured according to ranks or social classes. Relatedly, hunting-and-gathering societies are of two general types: Simple nomadic hunter-gatherers have the band type of social organization and are egalitarian, whereas complex sedentary hunter-gatherers are small-scale chiefdoms with social classes or status hierarchies.[14]

The Link Between Warfare and Social Organization

Approximately half the nonwarring cultures listed in Appendix 2 are hunter-gatherer band societies. This observation raises a question: Is the presence or absence of warfare related to social organization? A number of studies suggests that the answer is yes. Sociopolitical complexity and warfare do go hand in hand. After reviewing cross-cultural studies on this topic, Johan van der Dennen summarizes that "one of the most consistent and robust findings is the correlation between 'primitivity' and absence of war or low-level warfare, or in other words, the correlation between war and civilization." Reading the trends in the worldwide archaeological record, Jonathan Haas correspondingly concludes that "the level, intensity, and impact of warfare tend to increase as cultural systems become more complex."[15]

Even when aggression occurs in band society, it is relatively harmless. People sometimes fight, but grudges are personal affairs. In bands, most fighting is between individuals and nonlethal, although killings can occur. Violence, notes S. P. Reyna, is relatively ineffective for controlling people within the egalitarian band.[16] Turning to tribes, Reyna points out that aggression still stems from personal grudges, but now can involve kin militias, fighting groups that are temporarily assembled on the basis of kinship ties. In tribal societies, there are no professional standing armies and no hierarchical military structures. Fighting most often involves brawls and raids, and less often small-scale battles.

Reyna writes of tribes that "the organized means of violence in such polities, though more effective than those found in bands, were still harmless when compared to those found in centralized polities." For example, when the tribal Yanomamö go on a raid, no one has the power to command obedience. Typically, raiders drop out and return home with excuses such as having sore feet or a stomachache. Command structure and authority are very weakly developed within tribal society.[17]

Within the centralized polities of chiefdoms, chiefly militias come into play. The leaders and military specialists have authority to command obedience from the ranks, as illustrated in large chiefdoms such as Tahiti, Tonga, Fiji, and Hawaii.[18] With chiefdoms, battles become more common than within tribal social organization.

Margaret Mead describes warfare between relatively simple village chiefdoms in the eastern part of Samoa. Surprise attacks were preferred, but arranged battles also took place. When opposing sides met in combat, each group used distinctive headbands or face paint so as to differentiate friend from foe more easily. Clubs, spears, and shields of bamboo were employed during fighting.[19]

In some large-scale chiefdoms, such as Fiji with its six social classes, warfare involved large, bloody battles. Fijian chiefs tried to put as many men into combat as possible. Although standing armies did not exist and there was no formal draft, every man was expected to fight when ordered onto the field by his chief. Robert Carneiro explains, "Warfare among the Fijians was all-out and bloody, with no respect shown for sex or age. Women and children were killed ruthlessly and indiscriminately." The status and power of a chief could rise with success in war. Commoners were allowed to feast on slain enemies, and human flesh became a favorite delicacy of some Fijian chiefs. Perhaps the all-time record was held by a chief named Ra Undreundre, whose tally of people consumed came to nine hundred.[20]

As mentioned, complex hunter-gatherers are rare, exemplified most notably by a cluster of societies situated along the North American Pacific Coast between southern Alaska and northern California, such as the Bella Coola, Haida, Klallam, Kwakiutl, Nootka, Tlingit, and Tsimshian. Elman Service explains that nature provided these "hunting-fishing societies with an abundance of food and materials perhaps unsurpassed anywhere in the world."

Figure 6.2   This drawing of a Nootka house from 1778 by John Webber shows living units for multiple families. As complex hunter-gatherers from the Northwest Coast of North America, the Nootka stored food (note the supply of dried fish hanging from the rafters), lived in villages, had chiefs, and made war. Compare this large, solid Nootka residence to the Batek hut pictured in Figure 15.1, whose small size and comparatively basic construction are features typical of shelters constructed by simple nomadic hunter-gatherers. (© 2006 Harvard University Peabody Museum, Photo 2004.24.26744.)

The complex hunter-gatherers of this cultural area shared certain features: They subsisted largely on marine resources (such as highly valued salmon runs), lived in hierarchical class societies (consisting of chiefs or nobles, commoners, and often slaves), had highly developed arts, rituals, and economies based on the redistribution of goods, and, last but not least, engaged in warfare.[21]

In this region, archaeological evidence suggests warfare over at least 3,000 years. Attacks often were carried out by sea, as raiders paddled scores or even hundreds of miles carrying their provisions with them. Brian Ferguson writes, "War parties varied in size from a few canoes to huge flotillas with many hundred men. . . . Tactics were tailored to maximize enemy casualties and captives."[22] Wars stemmed from multiple motivations such as gaining access to salmon runs, acquiring slaves, exacting revenge for past wrongs, and gaining additional territory to support expanding populations.

Readers are probably intimately familiar with the state form of social organization, because today's world is divided into nation-states. State sociopolitical organization, which most people simply take for granted, is actually an extremely recent social development. The first archaic states arose only a few thousand years ago, and the birth of the nation-state is usually attributed to the signing of the Treaty of Westphalia in AD 1648—a mere three and a half centuries ago.

States, ancient and modern, tend to have large permanent armies led by military specialists operating within hierarchical command structures.[23] Under such conditions, elaborate military campaigns and protracted wars are possible. The recent military outlay of one current nation-state, the United States, is unprecedented in the history of the world, exceeding $400 billion a year.[24] The differences in fighting tactics between bands and tribal societies and those used by even small states are immense. The tribal Yanomamö's typical tactic is for raiders to hide outside an enemy village in the predawn hours, attempt to kill some unlucky person leaving the village at daybreak, and then run for their lives.[25] But returning to the military apparatus of the state, Reyna uses a specific case to illustrate a broader idea: "Caesar's legions did not ambush a few Gauls and then run for home. Rather, they stayed for the duration—the remaining five hundred years of the empire."[26]

A Comparison of Simple and Complex Hunter-Gatherers

It is imperative to highlight differences between simple hunter-gatherers (as archetypal nomadic bands) and complex hunter-gatherers (as low-level chiefdoms). Robert Kelly notes that the image of simple hunter-gatherers entails "small, *peaceful*, nomadic bands, men and women with few possession[s] and who are equal in wealth, opportunity, and status."[27] Kelly next generalizes that "complex hunter-gatherers are non-egalitarian societies, whose elites possess slaves, *fight wars*, and overtly seek prestige."[28] Some distinguishing points are summarized in Figure 6.3. One important observation is that lumping simple and complex forager societies together and then trying to make catchall generalizations about hunter-gatherer peace and war is an undertaking that is doomed to create confusion from the get-go.[29]

I decided to test statistically the generalization that warfare occurs in complex hunter-gatherer societies more regularly than

Variable	Simple Hunter-Gatherers	Complex Hunter-Gatherers
Primary food	Terrestrial game	Marine resources or plants
Food storage	Very rare	Typical
Mobility	Nomadic or semi-nomadic	Settled or mostly settled
Population	Low population densities	Higher population densities
Political system	Egalitarian	Hierarchical with classes based on wealth or heredity
Social structure	Absence of social heredity	Lineages in some cases
Slavery	Absent	Frequent
Competition	Not accepted	Encouraged
Warfare	Rare	Common

Figure 6.3   Contrasts Between Complex and Simple Hunter-Gatherers.

Source: Adapted from Robert Kelly, *The Foraging Spectrum: Diversity in Hunter-Gatherer Lifeways* (Washington, D.C.: Smithsonian Institution Press, 1995), 294, Table 8.1.

in simple hunter-gatherer bands. Recall that a worldwide cross-cultural sample of 186 societies, the SCCS, exists. Separately, George Murdock has published coded information (ratings) for certain features of hundreds of societies, for instance, how people make a living, what type of settlements they live in, whether or not a society has a class system and if so what type, whether horses are used in the society, and so forth.[30]

If we define hunter-gatherer societies as those rated by Murdock as having at most 5 percent subsistence dependence on agriculture and animal husbandry, the SCCS contains thirty-five hunter-gatherer societies. By examining other Murdock codes, these hunter-gatherer societies can be divided into three subgroups.[31] Simple hunter-gatherers are those societies rated as nomadic or semi-nomadic, lacking domestic animals including horses, and lacking class distinctions. Complex hunter-gatherers are those rated as not being nomadic or as having social class distinctions. Equestrian hunter-gatherers, those societies relying on horses for hunting, are a third type of society of very recent origin. These ratings yield twenty-one simple hunter-gatherer societies, nine complex hunter-gatherer societies, and five equestrian hunter-gatherer societies. It is possible to use ethnographic information for each society to classify it as warring or nonwarring according to the definition of war we adopted in Chapter 2.[32]

The essential finding is that all the complex hunter-gatherers and all the equestrian hunter-gatherers make war, whereas a majority of the simple hunter-gatherers do not. Both social complexity and adoption of the horse go along with warfare. Combining the relatively small number of complex and equestrian groups together allows a statistical comparison to be made between simple nomadic hunter-gatherers versus the other types of hunter-gatherer societies, and the results are very significant (see Figure 6.4).[33]

Hunter-Gatherers	Nonwarring (13)		Warring (22)	
Simple	!Kung Hadza Mbuti Semang Vedda Tiwi Slave	Aranda Copper Eskimo Andamanese Saulteaux Paiute Yahgan	Montagnais Ingalik Botocudo Aweikoma	Gilyak Micmac . Kaska Yukaghir
Others			Bella Coola Gros Ventre Comanche Chiricahua Tehuelche Klamath Eastern Pomo	Haida Yurok Yokuts Kutenai Twana Eyak Aleut

Fisher's exact test (one-tailed) probability, p = .0001

Figure 6.4   Presence or Absence of Warfare and Type of Society

Simple nomadic hunter-gatherers are in the top row. Other types of hunter-gatherers are in the bottom row. War is defined as involving armed combat between political communities and not merely as feuding and revenge homicide (see Chapter 2). Statistically, the results are very significant.

A consideration of war intensity and severity in simple and complex hunter-gatherer societies reveals an additional intriguing pattern: Warfare among complex hunter-gatherers tends to be more serious than it is among simple hunter-gatherers. Eleanor Leacock writes of nomadic Montagnais-Naskapi bands, for example, that "warfare was minimal or nonexistent."[34] Similarly, Jules Henry's portrayal of the nomadic Aweikoma suggests more instances of murder and feuding than warfare, although Henry makes reference to ancient enemies: The Aweikoma "have no idea of coming together and forming a solid unit against an outside aggressor. For them there was safety only in wakefulness and flight. Whoever pursues them constantly has them at his mercy, for they become panic-stricken and never turn to face their pursuers until they are brought to bay like hunted animals."[35]

Regarding Gilyak bands, Lev Shternberg singles out two motivations for "war" among these simple hunter-gatherers: competition over a woman and avenging the death of a clan member. "Indeed, what the Gilyak called wars in ancient times were in fact nothing more than sporadic clan skirmishes motivated by vengeance or, even more frequently, were over women. The Gilyak have never known war as a profession."[36]

Turning to complex hunter-gatherer societies, we see, as a pattern, an increase in the severity of fighting. Murdock calls the complex hunting-and-gathering Haida "the Vikings of the coast" and reports that "they fight amongst themselves over real or fancied injuries, and they wage relentless war, partly for revenge but mainly for plunder, against the Tlingits, Tsimshian, and Bellabella." Marlene Martin reports that the Klamath—a hunter-gatherer society from Oregon and northern California that had given up nomadism, had chiefs, valued wealth, and evidenced a number of other cultural features typical of the complex hunter-gatherer societies of the Northwest Coastal region—warred for revenge, booty, and slaves. Their enemies included the Shasta, Takelma, Kalapuya, and other groups. The raiding and warring of equestrian groups such as the Comanche and Chiricahua Apache also are well known.[37]

In closing, we have a dual conclusion: Not only is war more likely to exist in complex and equestrian hunter-gatherer societies than in simple foraging bands, but also when warfare is practiced by simple nomadic foragers, it tends to be less severe than in other kinds of hunter-gatherer societies. Shortly we will see how these findings call for a revamping of some widely held assumptions about war and peace.

7

Seeking Justice: The Quest for Fairness

[Among the Omaha] this feast occurred when there had been a difference between two tribes and the chiefs wished to make peace. . . . As the guests were seen approaching, all the men who had contributed gifts mounted their horses and rode out to meet the coming tribe, charging upon them as if upon an enemy. The leader bore a pipe prepared for smoking and offered it to the leader of the guests, who, after it was lighted, accepted it. The gifts were then distributed, the feast eaten, and peace concluded between the tribes.
—ALICE FLETCHER AND FRANCIS LA FLESCHE, "THE OMAHA TRIBE"

Conflict is an inevitable feature of social life, but clearly violence is not the only option for dealing with conflict. Disputants can simply avoid each other, tolerate difficult situations, or negotiate mutually acceptable solutions. Other people very often become involved as mediators and arbitrators, judges and juries, or advisors and therapists. Although the violence of homicide, feud, and war grab our attention, an examination of cross-cultural data reveals that people usually deal with conflicts without using any violence at all. Humans have a tremendous capacity for getting along with each other peacefully, preventing physical aggression, limiting the scope and spread of violence when it does break out, and restoring peace following violence. A cross-cultural perspective reveals not

Unilateral and Bilateral Approaches

1. *Avoidance.* Disputants cease to interact or limit their interaction, either temporarily or permanently.
2. *Toleration.* The issue in dispute is ignored as the relationship is simply continued.
3. *Negotiation.* Disputants interact to form mutually acceptable compromises or solutions. Negotiation often involves the giving and accepting of compensation.
4. *Self-redress* (also called *self-help* and *coercion*). One disputant takes unilateral action in an attempt to prevail in a dispute or to punish another.

The Trilateral Approach

5. *Settlement.* A third party deals with a dispute. Settlement can take several forms, of which the following are common:

Friendly peacemaking. The third party merely separates or distracts disputants.
Mediation. The third party facilitates the negotiation process.
Arbitration. The third party renders a decision but lacks the power to enforce it.
Adjudication. The third party renders a decision and has the power to enforce it.
Repressive peacemaking. The third party uses force or the threat of force to stifle a dispute.

Figure 7.1 Major Approaches to Conflict Management

only a human capacity for war and other forms of violence, but also human potentials for seeking justice and for handling conflict nonviolently (see Figure 7.1).[1]

Negotiation often results in compromises or mutually agreeable solutions. Individuals, kin groups, and communities directly negotiate peace treaties to end personal disputes, feuds, and wars. Often one party agrees to compensate the other for damages. The Jívaro of Ecuador, famous for shrinking the heads of their victims, sometimes negotiate an end to a feud by paying "blood money," usually a shotgun or a pig, to the victim's family.[2]

Third-Party Involvement

Humans are social beings who live in groups, and conflict management often involves third parties as friendly peacemakers, mediators, arbitrators, judges, repressive peacemakers, and so forth.[3] The first two roles occur across various types of social organization, from forager bands to modern industrial states. The other roles, especially the last two, become more common as the complexity of social organization increases.

Friendly peacemakers simply separate or distract adversaries and do not delve into the particulars of the conflict. More often than not, friendly peacemakers have a close relationship with one or both antagonists and thus are concerned about their well-being. Robin Fox tells how friendly peacemakers separate enraged disputants on Tory Island in Ireland: "[The antagonists] were pulled back, dusted down, showered with nonstop advice, and implored to cool down and go home."[4]

While working in the Zapotec community of San Andrés, I witnessed various fistfights, generally between inebriated men.[5] After several blows were exchanged, friendly peacemakers, usually kinfolk, pulled the antagonists apart before either received serious injuries. Not once in perhaps a dozen witnessed fights did the relatives of the combatants join the fray as partisans—rather, their intention clearly was to stop the fighting.

Having realized the way this system worked, I nonetheless was caught by surprise during a saint's day celebration. A friend of mine, Samuel, drew my attention to a man who had returned to the community for the fiesta, telling me that this guy was an aggressive bastard. Samuel pointed out the long scar on the man's face and relayed the details of a particularly nasty fight in which

Figure 7.2   Guests dance during a San Andrés Zapotec wedding celebration. The bride, with a parasol, and groom are dancing together in the center. At weddings, funerals, and saint's day celebrations, guests are provided abundant quantities of alcohol. At such events, physical altercations are predictable and so is the appearance of friendly peacemakers who successfully separate and distract opponents. (D. P. Fry photo collection.)

the man's opponent had slashed him with scissors, allegedly in self-defense.

Later that evening, the inebriated scar-faced man was dancing with my former wife. Mid-dance, he made a drunken lunge at her, wrapping his arms around her waist as he dropped to a kneeling position, his face pressed into her pubic region. Clearly my wife was not a happy camper. I rushed over, grabbed the man from behind, and tried to drag him away, but he was latched on tightly.

I had no intention of getting into a fight with him; I simply wanted to pry him off my distressed wife. And here is when I received a surprise that made perfect sense only after reflection: Two or three of my Zapotec friends hauled me away, leaving the drunken guy still wrapped around my wife. In amazement, I thought: "Why in hell are you pulling *me* away?" Others then helped my wife out of her predicament.

In San Andrés, men are very jealous. In fact, many fights and some murders stem from jealousy. After the shock wore off, I realized that I had been the recipient of friendly peacemaking. Concerned for my well-being, my Zapotec friends were preventing me from doing what they thought was likely to be my next move, what a typical San Andrés husband seeing his wife in the lustful embrace of another man would likely do: go for blood. And since this particular guy already had a reputation as an aggressive troublemaker, their perceived need to protect me was all the more urgent. A couple of years later, this man was murdered.

Friendly peacemakers need not always separate antagonists by physical means—distraction also can be an effective technique. The Mae Enga of New Guinea make war regularly. During peacemaking negotiations, if tempers begin to flare, someone may launch into an irrelevant, even mildly humorous speech, consequently allowing overly excited members of the group to get their emotions under control and not derail the peacemaking process.[6]

In mediation, neutral third parties help disputants to reach agreements. Mediators do not make judgments, and they lack the authority to impose agreements, but they may use coercion to push for agreements. Mediation occurs in a large number of cultures. People in many tribal societies rely on mediation, often as an alternative to aggressive self-redress, while peasant agriculturalists sometimes use mediation in preference to pursuing a grievance through governmental courts.[7]

The nonwarring, nonfeuding Semai of Malaysia shun conflict. They avoid disputes whenever possible and suppress feelings of anger. When conflict cannot be avoided, a Semai headman convenes a dispute resolution assembly called the *becharaa'*. The disputants, their relatives, and any other members of the community who want to attend meet at the house of the headman. In turn, each disputant discusses the conflict. Others then join in, expressing opinions or perhaps asking questions.[8]

Clay Robarchek explains that during the *becharaa'*, all events related to the dispute are explored from "every conceivable perspective in a kind of marathon encounter group. Every possible explanation is offered, every imaginable motive introduced, every conceivable mitigating circumstance examined . . . until finally a point is reached where there is simply nothing left to say." The headman then lectures one or both of the parties, noting their guilt in the matter, instructing them in how they should have acted differently, and directing them not to repeat such mistakes. The headman and other elders make speeches reaffirming the importance of harmony within the group. Robarchek emphasizes that, through the *becharaa'*, the Semai are able to deal nonviolently with serious conflicts—involving property ownership, infidelity, divorce, land claims, and so on—so as to dissipate anger, deal effectively with the basis of the conflict, promote the reconciliation of the disputants, reconfirm the interdependence of the band members, and reiterate the need for social harmony.[9]

In arbitration, a third party renders a decision but lacks the power to enforce it. The pacification of blood feuds in Montenegro during the 1800s illustrates of how arbitration can restore the peace. The arbitrators were called *kmets*, and they assembled as the "court of good men." *Kmets* were of high status and had nonpartisan reputations. Christopher Boehm emphasizes that the central goal of the *kmets* was to bring about a compromise and contribute to the social harmony. A *kmet* states: "For us, the task is to see clearly with our minds and to make the decision that we see as being most appropriate, to ensure that two embroiled brastvos [clans] come to peace with one another and that other honorable men will not look askance at what we have done."[10]

In general, disputants abide by an arbitrator's decision for any number of reasons: due to the pressure of public opinion or influence from relatives, because they believe the arbitrator's ruling is fair, to maintain a good reputation, or to avoid facing harmful consequences such as the violence of blood feuding or the expense of pursuing the matter in court. Even though arbitrators lack direct power to enforce their decisions, the arbitration process can provide a viable alternative to violence.

Adjudication may be even better for delivering justice because judges not only make rulings but also possess the power to enforce them. Max Gluckman describes the judicial system of the Lozi kingdom in what is now Zambia. For at least two hundred years, this African kingdom has had a hierarchy of courts. The primary goal of the judges is to reconcile disputants and correct errant behavior. "Large parts of the judgments read like sermons. . . . The aim of the judicial process is that when the parties have had their rightdoings and wrongdoings indicated to them, they will be reconciled and live together harmoniously in the future."[11]

In Mexico, local community courts among the indigenous groups such as the Tarahumara, Huichol, and Zapotec stem from colonial times and further illustrate the process of adjudication. Every Tarahumara group, for instance, has a head official, called the *gobernador*. During trials, the *gobernador* is the true judge, while other officials sit in advisory capacities. The *gobernador* hears the evidence, rules on the guilt or innocence of the accused, and when necessary dictates a punishment. The typical punishment is a public whipping. Sometimes the court also rules that a defendant should pay compensation to a plaintiff. To a Tarahumara, appearing in court is a horrible experience, not simply because of the pain of physical punishment or damage to one's pocketbook if fined, but also because of the risk of public humiliation and harm to one's reputation. The social disgrace of receiving a public scolding from the *gobernador* "stings almost as sharply as the whip."[12]

Repressive peacemaking is the most authoritative type of third-party settlement and treats fighting itself as an offense to be punished, regardless of the reasons for the dispute. Repressive peacemaking occurs when colonial powers or national governments unilaterally impose peace on feuding or warring indigenous peoples. Among the Yukaghir reindeer hunters of northeastern Siberia, traditionally the brother of a murder victim or another relative could seek blood vengeance. "He does not kill directly, but requires from the murderer an explanation of his act, not infrequently letting him off with a ransom," explains Waldemar Jochelson. The repressive peacemaking concept is illustrated by the fact that after the Russians subjugated the peoples in this area, the Yukaghir discontinued the practice of seeking blood vengeance, fearing punishment by Russian authorities through the newly imposed court and penal system.[13]

A major reason for illustrating with cultural examples the diverse ways that humans deal with conflict is to highlight that violence, as a form of self-redress, is only one option among various possibilities. Undeniably, humans engage in acts of physical aggression, but they also regularly deal with conflicts in other ways. Other approaches may not be as noticeable as violence, but this means neither that they are unusual nor that they are ineffective for dealing with conflict. Indeed, toleration, avoidance, negotiation and third-party-assisted settlement often are less costly and more effective than aggression.

Clearly, the maintenance of valuable social relationships is important among humans. Aside from being dangerous, dealing with conflict through aggression may harm relationships in ways that other options do not. An overemphasis on violence, including warfare, by the dark-sided, demonic school of thought ignores and obscures how humans manage to live peacefully together most of the time. A more realistic perspective also takes into account restraints against violence, aggression prevention activities, nonviolent conflict management techniques, and reconciliation strategies that humans regularly practice. Certainly, warfare and other types of violence are part of the human species' profile, but only part of it. A balanced view of human nature also recognizes the substantial capability that people have for limiting and dealing with conflicts without force.

Social Organization and Seeking Justice

Informal friendly peacemakers and mediators are active everywhere. However, some approaches to conflict management and justice seeking, such as the use of courts, are deeply affected by social organization. In uncentralized bands and tribes, rarely does anyone command enough influence to enforce a judgment. Courts of law, judicial authorities, police, mental hospitals, and prisons are all lacking. Within chiefdoms and states, adjudication becomes feasible with the advent of the social hierarchy. Those at the top have the authority to judge and the power to enforce their rulings. It is not uncommon to read in ethnographic accounts of chiefs imposing judgments. After all, the power to make rulings and to sentence commoners is a mark of chiefly authority. On the Pacific Island called Tikopia, chiefs sometimes settle land disputes; among the Nootka of the Northwest Coast of North America, the head chief could sentence a malefactor to death.[14]

Taking Justice into One's Own Hands

What about violent approaches to justice seeking? Anthropologists use the term *self-redress* when a person with a grievance takes action against another individual. Self-redress is a coercive approach. If violence is not directly used, then the threat of force lingers in the background. The phrase "taking justice into one's own hands" catches the essence of self-redress, whether lethal or not.[15]

One problem with using self-redress is that the actor's "justice" may be perceived by the recipient as "unjust," as an unwarranted, overzealous attack. This is one reason why self-redress can lead to the escalation of conflict. Consider an example from Jan Brögger's fieldwork in southern Italy. To make charcoal, Domenico cut down some trees along the property line he shared with Giuseppe. Giuseppe requested some of the charcoal, thinking he had partial claim to this common resource, but Domenico refused to give him any. As a result of an ensuing argument, Giuseppe became furious and stole some of Domenico's rabbits. Domenico retaliated by cutting down Giuseppe's vineyard late one night. Ultimately, an enraged Giuseppe killed Domenico.[16]

Diverse ethnographic accounts suggest that people know the dangers set in motion by the use of self-redress and more often than not seek to avoid unbridled cycles of violence. Among tribal Montenegrins—a culture that placed great value on defending one's honor—disputes very rarely led to lethal blood feuds.

> As a self-assertive Montenegrin warrior, then, a man's mission was to maximize his own reputation and honor at the same time that he minimized the risk of getting himself killed from ambush or of getting his kinsman or tribe into deep trouble. . . . With a warrior people who played this game very hard, it would not be surprising if there were quite a large number of feuds; indeed, what is remarkable is that there were relatively few.[17]

Is there a relationship between the use of self-redress and social organization? Based on a careful examination of systems of justice in 650 societies representing different kinds of social organization, Leonard Hobhouse, Gerald Wheeler, and Morris Ginsberg reached a conclusion in 1915 that has stood the test of time. Self-redress is most common among hunter-gatherer subsistence systems and steadily decreases in use as patterns of subsistence shift toward agriculture or herding. In their large cross-cultural sample, Hobhouse and his colleagues found self-redress to be present in about 90 percent of the simplest hunter-gatherer societies but in less than 15 percent of the most agriculturally reliant societies. These researchers concluded that "as we mount the [economic/social organizational] scale there is more government and more of the public administration of justice within society."[18]

A half century later, Adamson Hoebel expressed a similar conclusion about how law and justice are painted across the wide canvas of social organization: "The tendency is to shift the privilege rights of prosecution and imposition of legal sanctions from the individual [as in self-redress] and his kin-group [as in feuding] over to clearly defined public officials representing the society as such [as in courts of law]."[19] The main point is that as social complexity increases, administrators of justice sequentially change from the individual to kin groups and eventually to public officials.

Based on data from the 186 societies in the SCCS, Karen Ericksen and Heather Horton corroborate these generalizations about vengeance seeking. They report that individual self-redress is about seven times more likely to occur in hunter-gatherer band society than in all other types of societies. Additionally, they compared the likelihood of self-redress in unstratified or egalitarian societies (that is, the pattern typically found in uncentralized bands and tribes) and in stratified or hierarchical societies (basically, chiefdoms and states) and found over five times the self-redress among the unstratified group. Finally, Ericksen and Horton found adjudication to dominate in the most complex type of political economies. In other words, well-developed chiefdoms and states usurp from individuals and kin groups the right to administer justice. In modern states, homicides rarely result in individual acts of self-redress or in feuding between kin groups. Instead, with only rare exceptions, citizens accept that the administration of justice lies in the hands of the state. In the event that a person takes the law into his or her own hands, the state judicial system treats the act of self-redress as a new offense, not as the legitimate administration of justice. States claim the right and duty to administer justice.[20]

Chagnon recounts an anecdote that highlights the difference between seeking justice via revenge, as in self-redress and feuding, and the adjudicatory mechanisms found in hierarchical societies such as states, as represented by Venezuela in this account.

A particularly acute insight into the power of law to thwart killing for revenge was provided to me by a young Yanomamö man in 1987. He had been taught Spanish by missionaries and sent to the territorial capital for training in practical nursing. There he discovered police and laws. He excitedly told me that he had visited the town's largest *pata* (the territorial governor) and urged him to make law and police available to his people so that they would not have to engage any longer in their wars of revenge and have to live in constant fear. Many of his close kinsmen had died violently and had, in turn, exacted lethal revenge; he worried about being a potential target of retaliations and made it known to all that he would have nothing to do with raiding.[21]

On Feuding

As the foregoing discussion demonstrates, individual self-redress is relatively more likely in band societies than in hierarchical societies. However, feuding that pits kin group against kin group in a series of reciprocal killings is *not* typical of foraging bands for the simple reason that most band societies lack cohesive kin organizations.[22] Band societies tend not to exclusively emphasize either matrilineal or patrilineal kinship segments, instead paying attention to both mother's and father's descent lines. What this means is that in a majority of simple forager societies, each person thinks in terms of his or her own unique set of relatives. Of course, the kin networks of two individuals may overlap, but even two brothers in most cases will have different kin networks after marriage due to each having different sets of in-laws. In short, the individually oriented patterns of kinship in band society cut across various nomadic groups, creating webs of interlinking ties among different bands.

Another way of putting this is that simple nomadic foraging bands are more likely to be unsegmented, or only weakly segmented, compared to other types of societies that have clear sub-units such as lineages or clans. Raymond Kelly points out that in unsegmented societies, "a homicide is consequently likely to be perceived and experienced as an individual loss shared with some kin rather than as an injury to a group." This is a main reason why the individual self-redress pattern dominates over a back-and-forth feuding pattern in simple band societies that tend to lack the types of well-developed social segments typically present in more complex societies.[23]

Once social segmentation enters the picture, a killing is perceived as a loss not only to the victim's immediate family, but more generally to members of the same patrilineage, subclan, clan, and so on. In seeking revenge, the victim's larger kin organization may target anyone belonging to the killer's social segment. Kelly refers to this phenomenon as "social substitutability." In segmented societies that allow payback killings, it is likely that the particular malefactor is no longer the only legitimate target of revenge.[24]

To highlight another recurring pattern among simple nomadic foragers, the targets of lethal revenge tend to be the killers themselves.[25] This tendency is clearly apparent, for example, in Ju/'hoansi homicide data. Of twenty-two homicides, eleven were initial homicides. Revenge was sought against four of the killers in attempts that ultimately led to eleven more violent deaths, including the four killers themselves, one relative of a killer, and several revenge seekers and bystanders. Much of the bloodshed revolved around repeated attempts to execute two of the original four killers, who were notoriously violent men.[26]

In simple nomadic band societies that either lack social segments or have only weakly developed ones, at times justice is achieved when a killer is killed. A balance is restored between two families, and this typically ends the matter. In segmented societies, whether tribes or chiefdoms, retaliatory justice seeking may alternate back and forth between feuding clans or lineages. Each killing prompts a retaliation, which in turn prompts a counter-retaliation and then a counter-counter-retaliation. In other words, social substitutability facilitates feuding. Among nation-states, social substitutability can facilitate war, as one act of violence (for instance, a terrorist attack) provokes retaliation not solely against the actual perpetrators, but against anyone labeled as belonging to the same national or religious group as the attackers. Clearly the idea of social substitutability has great relevance for understanding some types of warfare and intergroup violence in today's world.[27]

Figure 7.3 summarizes this cross-cultural model of how social organization relates to lethal self-redress, feud, and war. Individual self-redress killings, although not universally present, are typical of the band type of social organization, feuds are typical of tribes, and warfare is typical of chiefdoms and states. Figure 7.3 reflects relative *tendencies* that are apparent across numerous anthropological studies and thus reflects a general pattern, not absolutes.[28] Adding social

	Nomadic hunter-gatherer bands	Tribes	Chiefdoms	States
Self-redress revenge homicide	**typical**	variable	atypical	atypical
Feud	atypical	**typical**	variable	atypical
Warfare	atypical	variable	**typical**	**typical**

Figure 7.3   A Model of Lethal Aggression in Relation to Social Organization

Note: When lethal violence occurs, which is not necessarily very often, it tends to have different manifestations depending upon social organization. Specifically, individual self-redress homicide is typical of simple nomadic hunter-gatherer society, whereas feuding and warfare are not. Nomadic band societies tend to lack the corporate kin groups (e.g., clans and patrilineages) that typify tribal society. In tribal society, revenge-seeking shifts from individuals to kin groups and thus feuding becomes possible. Feuding, in turn, tends to be repressed once central authority develops, as within chiefdoms and especially states. A series of cross-cultural studies show that warfare is most likely and most fully developed in chiefdoms and states. This model is intended to reflect the broad cross-cultural patterns involving lethal aggression, not invariable, universal features.

organization to the equation and untangling individual self-redress, feud, and war from one another greatly expand our knowledge about the overall pattern of lethal conflict.

The case involving the Italian peasants Domenico and Giuseppe illustrates the danger of unilaterally seeking justice through revenge, whether by self-redress, feud, or war. One party's justice seeking may precipitate retaliation from the other side, leading to a spiral of escalating violence. Conflict resolution, a social art highly developed in humans, offers alternative paths to justice that make unnecessary the violence of self-redress, feud, and war. The cross-cultural data demonstrate the wealth of nonviolent approaches that humans regularly employ to make the balance— to attain just solutions to conflicts—without breaking the peace.[29]

A central challenge in the twenty-first century is to extend to the international level—among nation-states—the types of conflict resolution and judicial procedures that effectively provide justice and keep the peace within democratic nation-states today. The same inherent problems of attaining justice in band society occur within today's international system, which lacks overarching authority and accepts self-redress in the form of war among nations. As Hoebel points out, the seeking of justice through self-redress among the equestrian Comanche is "exactly comparable to that observed among nations which recognize certain practices of international law, but which reserve to themselves the sovereign right to resort to force if things don't suit them. Then, in the words of [a Comanche man named] Post Oak Jim, 'Lots of trouble, lots of people hurt.'"[30]

Implications

Patterns of fighting, conflict management, and justice seeking all relate to social organization. As we will consider in future chapters, some theorists of warfare have ignored social organization and in so doing have made a host of untenable assumptions. Overlooking social organization has led to speculations, for instance, as to the importance of military leadership among hunter-gatherer bands in the human past. Such ideas are dubious from the outset due to the virtual absence of authoritative leadership in band society. In theorizing about the nature of warfare and the nature of human nature, we ignore social organization only at our peril.

In nomadic band society, each person exercises a high degree of personal autonomy. Authority is minimal and leadership is weak:

no one has the authority to adjudicate disputes or hand down enforceable judgments, nor does anyone have the authority to order others into combat. A further ramification of high personal autonomy in band society is that each individual is largely left up to his or her own devices in pursuing personal grievances. Additionally, patrilineal and matrilineal kin segments usually are lacking, and this is one of several factors that works against the development of social substitutability and kin-based collective military action. The other side of the coin is that individual self-redress is more likely at the band level of social organization than in other types of societies, and—not surprisingly, given the lack of lineage development—the usual target of self-redress is the actual perpetrator of a misdeed.

In tribal society, leadership is only slightly more developed than in bands. Individuals still have a high level of personal autonomy. Both bands and tribes lack social hierarchies and class stratification. However, tribal societies, in contrast to most bands, tend to be segmented into subunits on the basis of kinship. Individual grievances can become the basis for feuds between kin groups, spreading well beyond the original disputants themselves. It is this type of kin-based feuding that the Yanomamö man in Chagnon's story would like the Venezuelan nation-state to step in and stop.[31]

Stratified, centralized societies—chiefdoms and states—present a very mixed blessing. Social stratification and resulting positions of leadership open the door for a plethora of injustices and cruelties that come with warfare, slavery, and other types of exploitation by unchecked power wielders. As Reyna emphasizes, in centralized polities the power of some people to dominate and control others increases many times over what is possible at the level of bands and tribes.[32]

Modern democracies attempt to prevent the most flagrant abuses of power and to protect the rights of citizens. With increasing authority and leadership, adjudication of disputes also becomes feasible, largely eliminating justice seeking through individual self-redress and kin group feuding. Herein lies an important message: *The types of judicial principles currently used within nation-states theoretically could be applied among nation-states to create institutions for resolving disputes and assuring international justice that do not rely on each nation's self-claimed right to use force.* This judicial solution repeatedly has been implemented within democratic nation-states as an alternative to self-redress. The idea also offers a viable alternative to the current global self-redress war system, under which, to again quote Post Oak Jim, "lots of trouble, lots of people hurt."

8

Man the Warrior: Fact or Fantasy?

*For more than 99 percent of the approximately two million years since the emergence
of a recognizable human animal, man has been a hunter and gatherer. . . . Questions
concerning territorialism, the handling of aggression, social control, property,
leadership, the use of space, and many other dimensions are particularly significant
in these contexts. To evaluate any of these focal aspects of human behavior without
taking into consideration the socioeconomic adaptation that has characterized most
of the span of human life on this planet will eventually bias conclusions and
generalizations.*

—M. G. BICCHIERI, *HUNTERS AND GATHERERS TODAY*

What do the following descriptions of hunter-gatherer aggression
have in common? In the *Handbook of South American Indians* under the
heading "Warfare," Junius Bird writes of the Alacaluf:

> Crude spears, arrows, and clubs painted red were stuck into
> the ground around a roughly carved figure of wood as a
> declaration of war or as a warning of attack. . . . A man once
> stole another man's wife. The husband tried to get her back
> by force, but was beaten off by his competitor. He returned
> in the night with his brother and placed one red wooden

replica of the *tant-tarrb* [spear] . . . at either end of the hut and behind it. Thus, having given a warning that he would try to kill the man, the latter's relatives could not hold him accountable. The two brothers subsequently ambushed the rival and killed him with a spear. The woman was blamed and beaten.[1]

Jane Goodale describes how a Tiwi husband might react if his wife ran off with another man:

> If necessary, he would send a messenger to invite distant members of his sib and phratry to join the battle. The "enemy" (the lover's "people": his sib and phratry) would also be sent a message. . . . When everyone had arrived, my informant continued, they lined up on opposing sides and the battle began.
>
> First a young boy from each side advanced and threw a spear. Then two more youngsters exchanged spears, and then a third pair. After this exchange of spears everyone threw his spear. When one side decided that they had had enough, an old man carried a white flag between the two lines and said, "You have won, we lose." Then they all camped. . . . [Goodale's informant added that] the lover kept the wife, for the fight was not over who got to keep the woman but only for the husband's "honor," and after the fight the trouble must be forgotten.[2]

In these cases, the disputes are basically between *individuals*. In the Alacaluf case, a dispute between two men over a woman is labeled as something that it clearly is not: warfare. Despite the use of the phrase "declaration of war," this is a case of homicide, clear and simple. Furthermore, the homicidal self-redress is apparently conducted in accordance with Alacaluf legal procedure so as to prevent retaliatory violence. The bloodshed could have been averted, supposedly, if the woman had returned to her husband.

Similarly, in the Tiwi example, the use of words such as *enemy* and *battle* again suggests a warlike nature to a dispute that is in reality a dispute between two men over a woman. The informant sees the so-called battle as being for the honor of the deserted husband. It is important to explain that throwing spears in the manner described is not as serious as it might seem to a reader from another culture. Most male Australian Aborigines are skilled both at "throwing to miss" and, on the receiving end, dodging spears—a response that may not occur to someone accustomed to thinking in terms of guns and bullets.[3] Victoria Burbank reports that in a settled Aboriginal community, "when men take up spears, more often than not, no one is injured."[4] Even young boys throw spears in the described event; there is no loss of life or even bloodshed, and the two groups camp together overnight. Along with the initial observation that the dispute is between two individuals, all these points combine to show that something very different from warfare is actually going on here.

The broader point is far from trivial. Whether due to misperceptions, projections, or poetic descriptions, conflicts in band societies are regularly presented as "warfare." It is not difficult to find examples of this "war-ification" phenomenon when reading ethnographic material, especially if written by nonanthropologists such as colonial administrators, missionaries, or early travelers.[5] Many descriptions penned by Westerners contain vocabularies of war—*warfare, battle, enemy, declaration of war, war parties, war paint, war dance*, and the like—that are imprecisely or inappropriately applied to disputes. This use of language implies warring when in actuality two individuals, perhaps aided by kin, are fighting, or, ironically, engaging in procedures to settle disputes without bloodshed—to satisfy a deserted husband's honor, for instance. Descriptions of this kind help to re-create the "savage" in our own preconceived warlike image, as the Western concept of war is projected onto indigenous activities that are not really war at all.

As an undergraduate student at the University of California in Santa Barbara, I took an anthropology course from Elman Service called "Law and War." Recently my class notes surfaced and I looked them over with fond amusement. I had enjoyed Service's lectures. My notes now reminded me that Service had emphasized, "People have lived in hunter-gatherer bands for 99.87 percent of human existence." (I gather the .87 part was Service's way of having a little fun as he highlighted the magnitude of humanity's nomadic hunter-gatherer heritage to his students.) He had explained that in simple hunter-gatherer bands, leadership is weak and based on charisma, not authority. Everybody knows everybody else in band society. Generosity is highly valued. And when it comes to "warfare," hunter-gatherer bands engage in little more than, in Service's words, "feuds and Saturday night brawls." Later, I discovered that Service also had emphasized the personal nature of simple hunter-gatherer disputes in *The Hunters* as "often caused by an elopement, or an illegal love affair of some kind, or simply an insult."[6]

Service's observation that in hunter-gatherer band society disputes are personal has major implications, because it suggests that those who attempt to explain the biological evolution of human warfare are asking the wrong question. They are starting with the assumption that ancestral hunter-gatherer bands actually had wars, and then are going on to explain warring as an evolved adaptation.

Two Kinds of Assumptions

My sister, Mollie, once told me a joke about a chicken farmer who was eager to increase egg production. Hoping to benefit from the latest scientific knowledge, the farmer paid a visit to the university and eventually ended up talking with a good-natured physicist. After hearing the problem, the physicist said, "Let me work on this for a while. Can you come back in a week or two?" The farmer agreed and returned two weeks later. "Good news. I solved your problem," announced the physicist. Producing a thick pile of papers filled with equations and calculations, she continued, "First of all, we assume a two-dimensional chicken. . . ."

In science, whether designing an experiment or developing a theoretical model, we make certain initial assumptions because we can't investigate everything all at once. The physicist in my sister's joke begins by stating an *explicit* assumption, which has the advantage of holding it up for review. Obviously, making unrealistic assumptions can lead to unrealistic conclusions. We can assess at the onset that the physicist's recommendations for increasing egg production are based on a seemingly dubious assumption about the two-dimensionality of chickens.

Another class of assumptions, *implicit* assumptions, can be even more problematic in scientific endeavors because they are simply taken for granted. Implicit assumptions creep stealthily into theoretical modeling, research design, and scientific interpretations. We have already considered some cases involving implicit assumptions, such as when Blanc assumed that prehistoric hyenas had no bearing on the Neanderthal skull from Monte Circeo cavern. I suspect a similar process led Wright to ignore the flight option and instead to presume that *all* societies, even those with no evidence of war, would fight back if attacked.

Overall, the greater the number of implicit assumptions we can identify, the better, because this allows us to assess whether they are in fact realistic. I now will attempt to bring out into the open some of the typical assumptions that lie behind recent writings on warfare and human evolution.

The "Man the Warrior" View of the Past

Biologist Richard Alexander proposes a "balance of power" hypothesis.[7] "At some early point in our history the actual function of human groups—their significance for their individual members —was protection from the predatory effects of other human groups. . . . Multi-male bands . . . stayed together largely or entirely because of the threat of other, similar, nearby groups of humans."[8] Assumptions underlying Alexander's thinking are that prehistoric groups were hostile and predatory toward their neighbors.[9] Pervasive intergroup hostility, in turn, accounted for groups staying together. His model also implies that group membership would have been largely fixed and stable due to the inherent hostility among different groups.

Economists Paul Shaw and Yuwa Wong assume that "warfare propensities are deeply entrenched in human nature."[10] Referring to the last million or two million years, Shaw and Wong describe the ancestors of present-day humans as living in "small, tight-knit groups" of kin, numbering at most a hundred people, which they call "nucleus ethnic groups."[11] In their view, "relationships between nucleus ethnic groups were shaped largely by conflict in an environment of scarce resources," and "intergroup competition and warfare over scarce resources would have had to be widely prevalent throughout evolution."[12] In short, Shaw and Wong presume that tight-knit kin groups with propensities for war were engaged in ongoing fighting with one another. They also assume that resources were scarce and that humans regularly fought over them.

Biologist Bobbi Low continues in the same vein, asserting for example that "through evolutionary history, men [in contrast to women] have been able to gain reproductively by warring behavior." Like Alexander and like Shaw and Wong, Low assumes that war existed over long expanses of evolutionary time. Low explicitly asserts that in the evolutionary past, lineages of related men lived together and fought with other lineages. Reasons for past and present war include, according to Low, "women, revenge, agricultural lands, new territory, or any devised reason." For Low, the key assumptions are that engaging in war has led to reproductive rewards for men during the evolution of the human species and that warring is facilitated when genetically related men live together.[13]

Richard Wrangham and Dale Peterson echo the themes of the previous authors, using the term *male bonded* to refer to aggressive coalitions of patrilineal males—that is, individuals that are descended from a common ancestral male. These authors compare humans and chimpanzees and focus on apparent similarities regarding male-initiated territorial aggression. They generalize the pattern to all human communities: "In short, the system of communities defended by related men is a human universal that crosses space and time."[14]

Michael Ghiglieri assumes that warfare is ancient ("Wars are older than humanity itself"), that warfare is natural (*"Wars erupt naturally everywhere humans are present"*), and that warfare has been critical in human evolution ("War vies with sex for the distinction of being the most significant process in human evolution").[15] By war, Ghiglieri means *"conflict between social groups that is resolved by individuals on one or both sides killing those on the opposite side."*[16] According to Ghiglieri, war is a male reproductive strategy that was favored during human evolution. He writes, "Sexual selection and kin selection have designed human males—*compelled* human males—to wage war as a strategy to cooperatively seize the territory, resources, and women of other men and to use them reproductively. . . . According to the primeval conditions under which war evolved, a man could accrue more wives through war and thus raise his reproductive success by an order of magnitude."[17] In other words, Ghiglieri assumes that war is an evolutionary adaptation and asserts that, among other traits, male bonding—especially among groups of related males—and leadership "blend in natural selection's recipe for war."[18]

In these scenarios of prehistoric life, war is assumed to result from selection pressures operating over a long expanse of evolutionary time.[19] A careful analysis of such works, which I will refer to collectively as the "man the warrior" model, reveals interconnected assumptions about the human past.[20] War is extremely ancient. Intergroup relations tended to be hostile in the past. Group membership was largely fixed—the exception being that women were captured from neighboring groups as a goal of war. The males in a group were genetically related to one another, perhaps as members of a patrilineage. Related males readily bonded and cooperated with each other in warfare. Effective male bonding and cooperation in war paid off in terms of increased reproductive success for males engaging in these behaviors. Critical resources were scarce. War was waged to acquire scarce resources, territory, and women. Leadership and warrior behavior correlated with reproductive success and thus were evolutionarily favored.

This evolutionary scenario might seem reasonable. First, the model seems internally coherent and logical. Second, when scientists invoke concepts such as "sexual selection" and "nucleus ethnic group," their status as experts and use of impressive jargon contribute a scientific air to the model. Third, the model may simply "feel right" in many ways. That is, it seems to be in agreement with our own everyday observations about the nature of warfare and human societies. We know from history and politics, for example, that intergroup hostilities often exist, social groups are bounded, relatives tend to support each other, wars are fought to conquer and defend territory or over scarce resources, leadership in war is important, and so on.

Despite the apparent plausibility of this scenario, I am going to propose that the assumptions underlying the "man the warrior" model are about as realistic as a barnyard filled with two-dimensional chickens. Of course, that a model might "feel right" is insufficient grounds for uncritically accepting the host of assumptions upon which it rests. For centuries, the model of a flat earth "felt right" to many Europeans. Instead, we must ask: Does the model match our best available observations of the facts? Are the implicit and explicit assumptions inherent in the explanation really reasonable when checked against observations of the real world? Additionally, we can question whether some of the evolutionary principles are really being applied in a sensible, logical manner. Instead of simply *presuming* that warfare has existed as a typical pattern in band society over countless millennia to gain territory, capture women, obtain scarce resources, wipe out the enemy, or whatever, wouldn't it make more sense to put the horse back in front of the cart by asking: What types of disputes do nomadic hunter-gatherers actually have? How do they deal with them?

I propose that by carefully examining the nomadic forager data for patterns—for recurring themes—we can reconstruct in broad outline the typical social features of ancestral humans. Bringing together the important features of this reconstructed social environment, on the one hand, and evolutionary theory, on the other, leads to the suggestion that certain types of aggression and associated behaviors, *but not warfare*, were favored by natural selection over millennia. It is also likely, as we shall see in future chapters, that in ancestral hunter-gatherer bands, overly aggressive individuals were selected *against*, that is, disfavored in comparison to less aggressive individuals.

Time for a Reality Check

Insights about behavior and society during the evolutionary past come from three sources: archaeology, primate analogy, and hunter-gatherer analogy. Each method has its strengths and weaknesses. Archaeology's contributions to understanding the past are significant and obvious. Archaeology provides material evidence but unfortunately leaves out much detail. Related to warfare, we have already discussed in Chapter 5 how war leaves an archaeological trail and how the worldwide archaeological record shows a steady spread and intensification of warfare only in the most recent millennia, the period corresponding with a multitude of major changes in human social life following the agricultural revolution. We also have considered several cases that highlight the necessity of maintaining vigilance against accepting reconstructions of the past that deviate greatly from observable archaeological facts.

Primate analogy attempts to glean insights about the life of human precursors by studying living nonhuman primates, especially those species most closely related to humans. Features that are widely shared among primates—for example, living in social groups—are thought to be evolutionary ancient patterns. When two species such as humans and chimpanzees share certain features, it is often supposed that members of a common ancestral species also had these characteristics. However, this assumption may or may not be true depending on the feature in question. Similar features with similar functions also can evolve separately in different evolutionary lines. Wings used for flight provide a classic illustration, as they have evolved independently among birds (the feathered model) and among certain insects (the "cellophane" model). Furthermore, features that appear similar may have evolved to fulfill different functions from one species to the next. And some similarities between species may not constitute evolved adaptations at all, but instead are mere fortuitous effects. For example, the observation that both chimpanzees and humans can offer skilled comic performances in front of large audiences at the circus does not suggest that comic circus performing is an ancient evolutionary adaptation stemming from an ancestral species common to chimpanzees and humans.

In this book, rather than speculating about common ancestral features among humans and their closest living primate relatives —chimpanzees, bonobos, and gorillas—I am going to keep the focus directly on humans. My premise is that we will learn a great deal more about human warfare and society by studying humans than by studying other species. Insights gained through hunter-gatherer analogy relate directly to the human line. The rationale for drawing hunter-gatherer analogies is that the social and physical environments of current-day simple nomadic foragers are similar in many ways to those under which early humans evolved. The lifestyle patterns that recur across contemporary hunter-gatherer bands approximate past patterns better than those of any other type of society, a point emphasized in the chapter epigraph by Bicchieri. As Chris Boehm expresses it: "Such people can serve as rough proxies for the foragers in whose groups our genes evolved."[21] Thus the challenge is to assess recurring patterns, or themes, apparent in simple hunter-gatherer societies, rather than to grab idiosyncratic ethnographic tidbits from a few cultures.

We must not assume that today's nomadic foragers live exactly as our ancestors lived. Various forces in world history have influenced current-day nomadic hunter-gatherers. Over recent millennia, many simple hunter-gatherers have had varying degrees of contact with sedentary neighbors.[22] Nonetheless, compared to other choices for comparison, ranging from tribal peoples such as the much-discussed Yanomamö to the citizens of modern nation-states—or, for that matter, chimpanzees and bonobos if we engage in primate analogy—*the most basic, nomadic hunter-gatherer societies clearly are the best choice for gaining insights about the societies of our ancestors.* As members of the same genus, *Homo*, existing nomadic hunter-gatherers are much more closely related to ancestral humans of the last one million or two million years than are any living apes. Additionally, band social organization and reliance on foraging are critical features that most closely match those of ancestral humans.

In further considering hunter-gatherers, our focus will be on the "simplest of the simple," the nomadic bands, as our best model. Thus we will favor information on nomadic bands over societies that have adopted a sedentary lifestyle, on horseless hunter-gatherers over those that have adopted the horse for hunting—an extremely recent practice, by the way—and nonhierarchical groups over socially ranked cases.[23] To best re-create the past, in coming chapters we will focus on the types of forager societies that most closely mirror the types of social organization and subsistence patterns of ancestral hunting-and-gathering humans, the way of life for all humanity over the numerous millennia prior to the recent development of agriculture.[24]

In the next chapter, we will start with Australian Aborigines because they present us with some critical insights about war and peace. The entire continent of Australia constituted a hunter-gatherer social system before the Europeans arrived, thus offering a glimpse of how neighboring bands got along in a world without agriculture. We will explore some intriguing examples of justice seeking and conflict management among Australian Aborigines. Periodic violence, such as socially sanctioned executions and the practice of revenge homicide, occurred. But we will discover that warfare did not figure prominently in the lives of native Australians.

9

Insights from the Outback: Geneva Conventions in the Australian Bush

First encounters with the desert people are vividly remembered: the rapid realization, as you are touched, squeezed, and discussed, that as one of the first whites they have seen, you are at least as interesting an oddity to them as they to you; their complete unselfconsciousness about nudity (and on a winter's morning you wonder how can they be so warm in their bare skins while you're freezing in every piece of clothing you have with you); the pungent smell of grease and ochre [used as body lotion for medicinal-spiritual reasons], the matted hair, the wads of tobacco that are taken from the mouth or from behind the ear and generously offered (Will refusal offend? Is this what our teachers meant when they said rapport must be established regardless?); the way they constantly use their lips in indicating direction, which will soon become so habitual that you continue to do it back in "civilization," providing further proof that anthropologists are crazy (or become so, after fieldwork).

—ROBERT TONKINSON, *THE MARDUDJARA ABORIGINES*

The island continent of Australia is immense—about as large as the contiguous forty-eight United States—and before the arrival of the Europeans, Australia supported an Aboriginal population up to 750,000 people, speaking well over two hundred distinct languages.[1] In an area this large, it is not surprising that numerous ecological zones exist, from tropical to temperate forests and from prairies to deserts. Nonetheless, there was great similarity in the cultures of the native Australians.[2] Of central importance, Australian Aborigines shared the same basic economic strategy: hunting and gathering. Of course, local variations existed in the types of food eaten and the specific techniques used to obtain their meals, but all of Australia's hunter-gatherers lived in bands and shared food.[3] Australian Aborigines believed that they should follow a system of rules, "the Law," that originated from the part-human, part-animal spiritual beings active during a Dreamtime period of creation. A whole range of proper, customary activities stemmed from Dreamtime and were thus in accordance with the Law.[4]

Aboriginal Australia is intriguing to consider because over the millennia predating the arrival of colonizing Europeans, the entire population on the continent lived as hunter-gatherers. Thus Australia provides an example of how hunter-gatherer bands interacted with each other in the absence of changes brought about by the development of agriculture and ensuing new forms of social organization beginning, as we have seen, about 10,000 years ago elsewhere in the world. An entire continent exclusively comprised of hunting-and-gathering bands has relevance for understanding how prehistoric bands of humans—during the long hunter-gatherer stage of human existence—interacted with each other prior to the rise of tribes, chiefdoms, states, empires, colonialism, nationalism, and, most recently, globalism.

Australian Aborigines are important to our consideration of peace and war for at least two reasons. First, an examination of the Aboriginal cultures of Australia shows warfare to have been the rarest of anomalies. On this point, the anthropological evidence is unequivocal. In Aboriginal times, lethal violence took the form of murder, vengeance killings, and feud (more accurately called individual self-redress in most cases). Some deaths also occurred in the administration of Aboriginal law: during juridical fights, duels, and the punishment or execution of wrongdoers. However, lethal intergroup violence that could be considered warfare was truly the exception to the well-established peace system of the Australian Aborigines.

The second point of importance is that Aboriginal Australians employed a rich set of social and legal mechanisms to resolve disputes within and among social groups.[5] Much physical aggression was controlled and loss of life prevented. Let's be clear: By no means was Aboriginal society free of aggression.[6] However, the natives developed creative ways to limit and minimize the seriousness of fighting and to keep revenge killings and feuding in check. Almost a hundred years ago, Edward Westermarck explained: "Contrary to generally held ideas on the subject, war is not the normal condition . . . [among] the Australian Aborigines; . . . there are among them germs of what is styled 'international law'; . . . there has been something like an anticipation of the Geneva Convention even in the Australian bush."[7]

The Paucity of Warfare

As a generalization, David Horton points to the prevalence of symbolic, controlled displays of aggression in Aboriginal Australia and the *absence* of typical causes of warfare such as "territorial expansion, securing economic advantage, differences in political and religious ideologies, and the urge to devastate and annihilate."

Maurice Davie concludes that "real war does not exist among Australians because 'they have no property that is worth pillaging; no tribe has anything to tempt the cupidity of another. They have no political organization, so there can be no war for power.'"[8]

In reference to the Yolngu (also called Murngin) from Arnhem Land in northern Australia, Nancy Williams explains that the term "Yolngu war" actually refers *only* to blood revenge.[9] As we considered in the previous chapter, the loose application of martial vocabulary such as *war* and *battle* to individual self-redress, feuds, punishment of wrongdoers, and even regulated fights that serve as a form of conflict resolution occurs with some regularity in the literature on Australia and elsewhere. For example, W. Lloyd Warner tallied up violent deaths among the Murngin, lumping together those that resulted from individual fights, group fights, revenge homicides, and even capital punishment. Compounding the confusion, Warner titled his chapter "Warfare" and therein stated that "there are six distinct varieties of warfare among the Murngin."[10] Such labeling muddles the issue, for as Ronald and Catherine Berndt point out about Warner's six types, "not all can be termed warfare." Corresponding with Williams' statement that Murngin "war" is actually blood revenge, Warner reports that the majority of the killings stemmed from revenge seeking. One of Warner's six types of so-called warfare, the *makarata*, actually was, in his own words, "a ceremonial peacemaking fight." Warner's observations over a twenty-year period showed that no deaths resulted from *makarata* ceremonies. It is very odd to call a nonlethal peacemaking ceremony "warfare."[11]

Only one type of Murngin fighting, called the *gaingar*, actually resembled warfare. Tactically, men from different clans faced off and threw spears to kill. Seeking revenge for previous unavenged killings was a major motivation for this "spear fight to end spear fights," hence once again personal grievances entered the picture. Over the twenty-year period investigated by Warner, two *gaingar* fights took place, which resulted in a combined total of twenty-nine deaths. The Murngin *gaingar*, whether labeled war or feud, represents perhaps the bloodiest exception to the typical Australian Aborigine pattern, characterized by a dearth of lethal intergroup encounters.[12]

For another desert culture, the Walbiri, Mervyn Meggitt documents how one group challenged another over a water hole—an event Meggitt refers to as a "war of conquest." Birdsell points out that by the time the incident occurred, European colonists had already disrupted the Walbiri population, and he suggests that such fights were "unlikely to have been frequent in pre-contact times."[13] Meggitt himself makes clear that this event is at odds with the overall pattern of intergroup interaction among Australian Aborigines. Meggitt's description of Walbiri culture reflects the pattern of feuding and blood revenge, as opposed to struggling over territory. Meggitt explains that numerous factors counteract warfare, and his observations on the Walbiri also are relevant to the majority of Australian Aborigine societies:

> Walbiri society did not emphasize militarism—there was no class of permanent or professional warriors; there was no hierarchy of military command; and groups rarely engaged in wars of conquest. Every man was (and is still) a potential warrior, always armed and ready to defend his rights; but he was also an individualist, who preferred to fight independently. In some disputes kinship ties aligned men into opposed groups, and such a group may occasionally have

comprised all the men of a community. But there were no military leaders, elected or hereditary, to plan tactics and ensure that others adopted the plans.

... There was in any case little reason for all-out warfare between communities. Slavery was unknown; portable goods were few; and the territory seized in a battle was virtually an embarrassment to the victors, whose spiritual ties were with other localities.

... Communities usually respected each other's boundaries; and indeed the punitive party was likely to confine itself to performing sorcery at a distance. ... Raids and counter-raids usually concerned only specified groups of kinsmen and could thus be kept within manageable limits; rarely would the whole community arm. The members not directly involved often acted as informal referees; by inviting men of the other community to visit them for ceremonies, they created opportunities for the public settlement of grievances.[14]

In 1910, Gerald Wheeler thoroughly considered all of the material then available on Aboriginal society. Wheeler concluded that in Aboriginal Australia, there were no wars for conquest and few attempts to take women by force, and that what "war" there was amounted to blood feuding. Fifty years later, with additional ethnographic reports such as Meggitt's Walbiri material at his disposal, Elman Service likewise equated Aboriginal "war" with revenge killing. He also noted that exacting revenge "seldom results in much bloodshed and never involves taking land or any other possessions."[15]

The Berndts reach a similar conclusion, writing that "warfare in the broader sense is infrequent in Aboriginal Australia, and most examples which have been classified as such are often no more than feud." Adamson Hoebel concurs: "Among the Australians it is clearly a matter of feud."[16]

From this body of data on Australian Aborigine societies, an overall conclusion is clear: With very occasional exceptions, disputes that at first seemed to be between bands in fact turned out to be personal grievances between individuals who happened to be living in different bands. Sometimes such grievances led to revenge against particular individuals or their close kin, thus constituting personal self-redress, which if reciprocated amounted to feuding, not war between communities. Events that could be considered warfare were extremely few and far between in the ethnographic record of Aboriginal Australia, and in some exceptional cases may have been prompted by territorial loss and other changes caused by the arrival of Europeans.[17] At contact, the Aboriginal hunting-and-gathering societies on this island continent were functioning within a "peace system" wherein each society generally respected the territorial rights of its neighbors. Whereas it probably would be an exaggeration to claim that warfare never happened before European contact, the evidence clearly supports the conclusion that *warfare was a very rare anomaly among native Australian societies.*[18]

Conflict Management Down Under

Turning to a consideration of dispute prevention and resolution, some processes were similar within and across group boundaries. The first point to emphasize is that individuals were supposed to follow the rules of society, the Law, as decreed originally by the spiritual beings during Dreamtime and as passed down over the

Figure 9.1   A Mardu hunter from Australia's Western Desert in 1965 carries spears and a carving tool. The Mardu sometimes fight, verbally and physically, but they do not feud or wage war. Sometimes disputes are resolved at the beginning of "big meetings" as several bands come together to socialize and enact rituals. (Photo courtesy of Robert Tonkinson.)

generations. The rules specified correct ways to behave. Australian Aborigine society was egalitarian relative to class-differentiated societies; however, all members were not exact equals. Australian Aborigine societies tended to be less egalitarian than nomadic hunter-gatherers from other parts of the world. Women deferred to men, and young men obeyed certain decisions of older men. Elders played an important role in the maintenance of law and order in these societies where formal political authority was minimal.[19]

Typically, the most serious disputes between individuals stemmed from "corpse trouble" and "woman trouble."[20] To

Aboriginal thinking, most deaths were attributed to sorcery—hence the name "corpse trouble." Since deaths should be avenged, theoretically every death demanded another. However, as we shall see, the seeking of vengeance and counter-vengeance through feuding was generally kept in check. Disputes over women had multiple causes (jealousy, elopements, adultery, and unfulfilled betrothals) and had multiple solutions besides violence.

A recurring theme reverberates through the literature on native Australia: The seeking of vengeance through violent self-redress was the least favored path to justice. As a general portrait, alternatives to self-redress included the following:

1. Hearings, such as "big meetings," for accusers and defendants alike to make their cases before the juries of public opinion or to talk about a problem so that elders can arrive at a lawful solution[21]
2. Compensation of aggrieved parties for damages[22]
3. Duels, contests, and juridical fights[23]
4. The venting of emotions through public insults, harangues, and arguments[24]
5. Punishment of wrongdoers, often by administering a nonlethal spear wound to the thigh[25]
6. The reconciliation of antagonists via participation in joint rituals and ceremonies, such as the *makarata*[26]

A "Life" for a Life

As mentioned, most adult deaths were attributed to sorcery. In the Aboriginal system of thought, a death must be avenged, or balanced, ideally by the death of the sorcerer. There were many

ways to balance a death without bloodshed. The Lakes Tribes of
South Australia used a system of indebtedness called *kopara* to
prevent vendettas and preserve friendly relations among people
living in different groups.[27]

A typical pattern ran like this. A dying person dreamed of
a particular man and told his relatives. The person's kin then
suspected that that individual, or in some cases a clan, had caused
their relative's death by sorcery. They held an inquest by balancing
the corpse on the heads of two squatting men. An elder tapped
two inquest sticks together and asked the deceased whether the
person in the dream was responsible. The corpse answered in the
affirmative by falling off the two squatting men's heads. Once
the inquest had revealed the identity of the guilty party or parties,
the relatives of the deceased felt that they were owed a *kopara* debt
related to this death.

One option for paying the debt was for the accused murderer's
clan to give a woman as a wife to a member of the dead person's
clan, thus preventing a revenge expedition. We could call this
solution "a wife for a life." A more intriguing option of balancing
the books involved the exchange of a "life" for a life in a bloodless
ceremonial way. To become a man, a boy had to undergo an
initiation rite that included circumcision. Symbolically speaking,
the youth was "killed" and replaced by his new, more valued adult
identity. The *kopara* debt incurred by the original sorcery killing
could be balanced if one of the dead person's relatives circumcised
a youth from the accused killer's group, thus symbolically "killing"
the boy. A. P. Elkin writes: "This is a strange sort of punishment or
revenge, but the discipline associated with the period of initiation,
together with the increased importance and responsibility felt by
the individual is no doubt, in most cases, a very wise course and of

great social value. The Aborigines certainly prefer it to quarrelling and fighting."[28]

Letting Off Steam

Among the Tiwi of northern Australia, grievances were expressed at intergroup gatherings that allowed for the venting of emotions in a relatively harmless manner compared to initiating a revenge expedition. Wheeler calls this type of procedure a "regulated" or "juridical fight" and explains that participants "avoid any bloodshed other than that due to wounds; the first blood that flows puts an end to the fight and settles the dispute." Wheeler also emphasizes that juridical fights were a strictly regulated form of justice and occurred in many Australian Aborigine cultures.[29] C. W. M. Hart and Arnold Pilling describe how members of two Tiwi bands, the Tiklauila and the Rangwila, expressed their grievances against particular members of the Mandiimbula band. The disputes involved seduction accusations, the nondelivery of bestowed daughters, and other broken promises. The aggrieved visitors arrived carrying weapons and wearing white paint indicative of anger. After exchanging a few insults, both sides agreed to assemble the next day at a particular clearing. In the quotations that follow, I have added italics to emphasize certain points.

After a night mostly spent by both sides in individual visiting and renewing old acquaintances, the two armies met next morning in battle array, with the thirty Tiklauila-Rangwila warriors drawn up at one end of the clearing, and about sixty local warriors at the other end. Immediately the *familiar patterns* of the duel imposed themselves. A senior individual on one side began a harangue directed at an *individual* on the other. When he ran out of breath, *another individual* began his complaint. Since each accused Mandiimbula replied individually to the charges made against him, *the whole proceeding remained at the level of mutual charges and replies between pairs of individuals.* Angry old men on both sides often seemed to be trying to find a basis that would justify or provoke a general attack by one group upon the other, but always failed to find it because of the particularity of the charges. *The rules of Tiwi procedure compelled the accuser to specify the sources of his charges and his anger,* and those always turned out to be directed not at the Mandiimbula band, but at one, or at most two or three, individual members of the band. And when another old man took the center of attention, his anger would be directed at quite different individuals. *Hence when spears began to be thrown, they were thrown by individuals for reasons based on individual disputes.*[30]

A series of spear-throwing duels, mostly between elders, eventually resulted in someone getting injured. "Not infrequently the person hit was some innocent noncombatant or one of the *screaming old women who weaved through the fighting men, yelling obscenities at everybody,* and whose reflexes for dodging spears were not as fast as those of the men." As soon as someone was wounded, man or woman, all fighting ceased, and haggling over the new injury began.[31]

If the person wounded in the first flurry of spear throwing was a senior male, that similarly led the arguments off in some new direction since his kinsmen in *both* war parties [italics in original] felt compelled to support him or revenge his wound or inflict a wound on his wounder.

. . . The main outlines were quite clear. The bands were not firm political entities and therefore could not do battle, as bands, with each other. Everybody, on both sides, was interrelated in the same kinship system. An angry old Tiklauila, abusing and throwing spears at an angry old Mandiimbula, might have as the basis of his complaint the fact that the Mandiimbula father had promised but not delivered one of his daughters. Since Tiwi bestowals were from mother's brother to sister's son, the spear throwing was patently a case of a sister's son abusing his mother's brother, and the fact that the two men belonged to different bands was not germane to their dispute. The angry Tiklauila elder could not demand support from other Tiklauila *as Tiklauila* [emphasis in original] in the case at issue for it involved a dispute between kinsmen whose band affiliations were irrelevant to the subject matter. . . . *Tiwi interpersonal relations were primarily kin relations between members of all bands, territorial loyalties* [that is, band loyalties] *were shifting ones, temporary and necessarily quite subordinate to kin loyalties. Hence warfare, in the sense of pitched battles between groups aligned through territorial loyalties, did not occur and could not occur among the Tiwi.*[32]

From this example, we see how the development of warfare was frustrated by certain features of Australian Aborigine social life. Disputes were personal, not corporate, and kinship ties cross-cut band membership, meaning that everybody had relatives in other bands. The Tiwi case also illustrates a typical form of Aboriginal conflict management: the regulated or juridical fight. This widespread Australian procedure was not war; it was a way of expressing grievances and letting off steam without the loss of life. Finally, this example illustrates once again the confusing practice of using war terminology, such as *armies* or *war party*, to describe events such as conflict management procedures that in reality have nothing to do with warfare. Tiwi expressed grievances in juridical fights that, although superficially resembling warfare, actually amounted to the expression of individual grudges in accordance with established juridical procedures.

Making Amends: Penis Touching and Intercourse

Subincision was a critical aspect of initiation into manhood in some Australian societies. In this operation, traditionally conducted with a sharp stone flake knife, the underside of a youth's penis was cut so as to split the urethra all the way to the scrotum. Once his wound healed, the male was considered an adult.

Among the Aranda, a penis-touching rite was used to resolve a grievance. This type of rite demonstrated good fellowship and a lack of enmity among men from divergent groups. Each man belonging to one group approached each man belonging to a second group and invited each partner to touch the underside of his penis. The incisure on the underside of the penis, not the penis itself, was the important feature touched.[33]

If a particular man was suspected of a sorcery killing, a meeting sometimes was called to determine his guilt or innocence. Two groups gathered at a particular camp. In turn, each man in the group in which the death occurred carried out the penis-touching rite with all the men of the suspect's group, but not with the suspect himself. However, in all likelihood, one man of the suspect's group refused to participate in the rite until he had a chance to deliver a speech in defense of his fellow. As his speech progressed, the defender first moved toward an elder man of his own group and penis-touched with him, and then he moved to an elder man of the accuser's group and penis-touched with him as well. As the defender reiterated his arguments, he moved from man to man in both groups, engaging in the rite with all of them, except with the accused.

After the defender's speech, the entire group sat in silence. When the elders of each group reached a decision, the nature of the decision was relayed to the others by hand signal. If the accused had been acquitted, the leaders engaged in penis holding with his defender. All the other men then penis-touched with both the defender and the accused himself. With this outcome, the accused was considered to be cleared of the charges. "Later that night, the man who had previously been accused would come to his defender and offer his penis to the latter 'for saving his life.' The defender would in turn get up and offer his penis, at the same time saying, 'I could not see them accusing you wrongly'."[34]

If charges were brought against a woman, she might arrange for a male relative to stand for her, or she might defend herself. Berndt and Berndt explain:

> She would touch the arms of those men who had accused her; then, returning to her own group, she would touch those men who would if necessary be called upon to defend her. Later she would tell her friend's husband to notify all those men whose arms she had touched that she would be ready for them at some particular place. At the appointed time she would go alone to this spot, situated outside the main camp, and offer herself for coitus to each of the men concerned [both her accusers and defenders]. At the time of coitus, and during the actual act when they were lying close together, the man must tell her that "he won't kill her," or in any way accuse her again

in that particular affair (or should he be the defender, that he would stand by her). Should there be one man who did not appear at the arranged place for coitus, she would know that he still considered her to be in the wrong—i.e. "he won't give himself to her." . . . In this case another meeting might be called, a male relative of the woman standing for her. Should the matter not be settled in this way, the accuser might instigate a fight (i.e. should he consider himself to be in the right), or flee the camp, or be involved in a spearing (should he stubbornly refuse to accept the evidence of the woman or of her male defender). Should the accuser be in the wrong, and finally relent when matters have gone too far, he would arrange for his wife, a female relative, or a friend standing in relationship to him as a wife or sister, to stand for him. He would arrange matters with all the men concerned in the case so that at an appointed time they would go out, one by one, and copulate with the chosen representative of the man, at the same time telling her that the whole affair would be dropped; the matter would then be considered almost settled, the latter woman "squaring" the case, both parties having now put forth a woman. To finalize the affair completely, the original accuser must copulate with the first woman, telling her at the same time that he had wrongly accused her.[35]

Summing Up

Many features traditionally militated against warfare in Aboriginal Australia. First, no one held enough authority or coercive power to command military action.[36] Second, as nomadic hunter-gatherers, the Aborigines were regularly on the move in search of food.

Consequently, they had few material possessions or caches of stored food that others might be tempted to plunder.[37]

Third, groups were interconnected with one another through ties of kinship, religion, and trade.[38] Fourth, band membership was neither closed nor static. Individuals and families shifted band residence over both the short term and the long term. The fluidity of band composition is one feature that contributed to interconnections among bands. Virtually every person had relatives and contacts in other groups. These overlapping social and kinship networks that spanned the flexible bands served to damp intergroup hostility.[39]

Fifth, in the typical Australian Aborigine belief system, tribal territories originated in Dreamtime and theoretically were not changeable. Such beliefs were incompatible with conducting warfare for territorial gain.[40] Sixth, often resources were shared across band territories. A band with an abundance of some resource—a good harvest of a particular food plant, for example— might invite neighboring bands to come and share the windfall. Such generosity was reciprocated when another group experienced an abundance of some resource. In accordance with social custom, when use of a particular resource, whether abundant or not, was requested, permission was generally granted. The Aborigine belief system that promoted generosity and sharing, as well as the typical compliance with the social rules (the Law) regarding, for example, asking and granting permissions, helped to make trespassing, stealing, poaching, or fighting over resources all the less likely.[41]

Seventh, a well-developed legal system settled many personal disputes not only within bands but also between persons living in different bands or tribes. Aboriginal cultures generally shared certain emphases: obey the Law (the rules and customs) originating during Dreamtime, punish wrongdoers who disregarded the Law, attempt to obtain justice via sorcery, or try to resolve disputes through a variety of mechanisms such as duels, contests, juridical fights, meetings, discussions, balancing of debts, enactment of reconciliation ceremonies, and so forth.[42] Eighth, the most common grievances involved accusation of sorcery, rights to women, and, less often, trespass or poaching of a resource. Such grievances tended to be directed at particular individuals, not entire bands.[43] Ninth, the preferred means of dealing with grievances was to use the legal procedures available (point seven above), but the seeking of revenge through individual self-redress (which sometimes resulted in the counter-vengeance of feuding) also occurred in some Aboriginal societies. As discussed in earlier chapters, revenge killings and feuding stem from personal grievances and tend not to pit political communities against one another in the kind of intergroup combat that legitimately can be called warfare.[44]

The foregoing points suggest that with exceedingly rare exceptions, the types of physical aggression that traversed group boundaries cannot be called war. Instead, such aggression consisted on the one hand of seeking vengeance through violent self-redress, an activity that if reciprocated could become feuding, and on the other hand of a class of legal procedures consisting of physical punishment, duels, juridical fights, and the like, whose purpose was to deliver justice with a minimal amount of violence. These latter approaches were mechanisms for keeping the peace, not warfare.

The main point is not that we should return to a nomadic foraging way of life, but rather that the Australian Aborigine case illustrates the human capacities for creative conflict resolution and for coexisting without war. The actual data from this continent of foraging societies do not support the "man the warrior" view of human nature.

10

Void if Detached . . . from Reality: Australian "Warriors," Yanomamö *Unokais*, and Lethal Raiding Psychology

Their peacefulness is the real problem. I sometimes try to imagine what would have happened if we'd known the bonobo first and chimpanzee only later or not at all. The discussion about human evolution might not revolve as much around violence, warfare, and male dominance, but rather around sexuality, empathy, caring, and cooperation. What a different intellectual landscape we would occupy!

It's only with the appearance of another of our cousins that the stranglehold of the killer ape theory began to loosen. Bonobos act as if they have never heard of this idea. Among bonobos, there's no deadly warfare, little hunting, no male dominance, and enormous amounts of sex.

—FRANS DE WAAL, *OUR INNER APE*

In the previous chapter, I mentioned that the Murngin of Arnhem Land in northern Australia engaged in a ceremonial peacemaking fight called the *makarata*. Warner explains, "It is a kind of general duel and a partial ordeal which allows the aggrieved parties to vent their feelings by throwing spears at their enemies or by seeing the latter's blood run in expiation." Whereas the ceremony did not always succeed in restoring the peace, over the twenty-year period of Warner's study, no one was ever killed during a *makarata*. During the expiation ceremony, the elders continuously reminded those throwing spears "to be careful not to kill or hurt anyone." Clearly the *makarata* was not warfare; it was an example of conflict resolution, Australian Aborigine style.[1]

Exquisite rock art showing animals, humans, and mythological beings is spread across Arnhem Land. Dating to perhaps ten thousand years ago in the oldest cases, most of the human scenes portray tranquil daily activities, but some show figures amid flying spears and boomerangs. Archaeologists Paul Tacon and Christopher Chippindale advance the seemingly obvious interpretation that such scenes portray warfare. The main title of their article, for instance, is "Australia's Ancient Warriors." They explain that "some of the paintings depict fighting, warriors, aspects or the results of warfare, and even elaborate, detailed battle scenes."[2]

However, to question the seemingly obvious, there are at least two reasons to doubt whether most of the rock art actually portrays warfare at all. The first is the overall rarity of war among Aboriginal Australians, as documented in the previous chapter. The second stems from the scenes themselves and what is known about Australian Aborigine conflict resolution procedures. The majority of the rock art depictions of aggression are consistent with ethnographically described events that have nothing to do with warfare: revenge killings, the punishment of wrongdoers by delivering spear wounds to the thigh, and, especially, ceremonial expiatory duels such as the *makarata*. In one scene, a single figure has a spear penetrating its torso, an image more concordant with the aftermath of a killing than a battle—there is, after all, only one victim portrayed. In another case, a single figure has been speared in the thigh, an image consistent with an inflicted punishment.[3]

Significantly, most rock art scenes that portray aggression show only a few individuals, a pattern reminiscent of punishments and duels, not intergroup warfare.[4] In speaking of rock art called Dynamic Figures, Tacon and Chippindale write, "In most cases where actual combat is suggested only two or three figures are engaged in some sort of encounter. There are many examples of two opposed figures [see Figure 10.1]. . . . At a site above Jim Jim

Figure 10.1   As portrayed in Aboriginal rock art from northern Australia, boomerangs in flight between two figures suggest that the men are fighting. But are paired contests like this worthy of the label "war"? (Redrawn with permission from P. Tacon and C. Chippindale, "Australia's ancient warriors: Changing depictions of fighting in the rock art of Arnhem Land, N.T.," *Cambridge Archaeological Journal* 4 (1994): 211–48.)

Falls, two opposed Dynamic Figures appear to be engaged in a boomerang fight."[5] By contrast to the abundant two-person dueling scenes, images of groups facing off against each other are relatively rare. Additionally, recalling from the previous chapter the way that the Tiwi met in groups to haggle, throw spears, and vent their emotions, it would seem unwise to jump to the conclusion, on the basis of rock art alone, that bloody battles rather than juridical fights and duels are being presented, even in group scenes.

In short, the corpus of ethnographic data on Australian Aborigines contradicts the a priori assumption that most of these rock art fighting scenes are actually portraying warfare. Instead, even when multiple individuals are shown, the ethnographic data would suggest that, more probably, group-sanctioned punishments, expiatory duels, and similar grievance settlement procedures are being depicted.[6] When viewed from this ethnographic contextualizing perspective, certain speculations offered by Tacon and Chippindale about the supposed intensification of prehistoric warfare in this part of Australia become superfluous: There is not much point in speculating about an intensification of warfare if the events pictured are not actually warfare.[7] Given the individual nature of disputes in band society overall, the duels, contests, and other ritualized modes of conflict resolution regularly used by native Australians in particular, and the paucity of warfare in the Australian Aborigine context, shouldn't presumptions that rock art shows war elicit some healthy skepticism?

I suspect that the concept of war enters the picture not so much from the minds of the original artists themselves as from the interpretations imposed on the artwork by cultural outsiders. Westerners tend to take war for granted and, as we have seen, sometimes inappropriately project their martial conceptions onto indigenous situations. In their article, the Western archaeologists use the word *warfare* thirty-seven times, *war* twelve times, *warring* twice, *military* or *militarily* eight times, *battle* or *battles* twenty-two times, and *warrior* or *warriors* six times (which totals eighty-seven war words), whereas they refer to *resolution of disputes, settle grievances,* and *settling arguments* one time each and *conflict resolution* only twice (for a total of five dispute resolution terms). There also are many aggressive terms in the article that could be applied to individual or group aggression, such as *violence, fight, combat, skirmish, clash,* and *enemy.* The counting of particular words can provide only a rapid and rough reflection of which topics receive emphasis. By this count, Tacon and Chippindale employ unambiguous war terms about seventeen times more often they use conflict resolution terminology (eighty-seven versus five). This ratio is greatly out of step with what is ethnographically known about the widespread use of conflict resolution procedures in Australian Aborigine societies, on the one hand, and the paucity of war there, on the other. Could Tacon and Chippindale's decision to use *warriors* in the title of their article and the fact that their article overflows with war terminology, while virtually neglecting a consideration of indigenous conflict resolution procedures, reflect once again the influences of a cultural tradition on scientific interpretation in which the naturalness and antiquity of war are simply taken for granted?

Bursting the Warriors-Have-More-Kids Bubble

It has become almost obligatory to mention the South American Yanomamö in any evolutionary discussion of warfare. The fact that the Yanomamö are tribal horticulturalists, not nomadic hunter-gatherers, rarely enters the picture. Napoleon Chagnon has referred to the Yanomamö as "our contemporary ancestors." David Buss sees Yanomamö warfare as highlighting "key themes in the evolution of human aggression." And some proponents of the "man the warrior" view discuss the Yanomamö in support of their contention that war evolved as a male reproductive strategy.[8]

The Yanomamö live in sedentary villages, have a patrilineal system of descent, and sometimes raid other villages, occasionally but not usually abducting women in the process. The Yanomamö fit the "man the warrior" scenario rather closely, and this undoubtedly is one reason why their name so often appears in print.[9] Another reason involves a particular spectacular finding. In an article published in 1988, Chagnon announced that Yanomamö men who have participated in a killing have more wives and over three times the number of children as men who have not.[10]

When a Yanomamö man is involved in a killing, he must undergo a purification ritual. After the ceremony, the man is referred to as *unokai*.[11] Chagnon reports that the majority of *unokais* (about 60 percent) have participated in only one killing and the overwhelming majority (79 percent) have participated in one or two killings, but a minority of the *unokais* have participated in multiple killings. Almost two-thirds (243 of 380) of the men studied by Chagnon, however, never participated in killing anybody. Chagnon has repeatedly emphasized that in this society that allows polygyny, *unokais* average more than two and a half times the number of wives and more than three times the number of children as non-*unokais* of the same age.[12] Be sure to note the "same age" part of this claim.

The notoriety that this particular finding has achieved is really astounding. Immediately upon publication, the reports that killers have more children caught the attention of the popular and scientific press. The author of an article in *U.S. News and World Report* proposed that Chagnon's study "lends new credence" to the idea that "war arises from individuals struggling for reproductive success."[13] Almost two decades after the article's publication, citations of this particular study are simply too numerous to track.[14] The article has been republished in a book called *Understanding Violence*. Buss discusses the *unokai* reproductive success findings in his textbook *Evolutionary Psychology*. Judith Harris, in *The Nurture Assumption*, and Steven Pinker, in his best-selling *How the Mind Works*, summarize the findings. The article also is cited by several authors in the *Handbook of Evolutionary Psychology*, published in 2005.[15] The examples go on and on. Pinker explains that data suggesting differences in number of offspring between men who have participated in killing and those who have not are "provocative because if that payoff was typical of the pre-state societies in which humans evolved, the strategic use of violence would have been selected over evolutionary time."[16]

Examination of a sedentary, horticultural, tribal culture such as the Yanomamö certainly is not the best point of departure for making inferences about the evolutionary past. We have seen that bands and tribes differ when it comes to patterns of violence. Bands tend to lack social segments comparable to Yanomamö patrilineages and do not readily form coalitions. Differences in social organization should not be ignored. But this issue pales in comparison to the next problem: Contrary to Chagnon's assertions, the samples of *unokais* and non-*unokais* are *not* the same age.[17] This is readily apparent from glancing at Figure 10.2, which is drawn from Chagnon's own data.[18] A little calculating reveals that the *unokais* as a group are at least 10.4 years older than non-*unokais*. Not

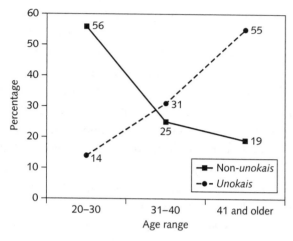

Figure 10.2 Age Distributions for Non-*unokais* and *Unokais*

Notice that 56 percent of the non-*unokais* are 20 to 30 years of age; by contrast, 55 percent of *unokais* are at least 41 years of age. As a group, *unokais* are older than non-*unokais*.

Source: Data used to make this figure are from Napoleon Chagnon, "Life histories, blood revenge, and warfare in a tribal population," *Science* 239 (1988): 985–92, Tables 2 and 3.

surprisingly, a group of older Yanomamö men average more offspring than do the younger men simply because they have had more time to reproduce.[19] But this is not the only problem with the original analysis.

Yanomamö headmen also tend to have more wives and more children than other men, and this fact must be taken into consideration so that our conclusions are not distorted. I have conducted a detailed mathematical reanalysis that demonstrates how neither the effects of age nor headman status were adequately controlled for in the original 1988 study. The most conservative corrections show that without a doubt the reported reproductive difference between *unokais* and non-*unokais* was greatly exaggerated.

It is quite possible in actuality that no difference in *unokai* and non-*unokai* reproductive success exists at all. But if some difference does exist, clearly it is only a fraction of the amount originally reported.[20]

An interesting question to ponder is why the study has gained such popularity in the first place. I propose that at least some of the enthusiastic reception and bountiful reiteration of these findings results from a perception that this study appears to offer a scientific confirmation of widely shared beliefs about violent, warlike human nature. (Remember the similar rush to relabel an entire population as cannibals based on one atypical coprolite discovered at the edge of the domain.) Perhaps another reason that these *unokai* findings continue to be so eagerly embraced is due to a rising interest in evolutionary explanations for behavior. Another consideration is that for some people these findings may have come to represent something much larger than the reported results of one study, namely, that an evolutionary perspective is important and valuable.

I wholeheartedly agree that an evolutionary perspective is important and valuable. But I think it is a mistake to place bets on a tribal-based model of the human past when instead we can wager on a nomadic forager model that more closely mirrors ancestral conditions. Furthermore, the proposal that war has evolved as an adaptation to enhance male reproductive success raises a pile of theoretical problems, which we will now begin to consider.

A Heap of Faulty Evolutionary Assumptions

In 1966, biologist George Williams attempted a theoretical house cleaning. His quest has much relevance today for evaluating the proposition that war is an evolutionary adaptation. Williams begins his discussion by proposing a ground rule: "adaptation is a special and onerous concept that should be used only where it is really necessary." Adaptations result from the evolutionary forces of natural selection operating over time; hence adaptations have evolutionary functions. Williams cautions that functions should not be confused with fortuitous effects. Take apples, for example. Observation and experimentation reveal that the reproduction and dispersal of apple trees are the evolved functions of apples. By contrast, as Williams explains, "the apple's contribution to Newtonian inspiration and the economy of Kalamazoo County are merely fortuitous effects and of no biological interest."[21]

Picking up on Williams' idea, Donald Symons discusses how functional explanations (or adaptations) can be assessed by investigating whether structures or behaviors are *designed* to produce predicted consequences. "For example, the detailed structure of the vertebrate eye provides overwhelming evidence of functional design for effective vision, and indicates continued selection for this purpose throughout the evolutionary history of vertebrates."[22]

A popular view of warfare, reflected in various recent writings, is that war has served evolutionary functions in the human past. This proposition, sometimes implied and sometimes stated, holds that either war itself or else psychological propensities for making war have resulted in higher fitness for individuals bearing such traits and *for this reason* have been favored by selection over past millennia.[23] For instance, Richard Wrangham sees "warfare as adaptive and rooted in genetic predispositions," and refers to such predispositions as "lethal raiding psychology." Wrangham writes that "our history of raiding has given us the tendency to attack whenever the costs appear sufficiently low." In a similar vein, Buss asserts that selection favored psychological traits "designed to lead men to war." Buss further proposes that "women would have been the key reproductive resource that selected for men to evolve a psychology of warfare," and tentatively concludes that "men have evolved specific psychological mechanisms for engaging in warfare."[24] What is the nature of the evidence that warfare itself or psychological mechanisms for warfare have evolved due to natural or sexual selection directly favoring such traits?

One frequently used argument in proposing evolved functions for war is to refer to its widespread occurrence across cultures and throughout history.[25] However, the mere fact that history and ethnography show a plenitude of wars does not prove war making to be an evolutionary adaptation. We must consider what can and cannot legitimately be concluded from the widespread occurrence of a trait. Paralleling adaptations, fortuitous effects also can be widespread. Consider, for example, that apples have economic value across many cultural circumstances; this is simply a fortuitous effect and not evidence that natural selection designed an economic function of apples. Similarly, the widespread use of computer keyboards, literally in every country of the world today, cannot be taken as evidence of a specifically evolved adaptation for keyboard use in humans. Obviously the ability to use computer keyboards is a fortuitous effect of various adaptations and not an evolved function in and of itself. The prevalence of a particular trait—selling apples, computer keyboard use, reading, or waging war—across various cultural landscapes (markedly different from those of ancestral conditions, by the way) does not in and of itself show that such traits are adaptations. The proposal that the widespread occurrence of war demonstrates its evolutionary function is fallacious.

A second, more specific argument for the evolutionary function of warfare alleges that raiding in humans and chimpanzees has a shared, ancient origin, dating to a common ancestor of both species. Wrangham argues that chimpanzees' and humans' warring behavior (coalitionary aggression) must be at least five million years old and therefore must have evolutionary functions.[26]

Several problems arise when using chimpanzees to reconstruct ancestral human behavior.[27] A series of lethal attacks on lone chimpanzee victims, documented at two African locations, Gombe and Kibale, nonetheless has prompted a plethora of speculation about what such behavior might show about the origin of human warfare. Obviously, chimpanzees and humans are different species. At best, chimpanzees provide only tangential insights about human behavior in the evolutionary past. Additionally, one problem with interpreting the acts of violence among chimpanzees, particularly at Gombe, is that killings may have been exacerbated by the destruction of chimpanzee habitats.[28] In locations other than Gombe and Kibale, the evidence for lethal raiding among chimpanzees is not clear-cut.[29] Wilson and Wrangham note, for instance, that "in contrast to Gombe, observers at Mahale neither directly observed intergroup killing nor found bodies of victims."[30]

Second, bonobos (an ape species, referred to in the chapter epigraph, that is about as closely related to humans as are chimpanzees) do not engage in raiding.[31] This raises a question: Why emphasize the common ancestry of humans and chimpanzees while neglecting a comparably close relationship with the peaceful bonobos? Linking humans to chimpanzees instead of to bonobos is an arbitrary decision that is begging for a convincing rationale. In any case, the data most relevant to understanding humans are on humans, whereas data on other species, while also useful at times, nonetheless provide less direct insights.

Third, as we have seen, the worldwide archeological evidence, including clear temporal sequences for the beginning of war in particular locations, contradicts the proposed scenario of five million years of warfare among human ancestors. Fourth, the fact that simple nomadic hunter-gatherers typically are nonwarring also poses a major problem for the assertion of a psychological predisposition for rampant raiding over millions of years.

Fifth, the proposed psychological mechanisms underlying war—what Wrangham calls "an evolutionarily selected 'propensity for lethal raiding'"—are derived merely from speculation, not from psychological research. Some proposed psychological mechanisms include, for example, "the experience of a victory thrill, an enjoyment of the chase, a tendency for dehumanization . . . ready coalition formation, and sophisticated assessment of power differentials."[32] It seems likely to me, partly based upon reading numerous ethnographies, that some or all of these proposed psychological mechanisms, rather than being universal human traits, more likely represent attitudes and ideas circulating within the culture of the theorist. Proposing that hunter-gatherers such as the nonfeuding, nonwarring Paliyan experience a "victory thrill" is totally at odds with their day-to-day peaceful behavior and the value they place on nonviolence and respecting other people.

To take another example, this time contradicting Wrangham's presumption of ready coalition formation as an aspect of so-called lethal raiding psychology, we have seen that Australian Tiwi do not readily form coalitions at all, and this is true for band-level society in general. The nature of band-level social organization—with its bilateral descent, crosscutting ties among bands, shifting band

Figure 10.3 A Batek father entertains his children with a beetle dangling from a string. "Warrior values" are far removed from Batek society. They neither feud nor war. As among nomadic foragers generally, kinship ties interconnect people across small groups with fluctuating membership. The psychology of lethal raiding idea gains no support from band societies such as the Batek. (Photo courtesy of Kirk Endicott.)

membership, and lack of social segments—actually makes coalition formation very difficult.[33]

According to Wrangham, selection favored tendencies "to regard members of out-groups as potential prey, to be alert to (or search for) power asymmetries between in-group and out-group parties, and to be ruthless in attacking out-group parties when the perceived power asymmetry is sufficiently great."[34] Do such traits even exist with any regularity in humans? Maybe some do and maybe others do not. Either way, Wrangham presents no evidence that such traits regularly exist. In fact, such traits do not match what we have observed among Australian Aborigines, the Siriono, and the Paliyan. The assertion that selection has favored such tendencies also lacks evidence. Listing psychological traits that might or might not be widespread in humans and that might or might not have evolutionary functions does not move scientific understanding forward. Such speculation that a "lethal raiding propensity" *might* exist should not be mistaken for evidence that it really *does* exist. Overall, the suggestion that propensities for warfare among chimpanzees and humans share an ancient origin and have been directly favored by selection lacks credibility on numerous grounds.

We have seen how the Yanomamö *unokai* findings continue to be cited to bolster the idea that, over evolutionary time, the risks of warfare must have been outweighed by fitness benefits that warriors are presumed to have accrued.[35] One problem with invoking the *unokai* findings in support of a functional interpretation of war is that these observations about reproductive success are derived from a type of social organization that did not exist in ancestral times. Ignoring for the moment the analytical flaws that call into serious question whether *unokais* have any reproductive advantage over non-*unokais* at all, findings reported on reproductive success from *one* sedentary tribal population provide a pretty weak foundation from which to propose an adaptation for killing or war making in humanity overall.[36]

A final problem arises when discussions of sex differences and adaptation shift back and forth from the aggressive behavior of individuals to the coalitionary aggression of groups.[37] Sex differences in aggression occur in many species that do not make war. Therefore, it is illogical to argue that if men on the average tend to be more aggressive than women, then warfare is an adaptation. In my view, as we will soon consider, a reasonable case can be made that a *potential* for aggressive behavior (but not some rigid inclination for it) has evolved in humans, but the existence of sex differences alone does not lend any support to an assertion that warfare is an evolutionary adaptation. Furthermore, switching back and forth between aggression and war, as if these types of behavior constitute a unified concept, further muddies the already murky waters swirling around evolutionary discussions of warfare.[38]

In sum, all four of the commonly used arguments that warfare is an adaptation have major problems. First, the widespread occurrence of warfare does not provide support for the war-as-adaptation argument, because fortuitous effects also can be widespread. Moreover, the widespread occurrence of warfare is almost certainly very recent in an evolutionary time frame. Second, the ancient common ancestor argument linking the presumed warring propensities of humans and chimpanzees is suspect for multiple reasons, five of which were mentioned. Third, the *unokai* reproductive success finding—major analytical shortcomings aside—relates to only one human society, which happens to be a tribe and thus is not the best choice to use in deriving a model of evolutionary function. Finally, sex differences in aggressiveness cannot logically be used to argue that war is an adaptation. The fact that similar sex differences exist among countless nonwarring animal species highlights that the mere existence of sex differences in humans provides neither a convincing nor a logical argument that warfare is an adaptation.

Writers who suppose that either war or psychological propensities for engaging in war are adaptations—that war has been directly designed by natural selection—are confusing functions with fortuitous effects. Clearly humans have a variety of attributes and capacities—from designing weapons to smoothly cooperating with each other—that make war possible. But this does not mean that such traits evolved specifically for warring. This would be analogous to suggesting that the design of human hands reflects an evolutionary adaptation expressly for using computer keyboards or that the vertebrate eye is an adaptation for reading. Observations that humans are *capable* of reading, keyboard use, chasing prey, being ruthless, and waging war are indisputable; however, such observations are not valid grounds for concluding that these actions have been designed through natural selection expressly to fulfill the specific functions of reading, computer use, or waging war. If we apply Williams' rule and reserve the concept of evolutionary adaptation for situations where it is really necessary, then we lack reasonable grounds for concluding that war is an adaptation.[39]

We soon will consider a new evolutionary perspective on human aggression that is more solidly grounded theoretically and in much closer agreement with observable facts than are proposals derived from either *unokai* findings or, more generally, the "man the warrior" view. In preparation, let's expand upon the conflict management data for Australian Aborigines by reviewing relevant facts on conflict, violence, and conflict management in some additional nomadic hunter-gatherer societies.

11

Returning to the Evidence:
Life in the Band

A dispute [among the Mbuti] may be stopped simply by making life intolerable for the disputants by miming them and throwing them into ridicule. If these measures fail and the dispute persists, the hunting automatically suffers, and if no reconciliation is effected, the band splits, either forming two subsections or remaining as a single band, with the splinter section joining another band, at least temporarily.

—COLIN M. TURNBULL, *WAYWARD SERVANTS*

In Chapter 3 we visited Siriono and Paliyan bands and saw relatively little interpersonal violence, no feuding, and no warfare. Later, we discovered a bounty of conflict resolution techniques and a paucity of war in Aboriginal Australia. Obviously these observations do not jibe with the "man the warrior" perspective. Now we will visit three additional nomadic band societies— the Montagnais-Naskapi, Netsilik, and Ju/'hoansi—and focus our attention on the types of conflicts that actually arise and how they are handled. The goal is to continue building a foundation of knowledge from which to erect a more realistic model of human nature and the potential for peace.

Montagnais-Naskapi

Broadly speaking, Montagnais-Naskapi refers to all the semi-nomadic hunter-gatherer peoples of the Labrador Peninsula in Canada that speak Algonkian languages. Frank Speck vividly portrays native life: "Sheltered only in draughty caribou-skin or bark tents, clad in caribou-skin raiment, using mostly bone and wooden implements, and processing neither political institutions nor government, they follow no occupation or industry other than hunting wild animals and fishing amid the most physically exacting and rigorous climatic environments of the continent."[1]

Jesuit missionary Paul Le Jeune spent the winter of 1633–34 with a Montagnais band and observed that goodwill, helpfulness, and a lack of jealousy characterized everyday life. Le Jeune also noted the high level of equality in social relations generally, as well as between men and women, and that leadership, as among the Siriono and Paliyan, was all but lacking.[2]

Observing that the native women participated in group decisions, went about their tasks unmolested by male supervision, and enjoyed sexual and other freedoms, Le Jeune became concerned. He lectured men to constrain the independence of the women and implored the women to obey the men. Le Jeune was vexed by the manner in which members of both sexes "imagine that they ought by right of birth, to enjoy the liberty of wild ass colts, rendering no homage to any one whomsoever," a poetic statement of what anthropologist nowadays call individual autonomy.[3]

In native legal thinking, the appropriate punishment for homicide is death. The death sentence ought to be carried out by the victim's close male relatives.[4] Furthermore, the murderer himself, not one of his relatives, is the only person subject to revenge. Julius Lips reports that "the kin feeling among the Naskapi is not strong enough to develop into a regular blood feud." In about 1850, a man named Chachiow killed Naytowcaneyoo "to get hold of the latter's wife." After sharing a meal, Chachiow simply stood up and shot Naytowcaneyoo as his wife looked on. Chachiow didn't even bother to bury Naytowcaneyoo properly, but simply piled some snow on the body. The next summer, several of his own band happened to pass by just as Chachiow was about to dine on a rabbit. They shot him in the leg but did not pursue him as he fled. Naytowcaneyoo's wife married another man.[5]

Each individual was more or less on his or her own in dealing with conflicts, since band leadership was ephemeral and no governing structures existed.[6] The strongest force was that of public opinion. Ideally, a person should be generous and cooperative, exercise self-restraint, and avoid disturbing the peace. Quarreling between spouses was exceedingly rare. Individuals avoided showing enmity, it seems, in part due to the pressure of public opinion and in part out of fear that by expressing anger toward another person they might subject themselves to retribution via supernatural means. Mutual dependency also seemed to inhibit the open expression of anger: "The toilsome and lonely life of the Indian in the woods made him inclined to accept a compromise in any legal dispute. His dependence upon his neighbor's aid and good will strengthened this tendency to work out an amicable solution, even with members of other bands."[7]

Social control was maintained largely by rewarding and encouraging positive behavior and also by applying ridicule as a reflection of public opinion. In response to serious transgressions such as incest, constant troublemaking, or murder (if not punished by the victim's kin), the guilty party could be ostracized from the band. "In Naskapi society, expulsion is equal to a death sentence," writes Lips. He recounts how a man named Ámechíchi was banished from his band in about 1870 due to his repeated violations of hunting rules; he starved to death.[8]

Regarding interband relations, Lips explains that borders "are respected by the neighboring bands. However, it is considered permissible to trespass the borderline and to pass through the territory of a foreign band, without any legal or bodily harmful consequences."[9] As is typical among nomadic hunter-gatherers, band composition is in a constant state of flux as families shift from one group to another.

"The different Montagnais-Naskapi bands maintain the friendliest relations with each other; they have never fought each other in any wars."[10] I did not rate the Montagnais-Naskapi as nonwarring in Chapter 6 because Lips reports that they defended themselves from Iroquois encroachment from the south and considered trespassing Eskimos their enemies as well. However, Eleanor Leacock clarifies that Montagnais-Naskapi warring amounted to "sporadic raiding," and her overall assessment is that "warfare was minimal or nonexistent."[11]

Moreover, Leacock points out that the hostilities between the Montagnais-Naskapi and the Iroquois originated from the introduction of the fur trade by Europeans, prompting the Iroquois to intrude into Montagnais-Naskapi territories in search of pelts. Gerald Reid adds: "Confrontations with European settlers and missionaries, the spread of epidemic diseases, the easy availability of alcohol through French traders, and the concentration of people at trading posts and mission stations all contributed to an increase in social fiction and conflict."[12] In sum, the hunter-gatherer bands of the Labrador Peninsula continued their tradition of interacting peacefully with each other, without war, following the arrival of Europeans. However, the encroachment of outsiders searching for furs prompted some fighting by the Montagnais-Naskapi against intruders.

Netsilik Inuit

The Netsilik Inuit are one of many groups in the Central Canadian Arctic that traditionally resided in small nomadic bands with variable membership and weak leadership. In the winter, the Netsilik harpooned seals on the frozen sea, and in the summer, they engaged in fishing and communal caribou hunts.[13] They had few material possessions and did not claim exclusive rights to natural resources. Asen Balikci emphasizes that a person had the right to hunt anywhere he pleased; the exclusion of others from hunting or fishing in a particular location was not allowed.[14]

"Men fight among themselves for a wife, for a simple consequence of the shortage of women is that young men must take women by force if their parents have not been so prudent as to betroth them to an infant girl."[15] As indicated in the quotation, wife stealing among the Netsilik was an individual affair involving a claim to a particular woman. Groups of Netsilik men did not raid other groups for women. Pertaining not only to the Netsilik but also to other Central Canadian Inuit, obtaining a wife by husband killing "was never done on a mass scale, involving war."[16] Only the most skilled hunters could support two wives. Occasionally two men attempted to share a wife. In contrast to the amiable relations between co-wives, sexual jealousy among co-husbands apparently was difficult to conceal and in recent history had contributed to two murders.[17]

Balikci reports that the most frequent cause of homicide was "the desire to steal a certain woman." In six out of seven Netsilik murder cases, the killers were male. The one female killer shot her sleeping husband apparently to get out of the marriage, although, generally speaking, Netsilik women were free to divorce. Netsilik killers used the element of surprise, murdering their victims while they slept or attacking them from behind.[18]

> Ikpagittoq encouraged [his brother-in-law] Oksoangutaq, who was single, to kill Saojori and take his wives. . . . The two men went out and found Saojori on the ice at the very moment when he was about to catch a seal. Saojori guessed the evil intentions of his visitors, and so he held the seal with one hand and kept the other free to grab his knife if he needed to defend himself. The visitors apparently were very friendly and helped to drag the seal to the shore, where Saojori extracted the liver for a quick meal. Then he went down to the beach to wash his hands, still holding his knife between his teeth, ready for defense. As he knelt down at the water, Ikpagittoq attacked him from behind, trying to throw him to the ground. A struggle developed, while Oksoangutaq stood by watching until the embattled Ikpagittoq shouted at him, "You said you wanted to kill this man, what are you waiting for?" Oksoangutaq stepped up and pushed his knife into Saojori's neck, killing him on the spot.[19]

C. Irwin notes that many Netsilik myths he collected focus on the wrongness of homicide and the certainty that a victim's relatives will seek revenge on the perpetrator. The clear moral of the story, that homicide doesn't pay, may discourage some potential murderers. In actuality, avenging a close relative's murder was a possibility, not a certainty. A frequently used alternative to physically killing a murderer was to exact revenge through supernatural means. Fear of supernatural retribution also may have prevented some contemplated homicides. Fearing revenge, murderers often fled to some distant area and did not return for several years, hoping that the passions of their victim's family would subside.[20]

The Netsilik language contains no word for war. Irwin concludes that warfare was nonexistent and that intertribal conflict among the Netsilik and their neighbors "was limited to murder, and revenge killing, or execution." Balikci describes several murders and kin-based revenge expeditions.[21]

Interpersonal conflicts were handled in many ways. Avoidance was practiced. Gossip and mockery were used to check deviancy. Quarreling and fighting were prevented or limited, because people feared aggressive retaliation, loss of beneficial relationships, or sorcery by an opponent. Moreover, the Netsilik utilized ritualized contests to settle disputes without bloodshed. If all else failed, the community could issue a death sentence against a person considered to be dangerously antisocial.[22]

Contests had definite rules. The opponents took turns striking each other on the forehead or shoulder until one man gave up. A Netsilik man explained, "After the fight, it is all over; it was as if they had never fought before." The song duel was another ritualized contest for settling disputes. Each opponent's wife sang the song her husband had composed as he accompanied her by beating a drum and dancing for the audience. The community-wide audience eagerly laughed and joked as they listened. Scathing lyrics included "accusations of incest, bestiality, murder, avarice, adultery, failure at hunting, being henpecked, lack of manly strength, etc."[23]

Killing once demonstrated a man's strength and courage; killing on multiple occasions showed that he was a danger to others. Decisions to kill dangerous deviants sometimes were made by the person's own family. The fact that a deviant's own kin removed the violent or otherwise antisocial person from society had the advantage of preventing revenge.[24]

[Arnaktark] . . . stabbed his wife Kakortingnerk in her stomach. She fled on foot with her child on her shoulders, and after arriving at the main camp she told what had happened.

They started to fear that he might stab again at someone they loved, and they discussed what should be done. The discussion was held among family, and it was felt that Arnaktark, because he had become a danger to them, should be killed. Kokonwatsiark [one of Arnaktark's brothers] said that he would carry out the verdict himself and the others agreed. . . . Kokonwatsiark said to him: "Because you do not know very well any more (have lost control of your mind), I am going to 'have' you." Then he aimed at his heart and shot him through the chest.[25]

In sum, the Netsilik engaged in homicide, revenge killings, executions, and occasionally feuds, but not war. Disputes generally were of a personal nature, and many were between two men over a particular woman. Occasionally, disputes led to homicide, but more often, conflicts were handled through ritualized fights, song duels, sorcery, toleration, and avoidance. "When camp stability was endangered by individuals who disregarded these community interests, or upset the social balance by disruptive aggressive activity or by evil sorcery or insanity, the community did take action—even to the extreme of execution, if it was needed."[26]

Ju/'hoansi

For many years, anthropologists have referred to the Ju/'hoansi of the Kalahari Desert in Africa as the Kung, !Kung, !Kung San, or !Kung Bushmen. Richard Lee suggests that it is more respectful to call the people by the name they use for themselves, Ju/'hoansi, which is pronounced "zhu-twasi" and means "real people."[27] Our focus here is on the traditional nomadic hunter-gathering lifestyle of the Ju/'hoansi, especially on the populations in the vicinity of Dobe and Nyae Nyae because they have been well studied.[28]

Disputes over food or land are rare and seldom entail aggression. They are much less common than quarrels over betrothals and adultery. Instead, the Ju/'hoansi have a nonexclusive, collective pattern of land ownership and reciprocally share resources. *"Among the! Kung [Ju/'hoansi] and other hunter-gatherers, good fences do not make good neighbors,"* emphasizes Lee.[29]

The nomadic Ju/'hoansi do not engage in warfare. "It is extremely interesting and significant," writes Lee, "that the traditional Ju/'hoansi did not attempt to fortify or stockade their village sites in any way. They slept in the open, protected only by their sleeping fires, which keep the carnivores at bay, and by their mutual trust of the peaceful relations with their human neighbors."[30]

Making war would be antithetical to the well-established system of reciprocal sharing wherein each person is linked to individuals in other bands as relatives, in-laws, trading partners, and friends. There is no reason to risk death by going to war over resources when one can exchange favors instead. Furthermore, each person has only a few personal possessions, so basically there is nothing to plunder.[31]

What about raiding other groups for women? As among the Netsilik, this simply does not occur. In parallel to the Alacaluf and Tiwi examples presented in Chapter 8, fighting over a woman is a personal matter among the Ju/'hoansi. Mislabeling this type of dispute as a "battle" or as "warfare" only confuses the situation and obscures the individual nature of such contests. Moreover, disputes over women are seldom lethal.

A lack of war does not mean that all other forms of lethal aggression are absent from Ju/'hoansi society. The Ju/'hoansi commit homicides. They sometimes avenge previous killings and may execute extreme deviants. These forms of violence, however, are not war. Failure to clearly distinguish between warfare and various other types of lethal aggression arising from personal grievances has contributed to confusion about the Ju/'hoansi.[32]

As a pattern, nomadic hunter-gatherers typically promote cooperation, sharing, and egalitarianism, including female–male equality.[33] The Ju/'hoansi are no exception. Marjorie Shostak relates the life story of a woman she calls Nisa. Certainly, Ju/'hoansi women are not at the beck and call of the men:

Sex with a lover [who] a woman really likes is very pleasurable. So is sex with her husband, the man of her house.

Figure 11.1   Among the Ju/'hoansi of the African Kalahari, women gather a variety of vegetable foods. The woman pictured is on a gathering expedition and carries her digging stick. The plentiful mongongo, which provides both fruit and nuts, is the most important vegetable food gathered. When away from camp on gathering trips, married women may rendezvous with their lovers. Richard Lee concludes that, on balance, neither sex exploits the other in Ju/'hoansi society, but to the contrary, there is relative equality between the sexes. (© 2006 Harvard University Peabody Museum, Photo 2001.29.284.)

The pleasure they both give is equal. Except if a woman has pulled her heart away from her lover, then there is little pleasure with him.

When a woman has a lover, her heart goes out to him and also to her husband. Her heart feels strong toward both men. But if her heart is small for the important man and big for the other one, if her heart feels passion only for her lover and is cold toward her husband, that is very bad. Her husband will know and will want to kill her and the lover. A woman has to want her husband and her lover equally; that is when it is good.

Women are strong; women are important. . . . [Ju/'hoansi] men say that women are the chiefs, the rich ones, the wise ones. . . . A woman can bring a man life, even if he is almost dead. She can give him sex and make him alive again. If she were to refuse, he would die! If there were no women around, their semen would kill men. Did you know that? If there were only men, they would all die. Women make it possible for them to live. Women have something so good that if a man takes it and moves about inside it, he climaxes and is sustained.[34]

Although Nisa mentions that a neglected husband might feel like killing, several fieldworkers who have studied the Ju/'hoansi conclude that they devalue aggression and usually avoid it. Based largely on work among a different Kalahari society, the !Ko San, ethologist Irenäus Eibl-Eibesfeldt argues, however, that verbal aggression such as mockery and insults, sorcery, sibling rivalry among children, and children's aggression refute Ju/'hoansi peacefulness. He points out that !Ko San, and by extension the Ju/'hoansi, are not aggression-free.[35]

The first observation is that Ju/'hoansi and !Ko are different societies. Second, the Ju/'hoansi are *relatively* peaceful, not *absolutely* nonviolent. Using terms such as *aggression-free* implies a dichotomy —that is, either having aggression or being aggression-free. By contrast, notice that Lee uses the word *relative*: "The Ju/'hoansi managed to live in relative harmony with a few overt disruptions." Patricia Draper concludes that physical aggression among the Ju/'hoansi is extremely rare but nonetheless does occur.[36]

The Ju/'hoansi themselves specify three types of conflict. The least serious is talking. Next comes physical fighting without deadly weapons. Finally, there is fighting with lethal weapons. Lorna Marshall concludes that talking helps to maintain the peace "by keeping everyone in touch with what others are thinking and feeling, releasing tensions, and keeping pressures from building up until they burst out in aggressive acts."[37] In the most serious verbal altercations, a plethora of sexual insults are exchanged.

Lee observed thirty-four physical altercations that lasted from less than a minute to five minutes.[38] Friendly peacemakers typically intervened. Adultery was the most common reason for the fights. Some features of verbal and physical fighting appear in Nisa's life story as told to Shostak. Nisa had separated from her husband, Besa, and was living with Bo.

I cursed him as he held me, "Besa-Big-Testicles! Long-Penis! First you left me and drank of women's genitals elsewhere. Now you come back, see me, and say I am your wife?" He pushed me toward the fire, but I twisted my body so I didn't land in it. Then he went after Bo. Bo is weaker and older than Besa, so Besa was able to grab him, pull him outside the hut, and throw him down. . . . My younger brother woke and ran to us, yelling, "Curses to your genitals!" He grabbed them and separated them. Bo cursed Besa. Besa cursed Bo, "Curses on your penis!" He yelled, "I'm going to kill you Bo, then Nisa will suffer! If I don't kill you, then maybe I'll kill her so that you will feel pain! Because what you have that is so full of pleasure, I also have. So why does her heart want you and refuse me?"

. . . The next time, Besa came with his quiver full of arrows, saying, "I'm going to get Nisa and bring her back with me."

. . . People heard us fighting and soon everyone was there, my younger and older brothers as well. Besa and I kept arguing and fighting until, in a rage, I screamed, "All right! Today I'm no longer afraid!" and I pulled off all the skins that were covering me—first one, then another, and finally the leather apron that covered my genitals. I pulled them all off and laid them down on the ground. I cried, "There! There's my vagina! Look, Besa, look at me! This is what you want!"

The man he had come with said, "This woman, her heart is truly far from you. Besa, look. Nisa refuses you totally, with all her heart. She refuses to have sex with you. Your relationship with her is finished. See. She took off her clothes, put them down, and with her genitals is showing everyone how she feels about you. She doesn't want you, Besa. If I were you, I'd finish with her today." Besa finally said, "Eh, you're right. Now I am finished with her."

. . . Bo and I married soon after that. We lived together, sat together, and did many things together. Our hearts loved each other very much and our marriage was very very strong.[39]

In the account, the sexual insults flow freely. Nisa's brother plays the role of friendly peacemaker by separating Bo and Besa, and later other people come to the scene of Besa and Nisa's verbal fight and thus are on hand to intervene if necessary.[40] Besa arrives with deadly arrows but makes no move to use them. Besa's own companion takes part in persuading him to give up and leave. Nisa exercises her rights to divorce and is not intimidated by Besa. She finally resorts to a dramatic genital display to get her message across. Judging from the way Nisa speaks about Bo, a husband and wife obviously can have very warm feelings for each other.

The third type of Ju/'hoansi fighting involves weapons and can result in injuries and death. Lee documents twenty-two homicides committed by twenty-five people over a thirty-five year period.[41] All killers were men, and all but three victims were men. Typically, victims were killed by spears or arrows. The Ju/'hoansi cover the tips of their hunting arrows with poison from Diamphidia beetles. Quite probably this practice increased the fatality rate. Furthermore, homicide victims were not always the adversaries themselves, but supporters, peacemakers, or unfortunate bystanders. Some homicides were conducted in revenge for a prior killing. Attempted and successful executions of killers also sometimes resulted in the unintended deaths of others.[42]

Close biological relatives tended not to kill each other. The closest biological relationship between killer and victim was when a nephew dispatched his uncle. Lee's data suggest that successful revenge killings and successful executions of recidivist murderers tended to bring an end to lethal violence. In other words, killing a killer restores a balance, preventing further violence.[43] For instance, the following revenge killing of a murderer provoked no counter-revenge:

One evening D2 walked right into G's camp and without saying a word shot three arrows into G, one in the left shoulder, one in the forehead, and the third in the chest. G's people made no move to protect him. After the three arrows were shot, G still sat facing his attacker. Then D2 raised his spear as if to stab him. But G said, "You have hit me three times. Isn't that enough to kill me, that you want to stab me too?"[44]

Draper explains that the Ju/'hoansi are uncomfortable around unpredictable persons or those with violent tempers. Aggressiveness is *not* appreciated.[45] As Christopher Boehm emphasizes regarding foragers overall, group members may execute "a bullying recidivist killer, possibly a psychotic, who in effect intimidates his group."[46] For instance, a Ju/'hoansi man named =/Gau was described as a lion who "ate people." After he had killed three people, a young in-law of =/Gau stabbed him in the heart as he slept. =/Gau jumped up to attack his assailant but dropped dead in his tracks. A second recidivist killer was named /Twi and, like =/Gau, was a notorious man and possibly psychotic. He was finally put to death by group action. "He had killed two people already, and on the day he died he stabbed a woman and killed a man. . . . No one came to his aid because all those people had decided he had to die. . . . Then they all fired on him with poison arrows till he looked like a porcupine."[47] In all, at least eleven homicides (50 percent of the total) stemmed directly or indirectly from the actions of only two overly aggressive men, =/Gau and /Twi. It is very understandable that the Ju/'hoansi do not like violent-tempered persons.

All this discussion of homicidal violence must be balanced by emphasizing that social relationships seldom involve physical aggression. Ju/'hoansi manage the overwhelming majority of their conflicts through talk, humor, short- and long-term avoidance, friendly peacemaking, and recently by appealing to non-Ju/'hoansi mediators.[48]

Conclusions

The Montagnais-Naskapi, Netsilik, and Ju/'hoansi, like the Siriono and Paliyan considered in Chapter 3, were selected for examination because ample data exist on conflict management in these band societies. What have we learned?

The first essential point is that group violence is minimal in all five of these nomadic hunter-gatherer cultures. Clearly none of these societies could be characterized as warlike. The data suggest that the "man the warrior" view is inaccurate in various ways. In none of the five cases do groups of men from one band attempt to capture women from other bands. Group-level fighting over natural resources is not reported and would appear to be most unusual. Revenge killings and executions occur in some cases. One factor that militates against warfare is that positions of authority are lacking.

Second, the fact that conflicts are personal deserves special attention. The case studies reinforce that disputes tend to be between individuals, not between entire bands. In simple foraging societies, characterized by high levels of individual autonomy, each individual is held personally responsible for his or her own behavior, including acts of violence, theft, adultery, incest, disrespect toward others, failure to share, and so forth. A typical conflict scenario is when two men compete for the same woman. Many, probably most, interpersonal disputes involve little or no actual violence. Homicides are sometimes left unavenged. Revenge killings, when undertaken, again show the personal quality of disputes in simple forager society: The predominant pattern is for family members of the victim to target the actual killer and no one else.

A third point to highlight is the variability among simple nomadic foragers regarding aggressiveness. The Paliyan exhibit extremely low levels of physical aggression, the Montagnais-Naskapi and the Siriono are slightly more aggressive but still rather peaceful, and the Ju/'hoansi and the Netsilik, while not overly violent on a daily basis, nonetheless are markedly more prone to periodic lethal violence than are the first three societies. Male sexual competition is often at the root of contests, song duels, and murders among the Netsilik and arguments, physical fights, and homicides among the Ju/'hoansi. The Montagnais-Naskapi, Siriono, and especially the Paliyan express rivalry and jealousy with far less aggression.

Fourth, when viewed in a broader cross-cultural framework, the kinds of aggression discussed in all these simple forager societies are relatively harmless. Sensibly, none of the anthropologists who have studied these band societies has called them aggression-free. However, the most lethal yet relatively rare form of violence involves the homicide-then-revenge sequence that originates from personal grievances. Some hunter-gatherers, such as the Siriono, are reported to attack foreign trespassers, whereas others, such as the Paliyan, simply avoid intruders. Warfare is absent among the Siriono, Paliyan, Netsilik, and Ju/'hoansi, and of not much consequence among the Montagnais-Naskapi. The Montagnais-Naskapi bands did not war among themselves, but following the changes set in motion by the arrival of Europeans in the New World, they sometimes attacked intruders.

12

Darwin Got It Right: Sex Differences in Aggression

It may metaphorically be said that natural selection is daily and hourly scrutinizing throughout the world, the slightest variations; rejecting those that are bad, preserving and adding up all that are good; silently and insensibly working, whenever and wherever opportunity offers, *at the improvement of each organic being in relation to its organic and inorganic conditions of life. . . . When we see leaf-eating insects green, and bark-feeders mottled-gray; the alpine ptarmigan white in winter, the red-grouse the colour of heather, we must believe that these tints are of service to these birds and insects in preserving them from danger.*

—CHARLES DARWIN, *THE ORIGIN OF SPECIES*

In this chapter and the next, we will consider an evolutionary analysis of the patterns of interpersonal aggression in nomadic hunter-gatherer societies. I will suggest that the forces of natural selection and sexual selection have shaped such behaviors in humans as they have in a great number of other species. Evolutionary theory, models of aggression based on game theory, studies of animal aggression, and data on nomadic band societies converge toward a similar assessment: During human evolution, restraint and limited interpersonal aggression have been favored by selective forces over more extreme aggression. This assessment pertains to interpersonal aggression. If we shift the focus to warfare, *neither the observable facts nor the application of evolutionary principles supports the notion that war is an evolutionary adaptation.* In short, widely publicized assertions by some evolutionary psychologists that war has evolved through natural selection cannot be substantiated by the evidence from nomadic forager studies.

Sexual Selection and Aggression

If the cases of protective coloration referred to by Charles Darwin in the chapter epigraph have evolved in these species due to selection favoring the survival and reproduction of the bearers of these particular traits over individuals lacking such traits, then these instances of protective coloration can be referred to as adaptations. The concept of adaptation applies to behavioral as well as physical traits. In other words, behavioral traits, such as those involving aggression, also are the products of natural selection operating on the variation in behaviors among individuals across past generations.[1]

George Williams points out that some adaptations are relatively fixed or invariable (obligate) while others are more flexible (facultative) in their expression depending upon environmental situations.[2] For instance, humans are adapted to walk upright and nearly always do so, as opposed to creeping, crawling, rolling along, or walking on their hands, regardless of cultural and ecological circumstances. Thus walking bipedally constitutes a relatively fixed adaptation in *Homo sapiens.* On the other hand, human language use is a more flexible adaptation. Whereas humans in every culture use language to communicate, which language or languages a young child begins to speak depends on the particular linguistic environment. Whereas obligate adaptations would be expected to occur across a wide range of social environments, facultative (more flexible) adaptations would be expected to show greater variability of expression across a range of different environmental conditions. Many adaptations in humans tend toward the flexible end of a flexible-to-firm continuum.

Sexual selection results from the variation among individuals in their abilities to acquire mates. Sexual selection can occur in two manners. First, the members of one sex can choose some members of the opposite sex over others; second, the members of one sex can compete with other members of their own sex for mates. The first type of sexual selection can be used to explain the evolution of ornamentation—the huge and colorful tail feathers of male peacocks being a classic example. The second kind of sexual selection accounts for the fighting structures and behaviors observed in many animal species, typically within the male sex. Larger body size in males than in females, greater muscle mass, and structures such as antlers are explained as adaptations for male-male competition evolved via sexual selection. Darwin writes, "It is the males that fight together and sedulously display their charms before the females; and the victors transmit their superiority to their male offspring."[3] Why do males tend to compete over females rather than vice versa?

Biologist Robert Trivers suggests that the answer lies in the unequal amounts of parental investment typically made by females and males in offspring. As Darwin noted: "The female often differs from the male in having organs for the nourishment or protection of her young, such as the mammary glands of mammals, and the abdominal sacks of the marsupials." Among mammals, a male at the minimum can mate and be gone, whereas the female continues to invest in offspring at the minimum through periods of pregnancy and nursing. Parental investment entails time, energy, and risk, and can be defined as any contribution "by the parent in an individual offspring that increases the offspring's chance of surviving (and hence reproductive success) at the cost of the parent's ability to invest in other offspring."[4]

Darwin suggested that the observable sex differences in humans, as in a variety of animals, resulted from sexual selection to a great extent: "There can be little doubt that the greater size and strength of man, in comparison with woman, together with his broader shoulders, more developed muscles, rugged outline of the body, his greater courage and pugnacity, are all due in chief part to inheritance from his half-human male ancestors." Donald Symons observes that in humans female body weight is 80 to 89 percent of male body weight on the average. "If one focuses on the anatomy that is primarily responsible for sex differences, it becomes clear . . . that human males have evolved roughly *twice* the aggressive apparatus of females." In accordance with the evolutionary concepts of sexual selection and parental investment, Symons proposes that men fight more than women because men are evolutionarily adapted to compete over women more than vice versa.[5]

I must emphasize one point to avoid any misunderstandings. The suggestion that certain sex differences in humans, including body size, muscular strength, and fighting ability, are in substantial part attributable to same-sex competition *cannot* be taken as evidence that warfare has evolved via sexual selection. After all, such traits have evolved in numerous animal species that lack any type of aggression remotely resembling warfare. Furthermore, these types of sex differences in humans, as in a host of other animals, are the evolutionary result of competition among *individuals*. It is not necessary, and in fact is theoretically problematic, to propose that sex differences evolved in humans as a result of competition among groups. Such a view, which is referred to as group selection, lacks empirical support.[6]

The cross-cultural evidence, including data from simple nomadic foraging societies, shows an overall pattern. Men tend to engage in more severe physical aggression than do women. With cross-cultural regularity—from the type of nomadic band settings that are most similar to those of the evolutionary past to a range of relatively recent social environments—men tend to commit more homicides than do women. In comparing male-male homicides to female-female homicides, Daly and Wilson conclude that "intrasexual competition is far more violent among men than among women in every human society for which information exists."[7]

Moreover, behavioral findings and crime statistics repeatedly show that physical aggression is both more frequent and more severe in men than in women.[8] Generally, even beyond simple nomadic hunter-gatherer society, it is virtually always men who exact violent revenge or engage in feuds, with great variation across cultures, as we have seen, and in social circumstances where war is present, with only the rarest exceptions, it is men who meet on the battlefields. The sex differences among humans, including larger male body size, greater strength, and overall pattern of disproportionate male participation in aggressive behavior of various types, suggest that Darwin was right: sexual selection in the form of male-male competition has operated on ancestral humans. Males have more potential to engage in physical aggression than do females, but obviously this does not mean that men everywhere are aggressive a lot of the time. The overwhelming majority of human males never commit a homicide, for example.[9]

From the simple nomadic hunter-gatherer case studies, we saw that two Siriono killers were both male, although one killing (and perhaps the other one as well) may have been accidental. In any case, males were the perpetrators in both incidents. In the Montagnais-Naskapi case, where homicides were not common, we considered an example involving a male killer. Homicides by women apparently were rare. Homicide was not reported among the Paliyan. Among the Netsilik, the killers of adults tended to be men. All twenty-two killers among the Ju/'hoansi were male. Again, the Ju/'hoansi rate may be atypically high for nomadic hunter-gatherers due to the ready availability of poisoned arrows.

Several conclusions about lethal aggression in simple hunter-gatherer societies are noteworthy. First, the case study material shows that men commit most homicides. Thus the cross-cultural pattern of sex differences in lethal aggression holds widely across social environments, from conditions resembling the evolutionary past to those markedly different from ancestral conditions. Second, rates of homicide vary, being low in some cases (for example, the Siriono, Paliyan, and Montagnais-Naskapi) and higher in other cases (for example, the Netsilik and Ju/'hoansi). Third, most disputes stem from individual grievances. Recurring reasons for homicide include competition between two men over a particular woman and close relatives of a victim avenging the death of a family member. *These types of dispute are not war; they are instances of individual aggression.* Fourth, it is important that only a small fraction of disputes actually end in homicide, even among the Netsilik and the Ju/'hoansi. Most disputes among simple nomadic hunter-gatherers are not lethal, being handled instead in a variety of other ways, as

Figure 12.1   Two Ju/'hoansi boys practice hunting. Like nomadic foragers everywhere, the Ju/'hoansi share meat. The "owner of the meat" has the right, and obligation, to distribute the meat to others, and ownership is determined by who made the arrow used in the kill. Since men avidly exchange hunting arrows, the owner of a kill is generally *not* the person who actually shot the lethal arrow. Thus a good hunter does not necessarily distribute more meat than does an average or poor hunter. This practice, interestingly, equalizes the glory of meat ownership and distribution among hunters, and reflects in a practical sense the Ju/'hoansi's strong ethos of egalitarianism. (© 2006 Harvard University Peabody Museum, Photo 2001.29.286.)

we have seen. As a generalization derivable from the ethnographic literature on simple forager band societies, the majority of men in such societies never kill anybody.[10]

As pointed out at the beginning of Chapter 5, the tendency for men to engage in more aggression than women does not prove "the ubiquity of warfare and violence across time and space." In a substantial assemblage of societies—the Saami, Sanpoil, Saulteaux, Semai, Semang, Sherpa, and Siriono, to supply a sibilant sample— neither men nor women engage in very much aggression. Thus, one major difficulty with this claim of ubiquitous violence is the existence of a substantial number of nonwarring cultures and societies with very low levels of internal aggression. The claim of ubiquitous violence simply collides with too much data to the contrary. At the same time, the evidence clearly shows that the male capacity for serious violence *is* greater than the female capacity for such violence, and this pattern both makes theoretical sense and corresponds with a great deal of data on animal aggression.[11]

There is a rather easy way to deal with both these observations that does not require a claim that warfare and violence are ubiquitous in the face of indisputable evidence to the contrary. The continuum between fixed, or obligate, adaptations on one end and flexible, or facultative, adaptations on the other can help us out of this conceptual cul-de-sac. Human aggression is a facultative adaptation, somewhat like the capacity to learn language, not a rigid, obligate adaptation like bipedal locomotion. Everywhere, human males tend to be larger in size, have greater strength, perhaps have a greater tendency as children to practice aggression, and as adults possess a greater potential to act aggressively than do females.[12] However, the adaptation for male-male aggressivity in humans is flexible and therefore significantly open to environmental influence.[13] Among the hunter-gatherer case studies, we have seen a range of variation, from the nonviolent Paliyan to the sometimes violent Netsilik. In other words, the implicit assumption that sexual selection has produced the rigid, obligate type of adaptation for human male-male aggressive competition is not defensible in light of the high degree of variability in levels of male aggression that occurs across cultural environmental conditions. Such an assumption runs into difficulty even among the five nomadic hunter-gatherer societies we have considered in some detail, even before referring to the dozens of very peaceful societies known to exist.[14]

Alternatively, if male-male competition is seen as a facultative, flexible adaptation that varies with ecological and social contexts, then theory and facts fit very well together.[15] The observation that some hunter-gatherer societies have very low levels of aggression and others have higher levels of aggression does not create any major obstacle for sexual selection theory. It is no longer necessary to turn a blind eye to the fact that many nomadic hunter-gatherer societies, as well as some other types of societies, have minimal amounts of physical aggression.

13

A New Evolutionary Perspective:
The Nomadic Forager Model

I want to hunt eland, kudu, and gemsbok, but hunting men is what gets you killed.
—JU/'HOANSI MAN, QUOTED BY RICHARD LEE IN *THE !KUNG SAN*

What are the evolutionary costs and benefits of aggressive behavior? Some likely costs include being injured, getting killed, harming relatives if fighting with them, losing friends, taking time and energy away from other necessary pursuits such as finding food or mating, and, among humans, getting yourself expelled from the group.[1] A central point is that engaging in aggression can be dangerous and has the potential for reducing an individual's fitness in various ways.[2] Animals sometimes die as a result of injuries sustained in fights, as observed, for instance, among hyenas, lions, and various primates, but as ethologist Robert Hinde assesses, "death and injury are less common than might be expected." Aggression researchers Caroline and Robert Blanchard explain: "In evolutionary terms . . . successful individuals will be those with techniques which enable them to avoid agonistic situations involving serious possibilities of defeat or injury, while leaving them to continue in more promising situations."[3]

Evolutionary benefits of aggression include, depending on species and circumstances, obtaining food, territory, or mates, protecting oneself and one's offspring and other relatives from injury or death, and gaining dominance and hence better access to resources or mates. Thus aggression seems to have various evolutionary functions. Furthermore, the severity, frequency, and specific functions of aggressive behavior vary from species to species. For instance, some species engage in territorial defense whereas others do not, and some species fight primarily during mating season whereas others are aggressive in other contexts.[4]

The essential point is that although aggression can be risky, clearly it can be beneficial to individual fitness in certain circumstances. Theoretically speaking, we would expect that *natural selection, operating over many generations, has shaped the aggressive behavior engaged in by the members of a given species, including humans, so as to maximize fitness benefits and minimize fitness costs under conditions of the ancestral evolutionary environment.*

Forager Aggression: Costs and Benefits

In considering costs and benefits of aggression, it may be useful to assess what the nomadic forager data show about reasons for conflicts. Among the nonviolent Paliyan, the most serious disrespect cases involved sexual jealousy between husbands and wives. In Siriono society, the majority of disputes involved food or sex. Among the Montagnais-Naskapi, a man murdered a husband to get his wife. A common cause of disputes in Ju/'hoansi society was adultery. Competition among Netsilik men over a particular woman was a typical reason for conflict and sometimes resulted in aggression. Thus the case studies suggest that much fighting at the band level of social organization stems from competition between men over a woman, and less often competition between women over a man, with the latter, when it occurs, being less injurious. This pattern is in accordance with predictions derived from sexual selection and parental investment theory.[5]

Additionally, among the Ju/'hoansi, Netsilik, and Montagnais-Naskapi, homicides at times led to revenge killings by close family members of the victim. The overall conclusion from the case studies is that serious aggression tends to result most typically from women and homicides, although of course a miscellany of other reasons also can underlie aggression in simple forager bands.[6]

The fighting of two men over a woman has obvious parallels in other species. We can speculate that the evolutionary benefits to be gained by defending or usurping a woman depend on a number of variables such as the age and health of the woman and an availability of other mates in the population. Interestingly, Netsilik society has a sex ratio imbalance, due largely to the practice of female infanticide, and among the Netsilik we see more lethal fighting over women than in the other four case study societies. In humans, belief systems regarding the acceptability or unacceptability of aggression also figure into the equation, as indicated by the rarity of physical aggression and the paucity of homicides among the Paliyan. Some Paliyan obviously feel jealousy, but the nonviolent values and patterns of respectful interaction that individuals internalize during socialization are highly successful at preventing homicide.

The fact that close family members of a victim sometimes avenge a murder in nomadic forager society, as far as I know, constitutes a uniquely human motive for killing. Revenge killings are reported for the Montagnais-Naskapi, Netsilik, and Ju/'hoansi. However, not all homicides are avenged.[7] It is important to emphasize a recurring pattern among nomadic foragers: *When revenge is undertaken, the tendency is for family members of the victim to target the killer personally.* This pattern is apparent in Ju/'hoansi homicide data. Recall that eleven out of a total of twenty-two killings were initial homicides.[8] Subsequently, revenge was sought against four original killers, whereas seven killings went unavenged. During retaliation attempts, the attacks sometimes went awry, resulting in the death of an attacker or a bystander rather than (or in addition to) the original malefactor. A cross-cultural study of vengeance by Karen Ericksen and Heather Horton also reflects the pattern among nomadic foragers wherein individuals, as opposed to kin groups, engage in self-redress against killers. In a majority of the nomadic band societies (eleven of seventeen) for which information was available, Ericksen and Horton report that a malefactor was either the only target or the preferred target of vengeance, or else that the society exhibited the "highly individual"—that is, *not* kin-group-based—pattern of individual self-redress.[9]

Killing is risky business, and nomadic hunter-gatherers certainly understand this, judging from the use of risk reduction tactics. Asen Balikci concludes that Netsilik "murderers were evidently careful to avoid a struggle." A prevalent homicidal tactic is to surprise the intended victim, as illustrated by Montagnais-Naskapi, Netsilik, and premeditated Ju/'hoansi homicides and numerous others in the ethnographic record. Killers attack their victims from behind or while they are asleep. For example, "/Toshe sneaked up on =/Gau in the dead of night while he was sleeping and stabbed him in the heart with a spear." A second risk reduction tactic involves outnumbering the victim, as illustrated by the murder by *two*

Alacaluf brothers of the man who was living with one brother's wife, the killing of a husband by *two* Netsilik brothers-in-law, and several planned Ju/'hoansi revenge killings that involved multiple perpetrators.[10]

Due to the possibility of becoming the victim of revenge, a common tactic used by killers in nomadic forager society is to flee or hide after committing a homicide, as was typical among the Netsilik.[11] Recall that the Montagnais-Naskapi killer hid in the woods with the wife of the man he had killed.

Inclusive Fitness and Forager Aggression

In 1964, biologist William Hamilton suggested that the degree of biological relatedness between individuals affects the manner in which they interact with each other. The more closely individuals are related, the more helping, sharing, and caring should be expected. Alleles are alternative forms of a particular gene, and due to common inheritance, relatives are likely to have many identical alleles. Helping relatives is an indirect way of enhancing one's own fitness—hence the concept is known as *inclusive fitness*.[12]

The inclusive fitness concept has the potential for elucidating some aspects of aggression among nomadic hunter-gatherers. Inclusive fitness theory predicts that close relatives will come to each other's aid during aggressive conflicts.[13] We have seen an example of such aid as an Alacaluf brother assisted his sibling in a murderous maneuver to recoup a wife.[14]

I think, however, the application of inclusive fitness theory to conflict situations in humans has been too narrowly conceived as fighting support. "Aiding" a relative in an aggressive situation should not automatically imply that fighting shoulder to shoulder is the only or best tactic as weighed by inclusive fitness enhancement. Perhaps a more effective aid-giving approach, in some circumstances, involves talking some sense into an infuriated relative and dragging him away from a risky situation. I am reminded of the idea behind a slogan used in the United States intended to reduce drunk-driving tragedies: "Friends don't let friends drive drunk." In this case, kin don't let kin fight foolishly. My speculation is based in part on a recurring theme in ethnographic accounts: In nomadic bands, and also in other types of societies, third parties routinely distract and separate disputants. How does inclusive fitness theory apply here? In nomadic band society, third parties are generally relatives to some degree of one or both antagonists.

Inclusive fitness theory also leads to the prediction that biological relatives should not kill or harm one another.[15] Seemingly counter to this prediction, we have seen that a Netsilik man killed his violent, insane brother and that one of the two Siriono killers threw a wooden club from a tree, killing his sister. In the Netsilik case, the entire family and other members of the band saw the act as necessary for the safety of everybody. In short, this is an unusual situation wherein the victim, while a relative, represents a deadly threat to all his other relatives. As mentioned, the Siriono killing may have been an accident. These two incidents reinforce a broader epistemological point. In attempting to assess overall patterns, we should not lose sight of the forest when confronted by an occasional exceptional tree. Unfortunately, ethnographic reports are often sketchy as to the degree of relatedness between killer and victim, but regarding the Ju/'hoansi, Lee specifies that the closest biological relationship between killer and victim was nephew and uncle: "Close kin do not kill one another."[16] Given the fact that biologically related family members are regularly in proximity to each other in band society, Ju/'hoansi killings would seem to disproportionately represent nonkin and distant kin over close family members.

Insights from Game Theory

Game theory provides us with a hawk-dove model, which, although simple, offers some tantalizing insights. John Maynard Smith and G. R. Price used computer simulations to model the evolution of aggression by comparing the relative success of different fighting strategies. They used the term *evolutionary stable strategy*, or ESS for short, to refer to a particular behavioral pattern, such that "if most of the members of a population adopt it, there is no 'mutant' strategy that would give higher reproductive fitness." An ESS is roughly comparable to a behavioral adaptation. The ESS concept rests on the idea that a particular behavioral response will evolve not because it is good for the group or species as a whole, but rather because the given behavior is best for any individual to engage in as a way to maximize individual fitness.[17]

The researchers found that neither belligerent (hawk) nor timid (dove) strategies are as evolutionarily successful as an approach dubbed the *retaliator strategy*. The retaliator strategy involves being nonaggressive unless attacked, in which case the retaliator fights back. In the evolutionary simulations, individuals who retreated too readily from a fight did not fare very well in comparison to more aggressive individuals; however, fighting entails risks, and thus bellicose individuals also accrued evolutionary penalties. The conclusion is that limited or judiciously applied aggression is more advantageous than either pacifistic or overly belligerent strategies.[18]

Game theorist Robert Axelrod used computer simulations to compare sixty-two different strategies for cooperation and defection between pairs of players matched in a cyberspace tournament. With a change of terminology, cooperation can be viewed as somewhat analogous to engaging in restrained, relatively safe fighting, whereas defection can be seen as employing injurious fighting techniques. Interestingly, one strategy, called tit for tat, outperformed all the other strategies. The tit for tat strategy entails always cooperating on the first move and thereafter doing exactly what the other player did on the previous move. If the other player defects rather than cooperates, tit for tat also defects next time. If the other player then cooperates, the tit for tat strategy then also cooperates. Thus the tit for tat approach parallels in some ways the retaliator strategy from the hawk-dove simulations, which never attacks (defects) first, but responds to an attack (defection) by fighting back. Axelrod explains tit for tat's robust success in outperforming a multitude of alternative strategies: "[It is] nice, retaliatory, forgiving, and clear. Its niceness prevents it from getting into unnecessary trouble. Its retaliation discourages the other side from persisting whenever defection is tried. Its forgiveness helps restore mutual cooperation. And its clarity makes it intelligible to the other player, thereby eliciting long-term cooperation."[19]

What is the typical pattern of aggression in nomadic forager bands? Does aggression tend to be restrained or of a no-holds-barred variety? In other words, in this natural context, is aggression typically hawkish, dovish, or retaliatory?

Human Hawks, Doves, and Retaliators

Computer simulations comparing different fighting strategies found that retaliators outcompete hawks and doves. In none of the five band societies that we have examined in detail is a hawkish approach popular or typical. Acts of gratuitous aggression violate the emphasis that nomadic foragers place on egalitarianism, sharing, and generosity.[20] In correspondence with the computer simulation, the occasional hawk does not fare very well. Among the Ju/'hoansi, the two notorious killers, =/Gau and /Twi, both met violent ends. Among the Netsilik, a man executed his own brother who had become mentally unbalanced and unpredictably violent. The Montagnais-Naskapi sometimes indirectly imposed a death sentence by ostracizing a serious malcontent.

In fact, the execution of violent persons and bullies is pervasively reported for band societies. David Damas' assessment for the Copper Inuit also applies to many other nomadic foragers: "Certain men were feared for their aggressiveness or violent tendencies, but they almost invariably met with violent ends themselves."[21] E. A. Hoebel explains the usual fate of the recidivist killer: "As a general menace, he becomes a public enemy. As a public enemy, he becomes the object of public action. The action is legal execution: a privilege-right of the executioner. The single murder is a private wrong redressed by the kinsmen of the victim. Repeated murder becomes a public crime punishable by death at the hands of an agent of the community."[22]

Based on an extensive consideration of the literature, Christopher Boehm writes that "reports of execution of individuals who behave too aggressively are available for Eskimos, North

American Indians, Australian Aborigines, and African foragers. . . .
My suspicion is that the pattern may be generalized to nomadic
foragers in general." To return for a moment to the tribal
Yanomamö and the "man the warrior" view, the recurring pattern
wherein recidivist killers are executed in nomadic hunter-gatherer
society and the fate of the hawks in evolutionary computer
simulations provide additional empirical and theoretical reasons,
respectively, for seriously doubting the plausibility of the scenario,
as often derived from Chagnon's *unokai* findings, that killers
have been favored over nonkillers (or warriors over nonwarriors)
during human evolution.[23] This proposal simply doesn't make
evolutionary sense.

Has the elimination of overly aggressive persons in band society
over millennia actually constituted an additional selection pressure
against hawks? And if so, does the execution of hawkish individuals
in band societies constitute an additional, perhaps uniquely human
selection pressure against overly aggressive individuals? I suggest
that it does.

What about the retaliator (or tit for tat) approach to life? Recall
that retaliators act peacefully unless attacked but then fight
back. The case studies suggest that nomadic foragers behave in
rough accordance with the retaliator strategy. The first part of the
retaliator strategy, to act peacefully, is clearly evident in everyday
social behavior. Most foragers interact nonaggressively most of the
time. None of these five societies places a high value on aggression,
and this generalization holds for most nomadic forager societies.[24]
To the contrary, generosity, calmness, and industriousness are
appreciated, reinforced, and emphasized during the socialization
of children and in social life overall. At the same time, these

societies are characterized by high levels of individual autonomy, wherein individuals defend their own rights. Recall how justice seeking among the Montagnais-Naskapi, Netsilik, and Ju/'hoansi is largely an individual affair. This constitutes a pattern in band society.[25]

While a certain amount of conflict among simple hunter-gatherers fits the retaliator strategy rather closely, at the same time these real life band dwellers are more flexible than computer-simulated retaliators. For example, instead of automatically retaliating, as in a computer model, nomadic foragers are renowned for "voting with their feet" and simply walking away in response to a conflict or attack. Furthermore, many grievances are resolved verbally, often with the involvement of third parties, rather than through physical retaliation. Dealing with conflict via avoidance, toleration, and other nonphysical means such as discussion and mediation suggests that in the real world of nomadic foragers, physical retaliation is only one option among others.[26]

Interestingly, the Paliyan, with their nonviolent belief system and corresponding peaceful behavior, at first glance might seem to be a population of doves. But are they true doves or are they really retaliators who rarely encounter any acts of aggression to retaliate against? The ESS simulations suggest that peaceful behavior among the Paliyan and similar nonviolent bands probably stems from retaliators engaging in the first part of their strategy, since a population of true doves theoretically would not fare well if invaded by hawks (but, of course, neither would the hawks in comparison to retaliators). Again we see that viewing aggressive behavior as a facultative, flexible adaptation is more consistent with the data than is viewing it in an obligate way.

Animal Aggression and Restraint

Additional insights about human aggression can be gained from evolutionary studies of animal aggression. Animal studies suggest that much of the aggression occurring within a species does not entail all-out fighting, but rather is restrained.[27] Rattlesnakes inject prey with deadly venom and may use their lethal fangs in self-defense against predators, including unlucky humans from time to time. However, when two male rattlers compete for a female they do not use their venomous fangs. Instead they wrestle with intertwined necks until one is pinned. The winner then releases the loser unharmed. Male mule deer "fight furiously but harmlessly by crashing or pushing antlers against antlers, while they refrain from attacking when an opponent turns away, exposing the unprotected side of its body." Overall, studies show that for the most part animals use nonlethal, restrained patterns of competition. By evolutionary reasoning, the use of threat displays in place of actual fighting, the employment of ritualized competitions (as is common among ungulates), and the display of submission and appeasement signals (as observed among many primates) exist because they have benefited individuals who have engaged in these kinds of restrained aggression over those who have not.[28] The same evolutionary logic can be applied to explain patterns of restraint observed among humans as well.

Restraint Among Nomadic Foragers

An examination of conflict and aggression in nomadic hunter-gatherer society, as among animal species, shows that individuals practice a great deal of restraint. Of Yahgan foragers, Martin Gusinde expresses: "A person will literally foam with rage. . . . Nevertheless, he can muster astonishing self-control when he realizes that he is too weak to stand against his opponent."[29]

The "voting with one's feet" approach to conflict, so widely practiced by nomadic foragers, obviously reflects restraint. Pertaining to the Netsilik, Balikci calls this technique a "very important strategy for conflict resolution."[30]

A second indication of the typicality of restraint is that a great number of disputes simply never escalate to the level of physical aggression. In evolutionary terms, if a conflict can be handled without incurring the risks associated with physical fighting, so much the better. Recall that animals sometimes employ low-risk threat displays in place of actually fighting. Humans, with language at their disposal, employ verbal threats in a parallel manner. We have seen that the Ju/'hoansi, for example, deal verbally with a great number of disputes.[31]

Third, the ritualized aggression of various animal species has analogs among nomadic foragers, as illustrated by the song dueling among the Netsilik, the formal pattern of spear throwing and dodging among the Tiwi, and the *makarata* peacemaking ceremony of the Murngin. Another example of ritualized restraint comes from the Siriono and their rules for fighting, which permit wrestling but not punching "like a white man." We saw that Siriono bystanders enforce the cultural rules of fair fighting. Such aggression-limiting rules and ritualized contests are regularly mentioned in the ethnographic literature on simple foragers.[32]

A fourth indication of restraint is that even within societies where revenge killing is socially allowed or advocated, as among the Netsilik, many killings simply go unavenged. The fact that

Figure 13.1   A group of Mardu from Western Australia in 1964. Self-restraint and ritualization are apparent in the way the Mardu handle grievances. Bob Tonkinson explains, "when men fight each other, the unstated aim of the many conventions surrounding their conflicts is to allow maximum opportunity for the dispute to be aired verbally. This takes place in an atmosphere of great public drama and menace, so that honor is seen to be satisfied, but with a minimum of physical violence." (Photo courtesy of Robert Tonkinson; the quote is from his 1978 book, *The Mardudjara Aborigines: Living the Dream in Australia's Desert*, 124.)

killers tend to flee in part accounts for this, but another reason may be due to restraint on the part of would-be avengers, a strategy that would seem to keep them out of risky situations. Alternatively, revenge is sometimes exacted through supernatural means, a very low-risk method, since it can be done from a safe distance and the target may never know that sorcery has been directed against him. Considerable patience may be required. The Netsilik, for instance, are aware that "the evil spell may take a long time, sometimes years, before reaching the culprit and accomplishing the original intention of revenge." Finally, the circumstances of the killing and the character of the victim come into play. Among the Yahgan— and I suspect also more generally—the danger of a revenge killing may be "even greater in the case of a murder for an insignificant reason." At the same time, there seem to be circumstances wherein family members of a homicide victim acknowledge that "he had it coming," or concede that a lethal duel "was a fair fight," and thus seek no revenge.[33]

As an important aside, I must comment that a focus on restraint also puts a new spin on tribal Yanomamö aggression. As among nomadic foragers, Yanomamö men minimize risks. They often take revenge through sorcery rather than by physically attacking an enemy, many disputes are handled through contests that curtail serious injury and the loss of life, raiding is undertaken in groups instead of individually, men find excuses to drop out of raiding expeditions, the ambushing of a single unsuspecting victim is a favored tactic, women usually are *not* captured during a raid because they slow down the rate of retreat and thus endanger the raiders, villages sometimes simply move away from aggressive neighbors, and so forth. Such features are rarely mentioned in descriptions that instead stress the valor of the allegedly fierce Yanomamö *unokais*. A film called *The Ax Fight*, by Tim Asch and Napoleon Chagnon, further illustrates that Yanomamö aggression is tempered with restraint. As the film begins, the self-restraint of two adversaries is clearly apparent during a long standoff following a very brief pole fight. Later, self-restraint is shown by a number of Yanomamö engaged in a melee. In the fast-paced brawl, attackers hit their victims with the flat side of machetes and with the dull sides of axes rather than using the chopping sides. Various third-party peacemakers appear in the footage, including the headman. When a young man is knocked to the ground as the dull side of an ax strikes his back, all fighting stops until the extent of his injuries can be determined.[34] As in many animal species, the use of restraint by humans is apparent across a variety of social environments. Exercising restraint during aggressive encounters may well be the outcome of strong selective forces operating over evolutionary time.

Assessing the Patterns and Themes

In summary, the anthropological material on patterns of aggression in nomadic hunter-gatherer settings is *not* consistent with an image of Hobbesian hawks. To the contrary and in parallel with studies of aggression in various animal species, *a great deal of restraint on aggression is evident in nomadic forager societies.* Conflicts are handled by toleration, avoidance, and a plethora of safer, nonphysical approaches such as verbal harangues, arguments, discussions, reprimands, song duels, and mediations assisted by others. Some groups have developed social rules that help to limit the severity of physical fighting or ritualized contests that allow for the venting of emotions without serious injury. In band-level societies, onlookers, as interested third parties who are often relatives, stand ready to intervene to enforce the rules or pull contestants apart should fighting escalate. Such interventions are often unnecessary because both contestants of their own accord simply follow the rules of restraint. It is in their interest to do so because following the rules minimizes risks to both of them.[35] As is observable elsewhere in the animal kingdom, the restrained or limited use of aggression among nomadic foragers is readily apparent.

The overall patterns of aggression observable in these five band societies, and reinforced by accounts of conflict in other band societies, show numerous similarities with aggressive behavior observed in other species. Furthermore, the typical patterns of aggression in nomadic forager social settings are largely consistent with predictions from evolutionary theory. In accordance with ESS modeling, for example, hawks do not fare well in these real-life settings. The majority of conflicts are dealt with without the use of physical aggression. Sex differences in aggression match predictions from sexual selection and parental investment theory. The reasons for disputing, whether through nonphysical or physical means, tend to be highly personal at the band level of social organization. Most disputes result from individual interests, often of a sexual nature. This corresponds with much aggression among animals. It seems likely that the patterns of interaction among simple foragers are in accordance with predictions of inclusive fitness theory, although data on this point are fragmentary. Close relatives sometimes support each other in aggressive actions, but perhaps of equal importance, close relatives, in third-party roles, help each other avoid and retreat from aggressive altercations, thus minimizing the risks. The intervention by friendly peacemakers, whether relatives or friends, is widespread. This pattern, by the way, also has been observed among other primate species.[36]

Aggression among nomadic hunter-gatherers also has some features unique to humans. First, language facilitates a vast array of options for dealing with conflict verbally, from threatening to apologizing. Second, the killing of someone is felt to be an abuse of the victim's family, and they sometimes kill the perpetrator in revenge.[37] Revenge killing, while not universal across simple band societies, is nonetheless a typical social feature associated with this type of social organization, in contrast to feuding and warfare, which are not typical of bands. And avenging the death of a close relative seems to be uniquely human. The exaction of revenge against killers would seem to represent an additional powerful selection force against killers, especially gratuitous killers, that can be hypothesized to have operated in the social world of ancestral humans.[38]

14

Setting the Record Straight

Hunter-gatherers are generally peoples who have lived until recently without the overarching discipline imposed by the state. . . . The evidence indicates that they have lived together surprisingly well, solving their problems among themselves largely without recourse to authority figures and without a particular propensity for violence. It was not the situation that Thomas Hobbes, the great seventeenth-century philosopher, described in a famous phrase as "the war of all against all."

—RICHARD LEE AND RICHARD DALY, INTRODUCTION TO *THE CAMBRIDGE ENCYCLOPEDIA OF HUNTERS AND GATHERERS*

Why do variations of the "man the warrior" perspective pop up faster than mushrooms after a good rain? Today, of course, we humans live in largely closed, socially bounded, territorial groups called countries. We all know that territorial integrity is paramount in our current world. We also know that relations between countries are sometimes hostile and that wars are always raging somewhere. With hardly an exception, nations have armaments, a military, and "prudently" prepare for the "next war." We identify ourselves as Mexicans, Finns, Americans, and so on. We wave literal and figurative flags, we are proud, and we set ourselves apart from people of other nations. Furthermore, many of us come to suspect from current events that competition for resources such as oil lies at the roots of at least some wars. We also take for granted that nations have leaders who manage affairs during peace and war. We honor our war heroes. Thus the "man the warrior" outlook corresponds closely with our current social and political world. Even the name Richard Alexander selected for his hypothesis about the function of human groups, "balance of power," is, of course, currently used in discussions of international relations.[1] One explanation for the appeal of the "man the warrior" idea is that it retells us a current-day tale that is comfortably familiar and easy to accept. The story line simply "feels right."

Are there other factors that might contribute to this blatant mismatch between the model and the facts? First, researchers who actually study nomadic hunter-gatherers—who know the relevant facts, in other words—are *not* the ones proposing "man the warrior" scenarios. Hunter-gatherer specialist Julian Steward has this to say: "There have been many contentions that primitive bands own territories or resources and fight to protect them. Although I cannot assert that this is never the case, it is probably very uncommon." Bruce Knauft reaches this overall assessment for simple hunter-gatherers: "With emphasis on egalitarian access to resources, cooperation, and diffuse affiliative networks, contrary emphasis on intergroup rivalry and collective violence is minimal." John Gowdy concludes, "Judging from historical accounts of hunter-gatherers, for most of the time humans have been on the planet we have lived in relative harmony with the natural world and with each other. Our minds and cultures evolved under these conditions."[2]

In contrast to researchers who actually study foragers, advocates of the "man the warrior" model tend to be from disciplines such as primatology and evolutionary psychology that are far afield from actual hunter-gatherer research. This observation might account, at least in part, for why "man the warrior" advocates are likely to reiterate the highly publicized Yanomamö *unokais* findings, place great emphasis on chimpanzees but not bonobos, and, at the same time, ignore the huge corpus of data on hunter-gatherers that contradicts their assumptions.

The picture of intergroup relations among nomadic bands is taking shape. First, in Chapter 6, an examination of the simple foragers in the SCCS showed the majority to be nonwarring. Second, the type of war practiced by the minority of simple hunter-gatherers in the sample seems relatively mild when compared with descriptions of fighting among equestrian and complex hunter-gatherers. Third, some so-called war reported for band societies in fact reflects nothing more than a misapplication of martial language to homicides, revenge killings, or juridical contests. Recall, for instance, how Jane Goodale refers to the noninjurious, ritualized exchange of spears—after a Tiwi wife deserted her husband—as a "battle."[3] Fourth, some warfare reported for simple foragers stems from an avalanche of social disruptions directly or indirectly caused by the spread of Europeans around the globe in recent centuries. Fifth, the data from Aboriginal Australia show warfare to be atypical of this continent of nomadic hunter-gatherers. Overall, the emerging picture is that warring at the nomadic band level of society is pretty rare and not very severe. This pattern is certainly reflected in the five nomadic band societies we have considered in some detail. All the forgoing observations cast doubt on the "man the warrior" presumption that warfare played a leading role in humanity's evolutionary past. However, before moving on, we must clear up an apparent contradiction between all the lines of evidence that support an unwarlike picture of band society and one particular cross-cultural study that continues to be frequently cited in support of "man the warrior" proposals.[4]

In 1978, Carol Ember wrote, "I wish to address myself to one other view of hunter-gatherers that I have reason to believe is erroneous—namely, the view that hunter-gatherers are relatively peaceful." Ember reported that only 10 percent of her "sample of hunter-gatherers . . . were rated as having no or rare warfare."[5] Many writers cite this study. Political scientist Joshua Goldstein, for instance, relies on Ember's findings to assert:

> The evidence from modern-day gathering-hunting societies, whose supposed peaceful nature was assumed to reflect peaceful human origins, in fact shows the opposite: modern gathering-hunting societies are *not* generally peaceful. Of 31 gathering-hunting societies surveyed in one study, 20 typically had warfare more than once every two years, and only three [10 percent] had "no or rare warfare." . . . If typical gathering-hunting societies found today represent the typical societies found before the rise of the state—as advocates of peaceful origins have claimed—then those original societies were warlike.[6]

Is Goldstein's conclusion really justified? There are two reasons why it is not. First, the original study defined war so as to include feuding and even revenge killings directed against a single individual.[7] Under this definition, personal grudges that result in a killing can be counted as acts of "war" if two or more persons commit the deed. This point alone, which is *not* clearly explained in the article itself, is sufficient to cast a totally different light on the findings.[8] The second serious complication is that, amazing as it might seem, *48 percent of the societies in the sample are not nomadic hunter-gatherers at all.* They are complex and equestrian hunter-gatherers, which, as we have seen, are very different from nomadic foragers. Therefore, the findings of Ember's study cannot legitimately be used to draw inferences about simple hunter-gatherer bands or the nomadic foraging past.[9]

The archaeological record shows that for most of humanity's existence, there were no villages or cities, no herding of animals, no horticulture, and no agriculture. These were the conditions under which the genus *Homo* appeared about two million years ago and more recently under which modern *Homo sapiens* emerged roughly 40,000 to 50,000 years ago. Therefore, if we want a window to the past, we should look for recurrent patterns among extant simple foragers. This decision is logical and defensible, even while acknowledging that simple current-day hunter-gatherers are not identical to ancestral groups. Combining archeological findings and a careful study of nomadic foraging societies represents our best bet for gaining useful inferences about our past.

My explicit assumption is that features that recur with great consistency across ethnographies of hunter-gatherer band societies also are highly likely to have occurred in band societies of the evolutionary past.[10] The overall patterns that emerge from nomadic forager studies are that simple hunter-gatherers live in small groups most of the time.[11] The membership of the small bands is flexible and changing. Individuals and families visit other bands, join other bands, and on occasion may forage as family units. At any given time, a person will have friends and relatives in various other bands.[12] The most common form of descent among simple hunter-gatherers is bilateral, a system that considers both mother's and father's lines rather than only one line as in a patrilineal system

Murdock Codes[a]	Knauft Sample[b] (n = 39)	SCCS Sample (n = 21)
Descent:		
Bilateral or ambilineal descent (col. 24, codes B or K)	59%	71%
Lack patrilineal kin groups of any type (col. 20, code O)	72%	86%
Residence:		
Patrilocal (col. 16, code P)	26%	10%
Virilocal (col.16, code V)	—	40%

Figure 14.1   Descent and Residence Data for Two Samples of Simple Foraging Societies

These findings run counter to the "man the warrior" assumption about the prevalence of patrilineal descent and/or patrilocal residence in ancestral band society. Very few band societies have patrilineages upon which to base male coalitions.

Note: Patrilocal residence is when residence is normally with or near a husband's male patrilineal relatives. *Virilocal* connotes a mixed pattern of residence in society that favors living near male kin, but in situations where paternal kin are neither aggregated into patrilineages nor patrilocal kin groups.[c] The sample of simple hunter-gatherers from the SCCS (see Chapter 5) includes the !Kung (Ju/'hoansi), Hadza, Mbuti, Semang, Andamanese, Vedda, Tiwi, Aranda, Gilyak, Yukaghir, Ingalik, Copper Eskimo, Montagnais,[d] Micmac, Northern Saulteaux, Slave, Kaska, Paiute, Botocudo, Aweikoma, and Yahgan. See *The Human Potential for Peace* for a more detailed discussion.[e]

Sources: (a) George Murdock, *Atlas of World Cultures* (Pittsburgh: University of Pittsburgh Press, 1981); (b) Bruce Knauft, "Violence and sociality in human evolution," *Current Anthropology* 32 (1991): 391–428 (Knauft does not report a percentage for virilocality); see also Frank Marlowe, "Hunter-gatherers and human evolution," *Evolutionary Anthropology* 14 (2005): 54–67; (c) George Murdock, *Atlas of World Cultures* (Pittsburgh: University of Pittsburgh Press, 1981), 94; (d) George Murdock, "Ethnographic Atlas: A Summary," *Ethnology* 6 (1967): 109–236; (e) Douglas Fry, *The Human Potential for Peace* (New York: Oxford University Press, 2006).

(see Figure 14.1). Bilateral systems tend to emphasize more kinship ties than do unilateral systems. This also means that each person has a unique kinship network. As was clearly evident in the Tiwi case explored in Chapter 9, the fact that each person's network of relations in band society differs to some degree from those of everyone else significantly hinders concerted group-versus-group fighting. In nomadic foraging groups, individual autonomy is emphasized and group leadership is minimal.[13] No one has the authority to order others to do anything, such as go to war. Sharing, cooperation, and egalitarianism are prevalent aspects of the simple hunter-gatherer ethos.[14] Reciprocal sharing crosscuts different groups; intergroup sharing is facilitated because people have trade partners, family members, and friends in other bands.[15]

The ethnographic patterns just summarized, which are clearly apparent in the band societies we are considering, show virtually all the assumptions of the "man the warrior" perspective to be flawed. Contrary to the assumption that patrilineages of related males live together, most simple hunter-gatherer bands lack patrilineal descent groups. Contrary to the closed group assumption, the bands are not tightly knit, but instead are flexible and fluctuating in membership. Contrary to the assumptions of pervasive hostile intergroup relations and recurring warfare over scarce resources, the typical pattern is for groups to get along rather well, relying on resources within their own areas and respecting the resources of their neighbors. Intergroup marriages contribute to positive ties within and across language boundaries that are augmented through gift exchange, visiting, and the reciprocal sharing of resources, the last pattern being especially important in times of scarcity. Contrary to the warring over women and territory assumption, disputes over women, when occurring between members of different bands, tend to be individual affairs rather than the foundation for warfare. Instances of nomadic bands fighting over territory are atypical. Contrary to the leadership assumption, high levels of individual autonomy and egalitarianism are hallmarks of forager bands. Militaristic or warrior values are rarely if ever emphasized. Some bands even promote nonviolent values and behavior. [16]

In sum, an examination of the actual ethnographic information on simple nomadic foragers suggests that the "man the warrior" view rests not on facts but on a heap of faulty assumptions and overzealous speculation. Furthermore, the "man the warrior" model is so out of step with reality that it makes no sense to evoke it in an attempt to explain warfare and other forms of violence in today's world. This conclusion may run counter to conventional wisdom— which cannot be considered wisdom when it so drastically diverges from observable facts. One benefit of using a scientific approach for gaining knowledge about the world involves the ongoing process of questioning assumptions, gathering information to test hypotheses, reaching tentative conclusions, and then starting over again.

15

A Macroscopic Anthropological View

*Kennedy proposed "that this nation should commit itself to achieving the goal, before
this decade is out, of landing a man on the moon and returning him safely to Earth."
... He recruited the best minds. Money was to be no limit. He used the media to rally
the voters behind the task. His is the perfect model for implementing our new vision.
The world needs a new John F. Kennedy who says, "I propose that within the next
25 to 35 years we end the use of war to resolve our conflicts, and here is the plan."
... The global community is at a pivotal, unique time in history. Given the will to
do it, we can create a warless future.*

—JUDITH L. HAND, *A FUTURE WITHOUT WAR*

Anthropology offers a broad perspective on humanity that
spans evolutionary time and crosses cultural space. In this sense,
anthropology is macroscopic—it helps us to see the big picture.
A macroscopic view, for instance, leads to insights about how
cultural belief systems affect our thinking. We have examined
how individuals tend to accept the belief system of their culture
without much question. Widespread beliefs that war is natural
and acceptable hinder the search for alternatives—and thus the
inevitability of war becomes a self-fulfilling prophecy. Such beliefs
may be detrimental both to preventing particular wars and to

abolishing the institution of war. Perhaps this insight can help us to overcome the problem.

The Human Capacity to Move Beyond War

A macroscopic perspective also helps us to see the current international "war system" within the broader context of conflict management alternatives. It is a self-redress system with all the usual problems: as the Comanche quoted previously put it, "lots of trouble, lots of people hurt." At the dawn of the twenty-first century, continuing to allow each Giuseppe and Domenico—now with missiles under their command—to fight it out on the international stage is simply too dangerous and too costly, not only for the disputing parties, but also for all the rest of us. The historical hour has arrived to shift from a state of imperfect security, as elusively sought through military means, to an effective system for providing justice through international legal structures and viable mechanisms of conflict management.[1]

Can such a transition be accomplished? For starters, the flexible nature of human behavior makes a transition from war to other forms of international conflict resolution conceivable. A macroscopic anthropological view reveals *Homo sapiens* to be an extremely flexible species. The fact that human beings are capable of living in a variety of markedly different types of social organization offers testimony to this behavioral and social plasticity. Consider the immense differences between life in a nomadic hunter-gatherer band and a modern industrial nation-state. Today's urban dweller could easily see over a thousand persons in a single day, more than a band member might see in her entire lifetime. And the modern

Figure 15.1   East of Oaxaca City in southern Mexico, a large mosaic tribute to Benito Juárez alludes to his role in implementing social reforms in the mid-1800s. Juárez's credo, "Respect for the rights of others is peace," appears in Spanish in the middle of the scene. On the right side of the mosaic, Justice, blindfolded, holds balanced scales in this familiar symbolic depiction of impartiality under the law. Courts of law and legal protection of individual rights typify today's democracies. Could the same principles also be implemented to protect human rights and provide impartial justice within the global neighborhood? (D. P. Fry photo collection.)

urbanite encounters numerous strangers, whereas the band member moves with a small number of relatives and acquaintances, only rarely encountering an unknown person. As we have seen, the members of nomadic band society are linked to one another through webs of reciprocity and kinship, place a high premium on sharing, and are egalitarian in their social relations. The socioeconomic hierarchy, generally taken for granted by citizens of modern states living in a world of ranked social roles—for instance, CEOs, middle management, and workers; school principals, teachers, and teachers' aides; generals, lieutenants, and privates; and doctors, nurses, and orderlies—is an alien concept in the social world of egalitarian nomadic foragers. Particular persons may be admired for certain abilities, but nomadic hunter-gatherer society lacks hierarchical positions of authority.[2]

The essential point is that members of the same species, *Homo sapiens*, are capable of living in the dramatically different social worlds of bands, tribes, chiefdoms, and states and within numerous cultural traditions. The transition from the millennia-old lifeways of the nomadic forager band to the conditions of the urban, industrial nation is truly staggering. Yet we high-tech folks of the twenty-first century rarely pause to consider the immense plasticity in the nature of our species that allows a hunter-gatherer primate to live in this Internet world of strangers, stock exchanges, and cruise missiles. A macroscopic anthropological perspective highlights the human capacity for creating and adjusting to immense social and institutional changes.

An appreciation of the immensity of social changes that humans have undergone in recent millennia leads to the observation that there is nothing sacred about the institution of war. The worldwide archaeological record, data on simple forager societies, and cross-cultural studies combine to suggest that warfare is a rather recent development, arising along with social complexity and greatly intensifying with the birth of states, as economic and political motives for war moved to the forefront. Nation-states and an international system that accept the waging of war are younger still.

In recent centuries, as Europeans colonized the world, warfare was exacerbated cross-culturally by a barrage of dramatic changes —the crowding and rearranging of native peoples; the usurpation of native land; the introduction of firearms, trade goods, and slavery; and the waging of wars of extermination against native peoples. The idea is not to blame the arrival of European colonial powers for *all* indigenous warfare, but rather to point out how time and again the flames of war have been fanned by social, political, and economic forces set into motion only within the last several centuries.[3]

A species as flexible as *Homo sapiens* certainly can create alternative ways of dealing with international conflicts. Humans have a solid repertory of conflict management skills to draw upon. Across societies, people are apt preventers and avoiders of violence. Over a vast array of societal circumstances, humans deal with most conflicts without any physical aggression at all. Regularly, the language-using primate "talks it out," airs grievances verbally in the court of public opinion, negotiates compensation, focuses on restoring relationships bruised by a dispute, convenes conflict resolution assembles, and listens to the wisdom of elders or other third parties who, acting as peacemakers, strive to end the tension within the group and among disputants. As we have considered, humans also routinely show a great deal of self-restraint against acting aggressively. Such restraint makes evolutionary sense and has numerous parallels in other animal species.

Breaking Out of Our Preconceptions

It is far too easy to become trapped by our own preconceptions and limited by cultural beliefs that we simply take for granted. A macroscopic view can increase awareness of this human tendency and may help to keep our minds open to new possibilities. Here are some illustrations of just how powerful assumptions and preconceptions can be.

Some men were out hunting and one spied a moose.[4] They shot through the brush until all sounds ceased. Upon investigation, they discovered only the body of a man. Then they remembered hearing, during their salvo, someone shouting, "Don't shoot. I'm not a moose." They also now realized that the "moose" had been waving a red cap, and it finally dawned on them what they had done. This tragic story illustrates dramatically that sometimes people can become so fixed in their ideas that they become oblivious to even blaring contradictory information.

A couple of years ago, my brother-in-law, Dale, and I were driving on a small country road and came across a Chevy van with its right wheels in the gully on the side of the road. Fortunately, no one had been hurt in this little mishap. Dale and I inspected the situation and determined that this was a job for a tow truck, since the underbelly of the van was lodged solidly on the pavement as the vehicle listed to the right.

While inspecting for damage, I realized that brake fluid was leaking from the *left* front wheel area onto the ground. This seemed just a little peculiar to me, because it was the *right* side of the car that was in the gully, but I didn't let this contradictory fact disturb my diagnosis. From my mechanical experience, limited though it is, I *knew* that the only fluid to be found in the wheel areas would be brake fluid. However, just to be sure that something such as windshield washer fluid wasn't dripping from a leak higher up, I checked. There was no dripping from above. Now I noticed something else that was a little bit odd. The brake fluid was on the hubcap side—that is, the outside—of the wheel with no obvious source from inside the wheel. Strange.

Provoked by creeping doubts about my brake fluid diagnosis, I now noticed for the first time that the liquid was yellow. I'd never seen yellow brake fluid before. "Come to think of it," I thought, "I *have* seen yellow liquid that looks like this." To gather more data, I got down on my hands and knees and smelled. Aha! Standing up, I looked around and verified a fact that previously had seemed irrelevant to the mechanical puzzle: One of the passengers of the stranded van was a male Labrador retriever, now joyfully running to and fro. Bingo! Life makes sense.

I imagine that all readers could tell a story or two of how they were absolutely convinced that something was one way when in fact is was not—their preconceptions blinded them to a more plausible interpretation of events. Such experiences can give us more empathy for the moose hunters and also may provide us with some humbling insights.

This returns us to the sleuthing analogy presented in the first chapter of the book. An initial "reading" of the evidence led to the conclusion that Holmes and Watson's new neighbor was a man. However, after gathering more data and weighing the totality of the evidence, Holmes and Watson reversed their conclusion.

Take a couple of seconds and think about the mental image that you formed of Holmes and Watson when reading Chapter 1. What were they wearing? Did they have accents? If you are picturing Holmes and Watson as British men, you probably are familiar with books and films featuring Arthur Conan Doyle's Sherlock Holmes and Dr. Watson. Were your images of Holmes and Watson male? Were your images a rendering of Doyle's famous sleuths?

The point of this thought experiment is to reinforce, in a personally subjective way, that our cultural background provides each of us with a host of initial, implicit assumptions that in turn affect our interpretations of the world. If you go back to Chapter 1 and look for any *factual* information about whether Watson and Holmes are male or female and what they look like, you won't find any. If you *assumed* that they were men without really giving the matter any thought, it is probably because we all know that Holmes and Watson are fictional male British detectives. This information is in our shared cultural fund of knowledge.

Many people in Western societies also already know, or just assume based on their cultural experiences, that warfare is extremely ancient, natural, and part and parcel of human nature. Many people also assume that war is inevitable—that there always has been war and there always will be war. They assume that there are no alternatives. But it's time to smell the brake fluid. It's time to look afresh at the available evidence and try to untangle the facts from implicit assumptions and preconceptions, for many of the so-called facts are actually culturally derived presumptions and lead to interpretations that are not necessarily very accurate.

Recall that a substantial number of university students in the United States agree that humans have "an instinct for war" and that "war is an intrinsic part of human nature." Such beliefs are manifested in many ways: in everyday conversations, in entertainment, and in politics. From television shows to motion pictures such as 2001: *A Space Odyssey*, from writings by scientists such as Raymond Dart to those of playwrights such as Robert Ardrey, these messages are reiterated in Western culture.[5] Sometimes people who question this prevailing view of human nature or the inevitability of war are even labeled as naive, foolish, unrealistic, or utopian.[6]

We have seen many examples in this book of how Hobbesian beliefs manifest themselves in science. In the case of Dart, his own explicitly stated views about human nature corresponded with his initial violence-laden interpretations of the australopithecine fossil material. According to Dart, humans bear the bloody mark of Cain, and so did the australopithecines. In a similar vein, C. Richards expressed openness to "the possibility of some built-in tendency towards war in man's genes or in some universal characteristic of human life" and in the same passage argued for the antiquity of warfare.[7]

Quincy Wright's cross-cultural classificatory scheme, which applied the label "war" to all societies, even nonwarring ones, would once again seem to reflect assumptions stemming from a Hobbesian cultural belief system. Under this labeling scheme, all cultures war. Carol Ember sought to disprove "that hunter-gatherers are relatively peaceful," lumping together complex hunter-gatherers and equestrian hunters with nomadic band societies to create a heterogeneous sample and defining "war" so broadly as to encompass feuds and some types of revenge killings. Not surprisingly, she discovered a lot of so-called war.[8] These problematic findings continue to be cited in support of Hobbesian views of the past.[9]

In a somewhat similar manner, Lawrence Keeley mixed archaeological evidence of homicide and some ambiguous cases of death with the evidence of prehistoric war to create an impression of more warfare and older warfare than actually exist. Paul Tacon and Christopher Chippindale filled their article on Australian Aborigine rock art with war words and labeled the human figures "warriors," while virtually ignoring a huge body of contextualizing information about the nature of conflict management in Aboriginal Australian societies.[10] "Man the warrior" scenarios basically project present-day beliefs and circumstances onto the past. We also have considered the fascination with Yanomamö *unokais* and the eager reiteration of the purported link between reproductive success and killing.

These examples simultaneously represent and reinforce deep-seated and largely taken-for-granted cultural beliefs about the antiquity and naturalness of war. Cultural beliefs creep into scientific and other writings, affecting perceptions, descriptions, and interpretations. In the real world of global politics, they may also affect decisions whether or not to wage war. They may also limit our view as to the possibilities of achieving security and justice without war.

My intention in this book has been to raise questions that have been largely ignored—to open this pile of implicit assumptions about war, peace, and human nature to more careful scrutiny. An initial reading of the facts pointed Holmes and Watson in one direction, but further investigation revealed that the weight of the evidence suggested a very different conclusion. One implication of the sleuthing analogy is the importance of considering *all* of the available data, not simply a few selected facts. Another implication is that some observations carry more theoretical weight than do others. In the analogy, observations about items inside the house deserved more weight than observations about a vehicle parked on the street. In regard to understanding warfare and human nature, the findings from one problematic article on *unokai* reproductive success, for instance, should carry much less weight than an entire body of research studies on nomadic forager societies. Similarly, the behavior of chimpanzees should carry less weight for understanding humans than does the actual behavior of humans. Obviously we should consider all of the available facts, not simply those that happen to fit preconceived ideas. Ultimately, we must base our conclusions on the facts, not on preconceived notions, as difficult as this may be. This is where it may be helpful to remember the lessons learned from Rudolf Virchow and his microscope, the moose-hunting tragedy, and the leaking "brake fluid," in order not to shut our minds to new ideas.

William Ury strikes a similar note:

> Perhaps the principal obstacle to preventing destructive conflict lies in our own minds—in the fatalistic beliefs that discourage people from even trying. The story that humans have always warred, and always will, is spread unchallenged from person to person and from parent to child. It is time, in our everyday conversations, to question and refute this story and its embedded assumptions about human nature. It is time to give our children—and ourselves—a more accurate and more positive picture of our past and our future prospects. From realistic hope springs action.[11]

If we step back and assess the big picture, the data suggest that humans, while very capable of engaging in warfare, also have a strong capacity for getting along peacefully. The view that warfare is ancient, natural, and an intrinsic part of human nature wilts under the light of fresh scrutiny. Warfare is not inevitable. When many different observations, experimental results, and data point to the same conclusion, support for the conclusion becomes overwhelming. Scenarios portraying the naturalness of war are contradicted across the board by the information we have considered in this book from archaeology, hunter-gatherer studies, comparative ethnography, the study of social organization, cross-cultural research findings on war and justice seeking, research on animal aggression, evolutionary theory, and, last but not least, a consideration of the powerful biasing effects that cultural belief systems continue to have on Western thinking about war and peace. *Findings and insights from these multiple areas complement and reinforce one another when viewed as a comprehensive body of relevant information.*

If we weigh the totality of the evidence, we arrive at a new conclusion: Humans are not really so nasty after all. Furthermore, we clearly are an extremely flexible species and capable of using numerous conflict management options. Given the huge social changes already experienced since our species began to give up a nomadic forager lifestyle a few millennia ago, it is not hard to envision that just a little more "social evolution" could move humanity beyond war. Now is the time to develop new security solutions, rather than clinging to the "same old, same old" of war-accepting beliefs and practices. A macroscopic perspective can help us move beyond conventional thinking and imagine new paths to a positive future.

16

Enhancing Peace

We share a planet and we need common rules to guide our actions.
—TARJA HALONEN, PRESIDENT OF FINLAND

Anthropology provides many insights on war and peace, but by far the most important, for it pertains directly to the future of the species, is that war, like slavery before it, *can* be abolished. With wars continuing to erupt in different quarters of the planet, this idea might seem implausible. The elimination of war, however, is starkly realistic in two senses of the word. First, an anthropological perspective suggests that the human species, realistically, has the capacity to accomplish this goal. Second, the serious challenges facing humanity, including the spread of weapons of mass destruction, suggest that realistically we must abolish war before it abolishes us. Replacing war with alternative ways to insure security and resolve conflicts is the only rational way to proceed into the twenty-first century and beyond.

As a means of ensuring a nation's safety and security, war is already obsolete, for it does little or nothing to protect people from the very real threats of global environmental degradation, human rights abuses, nuclear proliferation, and terrorism. It can be argued that the acceptance and the waging of war even contribute to these problems. The presence of nuclear weapons on the planet makes war increasingly risky, not merely for soldiers and civilians in combat zones, but for every person on Earth. For this reason also, war is obsolete. Alternative ways of handling conflict must be implemented and cooperation employed to deal effectively in the twenty-first century with problems such as global warming and the proliferation of ever-more-deadly weapons that threaten not only the citizens of particular countries but human survival overall.

In the twenty-first century, the price tag for dealing with intergroup conflict through war, as a form of self-redress, is shockingly high. Humanity simply must replace the dangerous, costly, and often ineffective practice of warfare with new international conflict resolution institutions—regional and global courts, for example. Within nations, this transition from seeking justice through self-redress to reliance on legal institutions has been made repeatedly in human history, offering hope that a similar transition is possible internationally. We are faced with the challenge of bringing the sheriff and the judge to the global Wild West.

We will now focus on some specific anthropological insights for building and preserving peace. Peace-promoting possibilities include the enhancement of crosscutting social ties; the recognition of global interdependence and the necessity of cooperative approaches to shared threats; the promotion of peace-oriented values, attitudes, and beliefs, as opposed to values, attitudes, and beliefs that support and encourage war; the implementation of new levels of democratic governance; and the greater utilization of conflict management mechanisms at the international level. Creating effective global governance and expanding conflict resolution in place of war are especially important. We cannot rely on fostering goodwill alone.

Crosscutting Ties

Humans often perceive themselves in terms of "us" and "them"—a feature that can be exploited to make killing "them" easier. However, the perception of differences among groups does not automatically lead to violence. Ethnocentrism is *not* equivalent to war. Who exactly constitutes "us" and "them" is flexible and subject to ongoing reevaluation and redefinition. Consider how in today's political world, countries that fought each other as bitter enemies during World War II—France and Germany or Japan and the United States, for instance—are now friends, allies, and trade partners. Furthermore, the ethnocentrism of "us" and "them" does not in and of itself cause warfare. Playing up differences can ferment conflict; building bridges and recognizing common interests can spawn peace.

Ilsa Glazer describes how special-purpose friendships can link members of agonistic ethnic groups, contributing to a common group identity that helps prevent violence. Using examples as diverse as New Guinea tribes and ancient Celtic clans, Kenneth Smail reports that leaders sometimes form crosscutting ties by sending their own sons to live in other groups to reduce tensions, deter aggression, and build friendly alliances.[1]

This anthropological insight is straightforward. Relationships that link groups tend to reduce intergroup violence. The greater the number of crosscutting ties, the smaller the chance of war. As Margaret Mead expresses it:

Our organizational task may then be defined as reducing the strength of all mutually exclusive loyalties, whether of nations, race, class, religion or ideology, and constructing some quite different form of organization in which the memories of these loyalties and the organization residues of these former exclusive loyalties cannot threaten the total structure.[2]

As Mead implies, crosscutting ties are relevant to reducing the threat of war and terrorism at different social levels within and among nations. Ways to encourage and promote crosscutting ties are as bountiful as human ingenuity itself. International student exchange programs could be increased manyfold (perhaps drawing on a fraction of the funds currently allocated to military budgets), especially involving the exchange of students between countries with a history of hostility. More generally, Smail proposes the utility of ongoing citizen exchange programs that include transferring substantial numbers of businesspeople, academics, political leaders, military personnel, artists, and so on among nations in order to reduce tensions and promote mutual friendship.[3]

Interdependence and Cooperation

Robert Tonkinson explains that nomadic hunter-gatherer Mardu bands need each other. The Mardu are interdependent for ecological reasons and are well aware of this fact. They strive to maintain positive relations among bands.

In the Western Desert, . . . there *is* an important underlying ecological factor, the irregularity of spread and unreliability of rainfall in a region having no permanent waters. . . . It necessitates a strong cultural stress on the permeability of boundaries and the maintenance of open and peaceful movement and inter-group communication within a huge area of desert. In these circumstances, to permit inter-group conflict or feuding to harden social and territorial boundaries would be literally suicidal, since no group can expect the existing water and food resources of its territory to tide it over until the next rains; peaceful inter-group relations are imperative for long-term survival. . . . It is not surprising, then, that the Mardu have no word for either "feud" or "warfare" and there is no evidence for the kinds of longstanding inter-group animosity one associates with feuding. The situation is one of small and scattered highly mobile groups moving freely within large territories rather than highly localized, solitary corporate groups contesting resources and maintaining boundaries.

Thanks to their open boundaries and the multiple linkages (shared values, religion, worldview, Law, kinship, friendship and marriage alliances) [that is, crosscutting ties] joining every Mardu band to all others in their society, the arena of shared understandings is huge when groups need to resolve their differences. Everyone is mindful also of how much their survival rests on mutual hospitality and unfettered access to their neighbors' natural resources in both lean and bountiful times.[4]

The Mardu recognize their state of interdependence. They understand that fighting would be extremely detrimental—potentially even suicidal—and avoid it. In this case, ecological factors contribute to interdependence and peace.

Common threats or economic specialization also can lead to interdependence and peaceful relations. For instance, solidarity within Comanche society was enhanced by the presence of hostile neighbors: "general fighting within the tribe was not to be countenanced when there were always outside enemies to be confronted." Similarly, feuding Montenegrins expeditiously enacted a truce if a common enemy appeared on the horizon. The intertribal trade in Brazil's Upper Xingu River basin provides a good example of economic interdependence. Each Xingu tribe produces and exchanges goods not manufactured by the other tribes, for instance, ceramics, hardwood bows, belts, necklaces, and salt. The Xingu people have created and nurture interdependent exchange relationships and do not make war on each other. The ties and interdependencies are viewed as positive and help to maintain peaceful relations among the villages.[5]

Interdependence has a huge potential for contributing to peace in the twenty-first century and beyond. Interdependence already exists among the peoples of the earth and continues to grow in the realms of economics, security, and the environment. Awareness that interdependence brings common challenges necessitating cooperation also is on the rise.

The reality of global economic interdependence is reflected in the growth and proliferation of transnational corporations and the effects that economic growth or decline in one region have on the economies of other world regions. The reality of global security interdependence also clearly exists. Nuclear weapons link the fate of all peoples of the world. Even a "small" nuclear exchange, if it set off a nuclear winter, would prove fatal for all humanity. Radiation from a nuclear war would encircle the globe. Use of biological and chemical weapons also could have broad-reaching, disastrous effects. Thus the very presence of weapons of mass destruction links the people of the planet in a shared fate that necessitates cooperative solutions to mutual problems.

Bulging military expenditures and the waging of conventional wars also relate to interdependence. Spending well over $2 billion *a day* worldwide on military expenditures diverts truly enormous amounts of financial and other resources from promoting sustainable development, protecting the environment, and fulfilling a host of human needs—issues that span borders and have major security ramifications. The waging of wars pollutes both local and common environments simultaneously, for war-caused environmental devastation can have ecological impacts regionally and even on the global ecosystem.[6]

A third reality of interdependence, just alluded to, involves the global environment. All individuals and nations on the planet are environmentally interdependent, being adversely affected by pollution of the oceans, greenhouse warming, ozone depletion, species loss, radioactivity, and so on.

Interdependence in the areas of economy, security, and environment already exists. Realization of the implications of interdependence lags behind. However, as sociologists Lester Kurtz and Jennifer Turpin explain, "no one is secure until everyone is, because we all live in the same 'global village.'" An important concept that is gaining a foothold in security deliberations is "comprehensive security"—the idea that military factors are only part of the story and that a host of nonmilitary influences, such as social inequities, ecological deterioration, poverty, and migration pressures, have major peace and security ramifications. Letting social inequities and injustices fester provides a rich breeding ground for terrorism.[7]

Figure 16.1   A Greek fishing boat returns to harbor in Heraklion, Crete. The overexploitation of the world's fisheries and pollution of the earth's oceans are but two critical issues that simultaneously reflect global environmental interdependence and the necessity of implementing cooperative solutions to shared problems. No nation, for instance, can unilaterally protect the seas. It is in the long-range self-interest of each interdependent nation to cooperate in solving common problems. (D. P. Fry photo collection.)

Anthropology suggests that replacing violent competition with cooperation is facilitated when individuals clearly perceive their interdependence.[8] Interdependence in and of itself may not promote cooperation.[9] The realization of interdependence is a critical variable. Thus one step toward doing away with war is to increase awareness, among leaders and citizens alike, that the current war system provides only a shallow illusion of safety and security. In actually, the continued acceptance of war imperils *all* people living on an interdependent planet. The rising awareness that all humans share the threat posed by terrorists with weapons of mass destruction, global environmental degradation, global warming, oceanic pollution, the worldwide loss of biodiversity, coupled with the realization that all of us on the planet are increasingly linked within an interdependent global economic system, leads to a rationale for resolving conflicts without war and for cooperatively addressing shared problems. It is in every person's and nation's self-interest to move humanity beyond war. In today's world, the institution called war can no longer provide the safety and security that people desire. The most pressing challenges to human survival in the twenty-first century simply are not amenable to military solutions.

Values, Attitudes, and Beliefs

Anthropological research clearly demonstrates the importance of cultural values, attitudes, and beliefs in influencing how conflicts are handled. Values, attitudes, and beliefs are internalized during socialization and reinforced in daily life. The nonviolent Semai and Paliyan, for instance, simultaneously shun violence and value harmony.[10]

The anthropological observation that attitudes, values, and beliefs can either promote peaceful, nonviolent behavior or, to the contrary, facilitate aggression and warfare has implications for abolishing war. A prevalent belief among national leaders and citizens is that the institution of warfare is permissible and at times necessary.[11] Such beliefs facilitate the waging of war. As David

Adams and Sarah Bosch demonstrate, holding such beliefs also discourages people from taking action for peace.[12] This pattern contributes to a self-fulfilling prophecy wherein the war institution continues in part because large numbers of people, believing that war is natural, even inevitable, and necessary, do not insist that intergroup conflicts be handled in new ways.

Albert Einstein noted that in the nuclear age "everything has changed, save our modes of thinking."[13] New attitudes, values, and beliefs—new modes of thinking—are critical for replacing war with other approaches to seeking security. The tremendous variation in cultural belief systems apparent in the ethnographic record, including those in peaceful societies, suggests that shifting to beliefs that favor nonviolent forms of conflict management instead of war are certainly within the range of human possibilities.

A new belief system should embrace common security and comprehensive security, placing cooperation over competition, in dealing with the shared threats to human safety and well being. A new belief system should highlight how all nations, all humans, share a common fate. A new belief system should acknowledge that warfare is an obsolete social institution. In short, "warfare must be de-legitimized as a means of settling disputes."[14]

It is possible to imagine a new global system that settles disputes without warfare and provides justice without violence. It is possible to imagine a global system that effectively addresses common environmental, developmental, and security concerns cooperatively. It is possible to imagine a global system based on law, not war, wherein effective judicial institutions provide the security that people in every society desire.[15] If implementing changes of this magnitude seems impossible, then a macroscopic time perspective may help to put the truly immense human potential for social change in focus. The same species that began as politically acephalous band-living hunter-gatherers has managed to create a system of nation-states, some operating as democratic polities with millions of citizens. The immensity of this shift in social and political complexity from band to nation is truly staggering. It shows without a doubt that humans are an amazingly flexible species fully capable of creating new social, political, and legal institutions.

The essential point is not that peace can be achieved simply through modifying beliefs, attitudes, and values, but rather that such modification is one ingredient in a complex recipe for abolishing war. Beliefs, attitudes, and values that promote peace can be fostered as alternatives to traditional views that war is acceptable, even inevitable. Elie Wiesel raises questions that challenge status quo thinking about war: "Why not glorify something else? Why not give a medal to those who oppose and prevent war? Give *them* a Medal of Honor! Why don't we write poetry, drama, and plays about the triumph of peace instead of victory in war?"[16]

The Benefits of Governance over Anarchy

Clayton and Carole Robarchek suggest that the absence of an overarching authority among the Waorani was one factor that contributed to feuding and that makes the marked reduction in fighting a "fragile peace." In Chapter 6, I related an anecdote about a Yanomamö man who enthusiastically realized the potential of police, courts, and a code of law for achieving justice without raiding and revenge killings. The point, which obviously excited the Yanomamö man, is that a superordinate authority with viable judicial institutions can replace the violent self-redress patterns of individual revenge killings, feuding, or warring.[17]

At this moment in history, the international war system is roughly analogous to the individual self-redress system typical of band society or the feuding system typical of tribal social organization. The scale is different, but the self-redress patterns are similar. In self-redress systems, third parties may intervene as friendly peacemakers or mediators and attempt to prevent bloodshed, but ultimately no one has the authority to prevent disputants from using force. Any nation in the current acephalous world system can seek justice via military means—in the same way that a wronged Alacaluf hunter pursues self-redress or a group of Yanomamö set out on a revenge raid in an attempt to even the score. As pointed out in Chapter 6, seeking justice via self-redress has the major disadvantage of potentially leading to the escalation and prolongation of violence, as occurs during feuding among socially segmented groups. *Anthropology shows that an effective way to stop violence within an acephalous self-redress system is to create or impose a higher level of judicial authority.* New mechanisms, such as courts, take over the administration of justice, and in the process reduce the violence inherent in seeking justice through self-redress. Thus the Yanomamö man eagerly realized the benefits of courts and police.

One variety of superordinate authority that halts warfare is what Donald Black calls "repressive peacemaking." Peace is imposed by an authority that treats killing, feuding, or warring as offenses punishable in and of themselves. The pacification of warring indigenous groups by a colonial power or national government exemplifies this type of superordinate approach to feuding or warfare. Repressive peacemaking, however, harbors the danger of replacing the devil with the witch, for its benefits may come at a cost: losses to rights, freedoms, and independence.[18]

Superordinate authority, however, need not be repressive.[19] An overarching authority structure can be formed when the participating parties create a confederation or a federation. In a confederate system, the locus of authority remains primarily in the constituent units. In a federal system, greater authority is transferred from the constituent units to an overarching institution.

Various authors have suggested that the United Nations could be reformed to make it more democratic and to shift it from a confederate system toward a federal model. The United States, it will be remembered, went through just such a transformation in giving up the ineffective Articles of Confederation in favor of the federal system of governance created by the U.S. Constitution. Is there a global lesson here?

The implementation of overarching authority structures also can occur at the regional level. The European Union (EU) is an example par excellence. The European Commission, European Parliament, and European Court of Justice provide an overarching level of governance to the twenty-five member countries that includes new political, legislative, and judicial mechanisms for handling disputes and for facilitating cooperation on shared concerns. A common currency, the euro, has already replaced national currencies within about half of the EU countries. The possibility of war within the EU has become about as unlikely as war breaking out between Indiana and Illinois. "Peace is therefore the primary achievement of the process of European integration."[20] Although presenting additional difficulties in scale, a global union through the United Nations or other global institutions could be implemented. Another lesson of European integration is that it does not occur

Figure 16.2 The European Union Parliament building in Brussels, Belgium, and the national flags of the member states. In 2004, ten new countries joined the European Union, which now consists of twenty-five member nations. In the wake of the devastating destruction suffered by Europe in World War II, postwar leaders envisioned how a more integrated Europe could prevent future wars. The European Union has not destroyed national traditions, but it has reduced the chance of war within the union. The European Union also has added a level of governance to benefit member countries in terms of enhancing commerce and trade, providing added food and product safety, limiting regional air and water pollution, preventing crime and terrorism, and so forth. (D. P. Fry photo collection.)

overnight; in fact, the "two steps forward and one step back" saying has been applied to the process. A similar view seems appropriate when considering the potential of creating greater global governance.

Enhancing Conflict Management

The human potential for peace is omnipresent. Conflict abounds in human societies, but even in the most violent societies, people handle most disputes without bloodshed. Some cultures have developed regulated contests that prevent serious injury, as illustrated by Netsilik song duels and the wrestling fights of the Siriono. In mediation, recall that a more or less neutral third party attempts to assist disputants in reaching a mutually acceptable agreement. Neil Whitehead tells of how one tribal group, the Yao, engaged in mediation between Aricoure and Carib warriors in 1624. The Yao intervened because they were friends of both groups; following the attainment of peace, they hosted both groups of warriors in their village for eight days.[21]

An anthropological perspective demonstrates that humans are capable of devising and employing a great diversity of conflict prevention and management techniques.[22] Warfare, a form of group-level self-redress, can be seen as just one option among others in a general conflict management typology that also includes avoidance, toleration, negotiation, and third-party settlement procedures of various types. Clearly there are alternative approaches for dealing with intergroup conflict besides war.

Moreover, as William Ury and his colleagues demonstrate, nonviolent systems for dealing with conflict can be designed and implemented. These practitioners show that it is possible to shift from power contests (and war is the ultimate power contest) to a system that focuses on reconciling the interests and rights of disputants. Ury and his colleagues suggest that an effective conflict management system should have a set of successive layers so that "if one procedure fails, another is waiting."[23]

There is no reason that third-party conflict management options such as mediation, arbitration, and adjudication could not be used in place of war. In an international system that has abolished war, trained mediators and arbitrators, operating under the auspices of the United Nations or other international and regional organizations, could assist with the handling of disputes among nations. International courts could be reserved for more serious cases, especially those dealing with violations of international law or human rights issues.

Although currently referred to as the International Court of Justice or the World Court, this United Nations–affiliated tribunal actually engages in arbitration, not adjudication, because it lacks enforcement power, relying instead on voluntary appearances and voluntary compliance with rulings. Shifting the procedure of this important international tribunal from arbitration to adjudication, a change that would also require shifts in attitudes and perceptions, would advance global governance.

Anthropological studies show that such shifts in thinking are indeed possible. The Waorani chose to give up their system of violence and counterviolence when presented with a new view of reality. The transition can serve as a parable for the overall abandonment of warfare by the peoples of the earth, who, we must remember, are still living under the ominous shadow of existing nuclear arsenals and weapons of ever greater mass destruction:

Once contact was established, they [more distant hostile Waorani bands] too were presented an alternative reality premised on peacefulness and a glimpse of a world without constant fear of violent death. . . . The result was that new cultural knowledge—new information and new perceptions of reality—allowed people to visualize new options and new goals. . . . The killing stopped because the Waorani themselves made a conscious decision to end it.[24]

Michael Renner provides some specific redesign proposals for improving the conflict prevention and resolution system of the United Nations. With an eye to prevention, an early warning office could monitor potential conflicts. Early warning reports spanning the globe could allow United Nations mediation and arbitration teams to respond quickly to prevent brewing disputes from escalating. Eventually, such teams should be prepared to defuse internal as well as external disputes.[25]

Humans use a variety of conflict management techniques that do not entail violence. Humans also are capable of designing and implementing new conflict management procedures.[26] As illustrated by the planned creation of the European Union, humans can exercise foresight and ingenuity to eliminate the threat of war through the design of higher levels of democratic government, complete with built-in conflict management procedures (see Figure 16.3). Although more complicated, the same process conceivably could be accomplished at the global level. To argue otherwise is to belittle human ingenuity.

Closing Thoughts

One important, general contribution that anthropology holds for ending the scourge of war lies in demonstrating that warfare is not

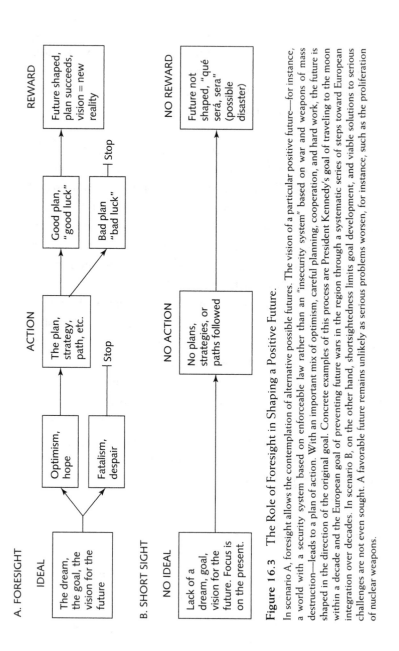

Figure 16.3 The Role of Foresight in Shaping a Positive Future.

In scenario A, foresight allows the contemplation of alternative possible futures. The vision of a particular positive future—for instance, a world with a security system based on enforceable law rather than an "insecurity system" based on war and weapons of mass destruction—leads to a plan of action. With an important mix of optimism, careful planning, cooperation, and hard work, the future is shaped in the direction of the original goal. Concrete examples of this process are President Kennedy's goal of traveling to the moon within a decade and the European goal of preventing future wars in the region through a systematic series of steps toward European integration over decades. In scenario B, on the other hand, shortsightedness limits goal development, and viable solutions to serious challenges are not even sought. A favorable future remains unlikely as serious problems worsen, for instance, such as the proliferation of nuclear weapons.

a natural, inevitable part of human nature. Brian Ferguson has stated clearly why this message is of paramount importance: "The image of humanity, warped by bloodlust, inevitably marching off to kill, is a powerful myth and an important prop of militarism in our society. Despite its lack of scientific credibility, there will remain those 'hard-headed realists' who continue to believe in it, congratulating themselves for their 'courage to face the truth,' resolutely oblivious to the myth behind their 'reality.'"[27]

In suggesting that war is an obsolete social institution that can and must be abolished, I have not dwelled on the current conflagrations raging in the world, the threat of terrorism, or the peril of nuclear holocaust (which has slipped into the background of daily consciousness but nonetheless remains a grave obstacle to long-term human survival). An interview project with environmental activists led to the conclusion that at least a glimmer of hope is critical to motivate an individual to try to bring about social change.[28] By adopting a macroscopic anthropological view, I have concentrated on many glimmers of hope that I think shine toward the same conclusion: *Potentially, war can be eliminated and replaced by effective and just conflict management procedures and institutions.*

In *The Descent of Man*, Charles Darwin observed, "No tribe could hold together if murder, robbery, treachery, etc., were common; consequently such crimes within the limits of the same tribe 'are branded with everlasting infamy;' but excite no such sentiment beyond these limits."[29] Anthropology has borne out Darwin's observation; murder, violence, and rape within a social group are condemned by the members of the group.[30] Darwin also observed that with the advent of nation-states, the constitution of the "tribe" broadened dramatically. This development suggested a new possibility to Darwin:

As man advances in civilization, and small tribes are united into larger communities, the simplest reason would tell each individual that he ought to extend his social instincts and sympathies to all the other members of the same nation, though personally unknown to him. This point being once reached, there is only an artificial barrier to prevent his sympathies extending to the men of all nations and races.[31]

Anthropology shows clearly that through millennia and across continents humans experience tremendous variation in ways of life and social organization. In foraging bands, individuals identify with their relatives and friends in their own and neighboring bands; in nation states, as Darwin noted, the level of identification generally rises to the country as a whole. This shows that both the social organization and the unit of identification (the "us" compared to the "them") are extremely malleable. A global identification, "all of us," in addition to lower-level "us" identifications, seems well within the realm of human capacities, especially when our common survival depends on at least enough common identification to put a halt to war and to cooperate to solve global problems that threaten all of us.

Immense social change on numerous dimensions is indisputably possible, as illustrated by the transformation from a nomadic hunting and gathering existence to a global system comprised of nation-state polities, by the institution of slavery being totally given up in Western thinking and practice, and by the creation of the European Union as a regional level of government complete with its own courts, legislators, and laws. And the existence of peace systems and numerous societies that do not engage in war illustrates the flexibility of humans and their social systems and demonstrates the human capacity to live without war. At a more specific level, anthropology suggests a full palette of often complementary approaches that could be implemented to move humanity beyond war: enhancing crosscutting ties; recognizing the new reality of global interdependence and the necessity of working together to effectively address common challenges; adopting new attitudes, values, and beliefs that are appropriate to an interdependent world and promote nonviolent conflict resolution; creating overarching authority structures for effective governance; and utilizing conflict management processes in place of war. Abolishing war in the twenty-first century is not only realistic in the sense that it is possible, but also realistically necessary for human survival and well being. The flexible, peacemaking primate has the capacity to do so.

Appendix 1: Organizations to Contact

Cultural Survival

Around the planet, many of the world's indigenous peoples, including some societies mentioned in this book, are struggling for survival. Readers who would like to find out more about the current challenges faced by indigenous peoples and what can be done to offer assistance may want to contact Cultural Survival at 215 Prospect Street, Cambridge, MA, 02139, USA (www.cs.org). The goal of Cultural Survival is to promote "the rights, voices, and visions of indigenous peoples."

Citizens for Global Solutions

Readers who would like to find out more about ongoing efforts to replace war with viable security alternatives can obtain useful information from Citizens for Global Solutions at 418 Seventh Street, Washington, DC, 20003, USA (www.globalsolutions.org). The group's mission statement reads: "Citizens for Global Solutions envisions a future in which nations work together to abolish war, protect our rights and freedoms, and solve the problems facing humanity that no nation can solve alone. This vision requires effective democratic global institutions that will apply the rule of law while respecting the diversity and autonomy of national and local communities."

Worldwatch Institute

"The Worldwatch Institute offers a unique blend of interdisciplinary research, global focus, and accessible writing that has made it a leading source of information on the interactions among key environmental, social, and economic trends. Our work revolves around the transition to an environmentally sustainable and socially just society—and how to achieve it." Worldwatch publishes the highly acclaimed annual *State of the World*, and can be contacted at 1776 Massachusetts Ave., N.W., Washington, DC, 20036, USA (www.worldwatch.org).

Appendix 2: Nonwarring Societies

Africa and the Middle East

Dorobo,[1] Fipa,[2] Guanches of the Canary Islands,[3] G/wi,[4] Hadza,[5] Ju/'hoansi (!Kung),[6] Mandaeans/Subba,[7] Mbuti,[8] Nubians,[9] Tristan da Cunha[10]

Asia

Andaman Islanders,[11] Badaga,[12] Baiga,[13] Batak Agta,[14] Batek,[15] Birhor,[16] Buid,[17] Central Thai,[18] Chewong,[19] Hanunóo,[20] Irula,[21] Jahai,[22] Kadar,[23] Kota,[24] Kubu,[25] Kurumbas,[26] Ladaki/Ladakhi,[27] Lepcha,[28] Malapantaram/Hill Pandaram,[29] Naikens/Nayaka,[30] Palawan,[31] Paliyan,[32] Penan/Punan,[33] Sama Dilaut/Bajau Laut,[34] Semai,[35] Semang,[36] Sherpa,[37] Subanun,[38] Toda,[39] Veddah/Vedda,[40] Yanadi[41]

Europe

Saami/Lapps[42]

North America

Central Inuit,[43] Columbia,[44] Copper Inuit,[45] Greenland Inuit,[46] Kawaiisu,[47] Kaibab and most other Southern Paiute groups,[48] Karok,[49] Mission Indians,[50] Point Barrow Inuit,[51] Polar Eskimo,[52] Sanpoil,[53] Saulteaux,[54] Shoshone,[55] Slave/Slavey,[56] Southern Paiute (*see* Kaibab Paiute), Wenatchi[57]

Oceania

Arunta/Aranda,[58] Australian Aborigines generally,[59] Ifaluk,[60] Mardudjara/Mardu,[61] Tikopia,[62] Tiwi[63]

South America

Cayapa,[64] Curetu,[65] Matsigenka/Machiguenga,[66] Panare,[67] Paumari,[68] Pemon,[69] Piaroa,[70] Siriono,[71] Waíwai,[72] Warao/Warrau,[73] Yahgan[74]

Sources

The following references are abridged from Douglas Fry, *The Human Potential for Peace: An Anthropological Challenge to Assumptions about War and Violence* (New York: Oxford University Press, 2006). For additional references, please refer to *The Human Potential for Peace*, Box 7.1, 92–93.

Notes

To reduce the number of notes, a single note at or near the end of a paragraph will supply all the references relevant to the paragraph in situations where this does not result in citation ambiguities. Source-hungry readers will find additional references in Douglas Fry, *The Human Potential for Peace: An Anthropological Challenge to Assumptions About War and Violence* (New York: Oxford University Press, 2006).

Chapter 1: Charting a New Direction

1. Throughout the book, the academic discipline of a researcher, if known, is provided the first time that the person's name is mentioned in the book (except for anthropologists, whose works constitute the vast majority of sources cited). Douglas Fry, "Utilizing human capacities for survival in the nuclear age," *Bulletin of Peace Proposals* 16 (1985): 159–66; Thomas Hobbes, *Leviathan: Or the Matter, Forme and Power of a Commonwealth Ecclesiasticall and Civil* (Oxford: Basil Blackwell, 1946, orig. pub. 1651).
2. Quincy Wright, *A Study of War* (Chicago: University of Chicago Press, 1942); Quincy Wright, *A Study of War*, 2nd ed., abridged by L. Wright (Chicago: University of Chicago Press, 1964) 40.
3. Napoleon Chagnon, "Life histories, blood revenge, and warfare in a tribal population," *Science* 239 (1988): 985–92. Critiques: Bruce Albert, "Yanomami 'violence': Inclusive fitness or ethnographer's

representation?" *Current Anthropology* 30 (1989): 637–40; R. Brian Ferguson, "Do Yanomamö killers have more kids?" *American Ethnologist* 16 (1989): 564–65; R. Brian Ferguson, *Yanomami Warfare: A Political History* (Santa Fe, N.M.: School of American Research Press, 1995); Jacques Lizot, "On warfare: An answer to N. A. Chagnon," trans. Sarah Dart, *American Ethnologist* 21 (1994): 845–62. And more generally on the Yanomamö controversies: Robert Borofsky, *Yanomami: The Fierce Controversy and What We Can Learn from It* (Berkeley: University of California Press, 2005); Leslie Sponsel, "Yanomami: An Arena of Conflict and Aggression in the Amazon," *Aggressive Behavior* 24 (1998): 97–122.

4. Frans de Waal and F. Lanting, *Bonobo: The Forgotten Ape* (Berkeley: University of California Press, 1989), 2; see also Frans de Waal, *Our Inner Ape* (New York: Riverhead Books, 2005), 3, 13, 30; Robert Sapolsky, "A natural history of peace," *Foreign Affairs* 85, 1 (2006), online at www.foreignaffairs.org.

5. Robert Ehrlich, *Nine Crazy Ideas in Science: A Few Might Even Be True* (Princeton: Princeton University Press, 2001), 11.

Chapter 2: Do Nonwarring Societies Actually Exist?

1. Michael Ghiglieri, *The Dark Side of Man: Tracing the Origins of Male Violence* (Reading, Mass.: Perseus, 1999), 246; David Buss, *Evolutionary Psychology: The New Science of the Mind* (Boston: Allyn and Bacon, 1999), 298; Richard Wrangham and Dale Peterson, *Demonic Males: Apes and the Origin of Human Violence* (Boston: Houghton Mifflin, 1996), 63; see also David Buss, *The Murderer Next Door: Why the Mind Is Designed to Kill* (New York: Penguin Press, 2005), 5, 9, 11, 231, 234–35; Steven LeBlanc (with

K. Register), *Constant Battles: Why We Fight* (New York: St. Martin's Griffin, 2003); Lawrence Keeley, *War Before Civilization: The Myth of the Peaceful Savage* (Oxford: Oxford University Press, 1996).

2. Keeley, *War Before Civilization*, 30–31; Wrangham and Peterson, *Demonic Males*, 75.

3. Edward Wilson, "On human nature," in D. Barash (ed.), *Understanding Violence*, 13–20 (Boston: Allyn and Bacon, 2001), 14; David Adams and Sarah Bosch, "The myth that war is intrinsic to human nature discourages action for peace by young people," in J. Ramírez, R. Hinde, and J. Groeble (eds.), *Essays on Violence*, 121–37 (Seville: University of Seville Press, 1987); Douglas Fry and James Welch, "Beliefs about human nature and conflict: Implications for peace education," paper presented at the meetings of the American Anthropological Association, December 1992, San Francisco; "Letters," *Time*, May 8, 2000, 11.

4. Marilyn Grunkemeyer, "Belief systems," in D. Levinson and M. Ember (eds.), *Encyclopedia of Cultural Anthropology*, vol. 1, 125–30 (New York: Henry Holt and Company, 1996), 126, 125; see also Clifford Geertz, *The Interpretation of Cultures* (New York: Basic Books, 1973); Florence Kluckhohn and Fred Strodtbeck, *Variations in Value Orientations* (Evanston, Ill.: Row, Peterson and Company, 1961), 11–12, 365–66.

5. David Barash, *Introduction to Peace Studies* (Belmont, Calif.: Wadsworth, 1991); Robert Carneiro, "War and peace: Alternating realities in human history," in S. Reyna and R. Downs (eds.), *Studying War: Anthropological Perspectives*, 3–27 (Amsterdam: Gordon and Breach, 1994); Thomas Huxley quoted in Rudolf Holsti, "The Relation of War to the Origin of the State," *Annales Academiæ Scientiarum Fennicæ*, ser. B, vol. XII (1913): 14.

6. Semai: Clayton Robarchek, "Hobbesian and Rousseauan images of man: Autonomy and individuality in a peaceful society," in S. Howell and R. Willis (eds.), *Societies at Peace: Anthropological Perspectives*, 31–44 (London: Routledge, 1989); Zapotec: Douglas Fry, "Multiple paths to peace: The 'La Paz' Zapotec of Mexico," in G. Kemp and D. Fry (eds.), *Keeping the Peace: Conflict Resolution and Peaceful Societies Around the World*, 73–87 (New York: Routledge, 2004).

7. Robert Ehrlich, *Nine Crazy Ideas in Science: A Few Might Even Be True* (Princeton: Princeton University Press, 2001), 11.

8. C. Ember and M. Ember, "Warfare, aggression, and resource problems: Cross-cultural codes," *Behavior Science Research* 26 (1992): 169–226; C. Ember and M. Ember, "Resource unpredictability, mistrust, and war," *Journal of Conflict Resolution* 36 (1992): 242–62; C. Ember and M. Ember, 1994, "War, socialization, and interpersonal violence: A cross-cultural study," *Journal of Conflict Resolution* 38 (1994): 620–46; C. Ember and M. Ember, "Violence in the ethnographic record: Results of cross-cultural research on war and aggression," in D. Martin and D. Frayer (eds.), *Troubled Times: Violence and Warfare in the Past*, 1–20 (Amsterdam: Gordon and Breach, 1997). For information about the SCCS, see Douglas White, "Focused ethnographic bibliography: Standard cross-cultural sample," *Behavior Science Research* 23 (1989) 1–145.

9. Ember and Ember, "Warfare," 172, italics added.

10. Ember and Ember, "Warfare"; Alfred Radcliffe-Brown, *The Andaman Islanders* (Cambridge: Cambridge University Press, 1922), 86; L. Hobhouse, "Part II. Peace and order among the simplest peoples," *British Journal of Sociology*, 7 (1956): 96–119, 105; Elman Service, *The Hunters* (Englewood Cliffs, N.J.: Prentice-Hall, 1966), 110.

11. See Keith Otterbein (ed.), *Feuding and Warfare: Selected Works of Keith F. Otterbein* (Langhorne, Penn.: Gordon and Breach, 1994); Keith Otterbein, "A history of research on warfare in anthropology," *American Anthropologist* 101 (1999): 794–805; Keith Otterbein, "Five feuds: An analysis of homicides in Eastern Kentucky in the late nineteenth century," *American Anthropologist* 102 (1999): 231–43; Keith Otterbein, *How War Began* (College Station, Tex.: Texas A&M University Press, 2004).

12. Keith Otterbein and C. Otterbein, "An eye for an eye, a tooth for a tooth: A cross-cultural study of feuding," *American Anthropologist* 67 (1965): 1470–82, 1470; see also Keith Otterbein, "Internal war: A cross-cultural study," *American Anthropologist* 70 (1968): 277–89, 279; Keith Otterbein, *The Evolution of War: A Cross-Cultural Study* (New Haven: Human Relations Area Files Press, 1970).

13. The coding of war among one society in the sample, the Tiwi of Australia, should be reconsidered, for, as will be discussed in Chapter 9, the material upon which the coding is based (in C. Hart and Arnold Pilling, *The Tiwi of North Australia* [New York: Holt, Rinehart, and Winston, 1960]; see also the 1979 fieldwork edition of the same book) does not pertain to "armed combat between political communities." A clarification of this issue and recoding of Tiwi society means that 10 percent of Otterbein's sample lacks war.

14. Harold Driver, *Indians of North America*, 2nd ed. (Chicago: University of Chicago Press, 1969), 310, 312–20, quote from 312.

15. Otterbein and Otterbein, "An eye for an eye," Table 3; Karen Ericksen and Heather Horton, "'Blood feuds': Cross-cultural variations in kin group vengeance," *Behavior Science Research* 26 (1992): 57–85.

16. Bobbi Low, "An evolutionary perspective on war," in W. Zimmerman and H. Jacobson (eds.), *Behavior, Culture, and Conflict in World Politics*, 13–55 (Ann Arbor: University of Michigan Press, 1993), 13.

17. Roy Prosterman, *Surviving to 3000: An Introduction to the Study of Lethal Conflict* (Belmont, Calif.: Duxbury-Wadsworth, 1972), 140.

18. Ibid., 140–41; Otterbein, *The Evolution of War*.

19. Some of the cultures on the nonwarring list have feuding, although most do not feud. When there was ambiguity in the ethnographic information as to whether violence was feud or war, I did *not* include the culture on the list even when feuding, not war, seemed to be the most appropriate classification. Likewise, if an ethnographer reported that a particular society is "not warlike" but failed to elaborate, I did *not* add that culture to the list. In situations where a source reported that a society is now peaceful but practiced war in the relatively recent past, I did *not* include the culture on the list. Thus I attempted to rule out cultures that are nonwarring due to relatively recent historical developments. See also Douglas P. Fry, *The Human Potential for Peace* (New York: Oxford University Press, 2006), Chapter 7; Bruce Bonta and Douglas Fry, "Lessons for the rest of us: Learning from peaceful societies," in M. Fitzduff and C. Stout (eds.), *The Psychology of Resolving Global Conflicts: From War to Peace*, vol. 1: *Nature Versus Nurture*, 175–210 (Westport, Conn.: Praeger Security International, 2006), "Peaceful Societies" appendix.

20. Thomas Gregor and Clayton Robarchek, "Two paths to peace: Semai and Mehinaku nonviolence," in T. Gregor (ed.), *A Natural History of Peace*, 159–88 (Nashville: Vanderbilt University Press, 1996), 161.

21. For the Mardu: Robert Tonkinson, *The Mardudjara Aborigines: Living the Dream in Australia's Desert* (New York: Holt, Rinehart, and Winston, 1978), 118. For the Arunta: Elman Service, *Profiles in Ethnology*, rev. ed. (New York: Harper and Row, 1971), p. 18. For the Sanpoil: Verne Ray, *The Sanpoil and Nespelem: Salishan Peoples of Northeastern Washington* (New York: AMS Press, 1980), 114. For the Saulteaux: A. Irving Hallowell, "Aggression in Saulteaux society," in A. I. Hallowell (ed.), *Culture and Experience*, 277–90 (Philadelphia: University of Pennsylvania Press, 1974), 278. For the Machiguenga: Allen Johnson, "Machiguenga gardens," in R. Hames and W. Vickers (eds.), *Adaptive Responses of Native Amazonians*, 29–63 (New York: Academic Press, 1983), 61, 63. For the Hanunóo: Frank LeBar, "Hanunóo," in F. LeBar (ed. and comp.), *Ethnic Groups of Insular Southeast Asia*, vol. 2: *Philippines and Formosa*, 74–76 (New Haven: Human Relations Area Files Press, 1975), 76; Harold Conklin, *The Relation of Hanunóo Culture to the Plant World*, unpublished doctoral dissertation, Anthropology Department, Yale University, 1954, 49. For the Subanun: Charles Frake, "The Eastern Subanun of Mindanao," in G. Murdock (ed.), *Social Structure in Southeast Asia*, 51–64 (New York: Wenner-Gren Viking Fund Publications in Anthropology, 1960), 52; Charles Frake, "Litigation in Lipay: A study of Subanun law," in A. Dil (ed.), *Language and Cultural Description: Essays by Charles O. Frake*, 132–43 (Stanford: Stanford University Press, 1980), 133. For the Veddahs: Van Goens quoted in Maurice Davie, *The Evolution of War: A Study of Its Role in Early Societies* (New Haven: Yale University Press, 1929), 50. For the Paliyan: Peter Gardner, "Respect for all: The Paliyans of South India," in G. Kemp and D. Fry (eds.), *Keeping the Peace: Conflict Resolution and*

Peaceful Societies Around the World, 53–71 (New York: Routledge, 2004), 58. For the Semang: Frank LeBar, Gerald Hickey, and John Musgrave, "Semang," in F. LeBar, G. Hickey, and J. Musgrave (eds.), *Ethnic Groups of Mainland Southeast Asia,* 181–86 (New Haven: Human Relations Area Files Press, 1964), 185. For the Jahai: Cornelia van der Sluys, "Jahai," in R. Lee and R. Daly (eds.), *The Cambridge Encyclopedia of Hunters and Gatherers,* 307–11 (Cambridge: Cambridge University Press, 1999), 307, 310. For the Andamanese: L. T. Hobhouse, "Part II. Peace and order among the simplest peoples," *British Journal of Sociology* 7 (1956): 105. For Costa Rica: Oscar Arias, "Esquipulas II: The management of a regional crisis," in D. P. Fry and K. Björkqvist (eds.), *Cultural Variation in Conflict Resolution: Alternatives to Violence,* 147–58 (Mahwah, N.J.: Lawrence Erlbaum Associates, 1997), 148.

22. Enclave societies: Bruce Bonta, *Peaceful Peoples: An Annotated Bibliography* (Metuchen, N.J.: Scarecrow Press, 1993); David Fabbro, "Peaceful societies: An introduction," *Journal of Peace Research* 15 (1978): 67–83. Sweden: Keeley, *War Before Civilization,* 32. Switzerland: Douglas Fry, "Utilizing human capacities for survival in the nuclear age," *Bulletin of Peace Proposals* 16 (1985): 159–66, 160; Keeley, *War Before Civilization,* 32. Iceland: E. Durrenberger and John Beierle, *Cultural Summary: Icelanders,* in the electronic Human Relations Area Files (New Haven: HRAF, 2004); David Levinson, *Aggression and Conflict: A Cross-Cultural Encyclopedia* (Santa Barbara: ABC-CLIO, 1994), 137. One hundred years without war: Levinson, *Aggression and Conflict,* 137. Costa Rica: Oscar Arias, "Esquipulas II: The management of a regional crisis," in D. Fry and K. Björkqvist (eds.), *Cultural Variation in Conflict Resolution:*

Alternatives to Violence, 147–58 (Mahwah, N.J.: Lawrence Erlbaum, 1997), 148.

23. Otterbein, "Internal war"; Otterbein, *The Evolution of War;* Ember and Ember, "Warfare"; Ember and Ember, "Resource unpredictability"; Ember and Ember, "War, socialization"; Ember and Ember, "Cross-cultural studies of war and peace: Recent achievements and future possibilities," in S. Reyna and R. Downs (eds.), *Studying War: Anthropological Perspectives,* 185–208 (Amsterdam: Gordon and Breach, 1994); Ember and Ember, "Violence in the ethnographic record."

24. Edwin Burrows, *Flower in My Ear: Arts and Ethos on Ifaluk Atoll* (Seattle: University of Washington Press, 1963), 421.

Chapter 3: Overlooked and Underappreciated

1. Douglas Fry, "Conflict management in cross-cultural perspective," in F. Aureli and F. de Waal (eds.), *Natural Conflict Resolution,* 334–51 (Berkeley: University of California Press, 2000); Agustin Fuentes, "It's not all sex and violence: Integrated anthropology and the role of cooperation and social complexity in human evolution," *American Anthropologist* 106 (2004): 710–18, 716.

2. S. Gardner and H. Resnik, "Violence among youth: Origins and a framework for prevention," in R. Hampton, P. Jenkins, and T. Gullotta (eds.), *Preventing Violence in America,* 157–77 (Thousand Oaks, Calif.: Sage, 1996), 169.

3. Bahram Haghighi and Jon Sorenson, "America's fear of crime," in T. Flanagan and D. Longmire (eds.), *Americans View Crime and Justice,* 16–30 (Thousand Oaks, Calif.: Sage, 1996), 20–21.

4. Clayton Robarchek and Carole Robarchek, *Waorani: The Contexts of Violence and War* (Fort Worth: Harcourt Brace College Publishers, 1998), 19, 20, 57, 58; Clayton Robarchek and Carole Robarchek, "Waging peace: The psychological and sociocultural dynamics of positive peace," in A. Wolfe and H. Yang (eds.), *Anthropological Contributions to Conflict Resolution*, 64–80 (Athens: University of Georgia Press, 1996), 66.

5. Douglas Fry, "Intercommunity differences in aggression among Zapotec children," *Child Development* 59 (1988): 1008–19; Douglas Fry, "'Respect for the rights of others is peace': Learning aggression versus non-aggression among the Zapotec," *American Anthropologist* 94 (1992): 621–39; Douglas Fry, "Maintaining social tranquility: Internal and external loci of aggression control," in L. Sponsel and T. Gregor (eds.), *The Anthropology of Peace and Nonviolence*, 133–54 (Boulder: Lynne Rienner, 1994); Douglas Fry, "Multiple paths to peace: The 'La Paz' Zapotec of Mexico," in G. Kemp and D. Fry (eds.), *Keeping the Peace: Conflict Resolution and Peaceful Societies Around the World*, 73–87 (New York: Routledge, 2004); Douglas Fry, *The Human Potential for Peace* (New York: Oxford University Press, 2006), Chapter 4.

6. Douglas Fry, "Peaceful societies," in L. Kurtz (ed.), *Encyclopedia of Violence, Peace and Conflict*, vol. 3, 719–33 (San Diego: Academic Press, 1999), 719, adapted from Jeffrey Rubin, Dean Pruitt, and S. H. Kim, *Social Conflict: Escalation, Stalemate, and Settlement*, 2nd ed. (New York: McGraw-Hill, 1994).

7. Allan Holmberg, *Nomads of the Long Bow: The Siriono of Eastern Bolivia* (New York: American Museum of Natural History, 1969, orig. pub. 1950), 1, 10, 13, 17, 144, 148.

8. Ibid., 138, 140, 141, 147, 161, 165.

9. Ibid., 151, 153, 154, 157.

10. Ibid., 158, 159, 160.

11. Ibid., 132, 151–53, 157.

12. Ibid., 152, 161.

13. Ibid., 166.

14. Ibid., 156.

15. Peter Gardner, "The Paliyans," in M. Bicchieri (ed.), *Hunters and Gatherers Today*, 404–7 (Prospect Heights, Ill.: Waveland, 1972), 407, 422; Peter Gardner, *Bicultural Versatility as a Frontier Adaptation Among Paliyan Foragers of South India* (Lewiston, N.Y.: Edwin Mellen Press, 2000), 23; Peter Gardner, "Bicultural oscillation as a long-term adaptation to cultural frontiers: Cases and questions," *Human Ecology* 13 (1985): 411–32, 413.

16. Gardner, *Bicultural Versatility*, 23, 33, 39; Gardner, "The Paliyans," 414.

17. Gardner, *Bicultural Versatility*, 103, 104–11; Peter Gardner, "The Paliyan," in R. Lee and R. Daly (eds.), *The Cambridge Encyclopedia of Hunters and Gatherers*, 261–64 (Cambridge: Cambridge University Press, 1999), 263.

18. Gardner, *Bicultural Versatility*, 3, 83, 85; see also Gardner, "The Paliyan," 263.

19. Gardner, "The Paliyans," 415–16.

20. Ibid., 425; Gardner, "The Paliyan," 263; Peter Gardner, "Respect and nonviolence among recently sedentary Paliyan foragers," *Journal of the Royal Anthropological Institute* (n.s.) 6 (2000): 215–36, 104–11, 224; Gardner, *Bicultural Versatility*, 93.

21. Gardner, "Respect and nonviolence," 225.

22. Gardner, "The Paliyans," 439; Peter Gardner, "Symmetric respect and memorate knowledge: The structure and ecology of individualistic culture," *Southwestern Journal of Anthropology* 22 (1966): 389–415, 402; Gardner, "Bicultural oscillation,"

413–16, 421; Gardner, "The Paliyan," 263; Peter Gardner, "Respect for all: The Paliyans of South India," in G. Kemp and D. Fry (eds.), *Keeping the Peace: Conflict Resolution and Peaceful Societies Around the World*, 53–71 (New York: Routledge, 2004).

Chapter 4: Killer Apes, Cannibals, and Coprolites

1. Francis Pottenger, *The Fight Against Tuberculosis: An Autobiography* (New York: Henry Schuman, 1952), 67, 68, 69–70, italics added.
2. Bobbi Low, "An evolutionary perspective on war," in W. Zimmerman and H. Jacobson (eds.), *Behavior, Culture, and Conflict in World Politics*, 13–55 (Ann Arbor: University of Michigan Press, 1993), 13.
3. To offer a brief overview, three broad trends are apparent in the fossil record over the last several million years of human evolution: a shift from walking on all fours to bipedalism, overall reduction in tooth size, and enlargement of the brain. From about five million years ago and continuing to about two million years ago, a variety of ancestral forms, collectively called australopithecines, lived on the African continent. As shown by fossilized footprints and anatomical studies, well before 3.7 million years ago these human precursors walked erect. Australopithecine brain size was close to that of the modern chimpanzee, and the australopithecine brain-to-body ratio was substantially smaller than that of modern humans. Slightly before two million years ago, larger-brained forms, the first representatives of the genus *Homo*, made their appearance. From this point onward, the brain-to-body ratio steadily increased over time, as did the sophistication of stone

tools in the fossil record. Teeth also continued to become smaller over the long haul within the genus *Homo*.

Specimens of hominids—a general term for likely human ancestors—that date roughly between 1.5 million and about 350,000 years ago are classified within the species *Homo erectus*. Later *Homo erectus* specimens had substantially larger brains than the earliest *Homo erectus* fossils. *Homo erectus* occupied parts of Asia and Africa, and some sites suggest the possibility that these hominids used fire. The facial features of *Homo erectus*, especially of the oldest specimens, were robust compared to modern humans.

Early forms of our own species, *Homo sapiens*, sometimes referred to as *archaic Homo sapiens*, follow and may overlap with the very last of the *Homo erectus* fossils. The fact that the species name *Homo sapiens* is used for this class of ancestors beginning with specimens that date somewhat more than 200,000 years ago reflects the fact that they were anatomically very similar to current-day people. From at least 40,000 years ago, modern *Homo sapiens*, or anatomically modern humans, are clearly represented in the archaeological record. The Neanderthals are a variation of *Homo sapiens* found in parts of Europe and the Middle East, dating roughly between 75,000 and 40,000 years ago. The Neanderthals have sparked much debate. Were these burly hominids ancestral to modern humans or were they off-shoots that became extinct? Did Neanderthals mate and merge with other groups of *Homo sapiens*, were they outcompeted in the search for game and eventually displaced, were they violently wiped out, or did they simply evolve more gracile (less robust, more modern) appearances? At least one point is clear: No archaeological evidence has been found to support the suggestion that the Neanderthals were victims of genocide.

One other point about the prehistoric world merits emphasis, an observation that may be difficult for people today, crowded on an earth populated by six *billion*, to visualize: Over several million years, hominids and then humans had a lot of space. It was not until about 11,000 to 12,000 years ago, just before the development of agriculture, that the entire population of the planet reached seven million.

4. Roger Lewin, *Bones of Contention: Controversies in the Search for Human Origins* (New York: Simon and Schuster, 1987), 47–84; Mark Weiss and Alan Mann, *Human Biology and Behavior*, 5th ed. (Glenview, Ill.: Scott Foresman, 1990), 317–22.

5. Joseph Birdsell quoted in J. van der Dennen, *The Origin of War*, 2 vols. (Groningen: Origin Press, 1995), 199; Raymond Dart, "The predatory implemental technique of australopithecines," *American Journal of Physical Anthropology* 7 (1949): 1–38; Raymond Dart, "The predatory transition from ape to man," *International Anthropological and Linguistic Review* 1 (1953): 201–18; Raymond Dart, "The minimal bone-breccia content of Makapansgat and the australopithecine predatory habit," *American Anthropologist* 60 (1958): 923–31.

6. Dart, "The predatory transition," 207; Dart, "The predatory implemental technique," 5, 13–14; see also C. K. Brain, "New finds at the Swartkrans australopithecine site," *Nature* 225 (1970): 1112–19; William Ury, *Getting to Peace: Transforming Conflict at Home, at Work, and in the World* (New York: Viking, 1999), 33.

7. Dart, "The predatory implemental technique," 12, 38; Dart, "The predatory transition," 209.

8. For example, Robert Ardrey, *African Genesis* (New York: Dell, 1961); Robert Ardrey, *The Territorial Imperative* (New York: Atheneum, 1966).

9. Marilyn Roper, "A survey of the evidence for intrahuman killing in the Pleistocene," *Current Anthropology* 10 (1969): 427–59, 432–33.

10. Brain, "New finds"; see also Donna Hart and Robert Sussman, *Man the Hunted: Primates, Predators, and Human Evolution* (New York: Westview Press, 2005).

11. Dart, "The predatory transition," 207–8.

12. Robert Foley, "Studying human evolution by analogy," in S. Jones, R. Martin, and D. Pilbeam (eds.), *The Cambridge Encyclopedia of Human Evolution*, 335–40 (Cambridge: Cambridge University Press, 1992), 335.

13. Ury, *Getting to Peace*, 33. The Taung child itself, by the way, may well have been the victim of a predatory attack by a large eagle—see Hart and Sussman, *Man the Hunted*, 6–7.

14. See Lawrence Keeley, *War Before Civilization: The Myth of the Peaceful Savage* (Oxford: Oxford University Press, 1996); Philip Walker, "A bioarchaeological perspective on the history of violence," *Annual Review of Anthropology* 30 (2001): 573–96; Maria O. Smith, "Osteological indications of warfare in the Archaic Period of the western Tennessee Valley," in D. Martin and D. Frayer (eds.), *Troubled Times: Violence and Warfare in the Past*, 241–65 (Amsterdam: Gordon and Breach, 1997); Herbert Maschner, "The evolution of Northwest Coast warfare," in D. Martin and D. Frayer (eds.), *Troubled Times: Violence and Warfare in the Past*, 267–302 (Amsterdam: Gordon and Breach, 1997).

15. Keeley, *War Before Civilization*, ix.

16. See also Joyce Marcus, *MesoAmerican Writing Systems* (Princeton, N.J.: Princeton University Press, 1992), 391–94.

17. Lewis Binford and Chuan Ho, "Taphonomy at a distance: Zhoukoudian, 'The cave home of Beijing man'"? *Current Anthropology* 26 (1985): 413–42.

18. Paul Bahn, "Cannibalism of ritual dismemberment?" in S. Jones, R. Martin, and D. Pilbeam (eds.), *The Cambridge Encyclopedia of Human Evolution*, 330 (Cambridge: Cambridge University Press, 1992), 330.

19. Mary Stiner, "The cultural significance of Grotta Guattari reconsidered. I. The faunal remains from Grotta Guattari: A taphonomic perspective," plus commentary, *Current Anthropology* 32 (1991): 103–17, 124–38, 116; Tim White and Nicholas Toth, "The cultural significance of Grotta Guattari reconsidered. II. The question of ritual cannibalism at Grotta Guattari," plus commentary, *Current Anthropology* 32 (1991): 118–38, 123.

20. Ury, *Getting to Peace*, 34; Tim White and Nicholas Toth, "Engis: Preparation damage, not ancient cutmarks," *American Journal of Physical Anthropology* 78 (1989): 361–67, 367.

21. Karl Reinhard, "A coprological view of Ancestral Pueblo cannibalism," *American Scientist* 94 (2006): 254–61, 254.

22. Ibid., 254, 259.

23. Ibid., 256.

24. Ibid., 256.

25. Leslie Sponsel, "The natural history of peace: A positive view of human nature and its potential," in T. Gregor (ed.), *A Natural History of Peace*, 95–125 (Nashville, Tenn.: Vanderbilt University Press, 1996), 105; Marilyn Roper, "Evidence of warfare in the Near East from 10,000–4,300 B.C.," in M. Nettleship, R. Dalegivens, and A. Nettleship (eds.), *War, Its Causes and Correlates*, 299–340 (The Hague: Mouton, 1975), 304–9.

26. C. Richards, "Comment," in M. Nettleship, R. Dalegivens, and A. Nettleship (eds.), *War, Its Causes and Correlates*, 342–43 (The Hague: Mouton, 1975), 342, 343, emphasis in original; Roper, "Evidence of warfare."

27. Richards, "Comment," 343.

28. O. Bar-Yosef, "The walls of Jericho: An alternative interpretation," *Current Anthropology* 27 (1986): 157–62.

29. Ibid., 161.

30. Ibid., 161.

Chapter 5: The Earliest Evidence of War

1. Richard Wrangham and Dale Peterson, *Demonic Males: Apes and the Origin of Human Violence* (Boston: Houghton Mifflin, 1996), 63, 108–9; Douglas Fry, "Anthropological perspectives on aggression: Sex differences and cultural variation," *Aggressive Behavior* 24 (1998): 81–95.

2. Douglas Fry, *The Human Potential for Peace* (New York: Oxford University Press, 2006); Bruce Bonta and Douglas Fry, "Lessons for the rest of us: Learning from peaceful societies," in M. Fitzduff and C. Stout (eds.), *The Psychology of Resolving Global Conflicts: From War to Peace*, vol. 1: *Nature vs. Nurture*, 175–210 (Westport, Conn.: Praeger Security International, 2006), www.peacefulsocieties.org.

3. Wrangham and Peterson, *Demonic Males*, 84; J. van der Dennen, *The Origin of War*, 2 vols. (Groningen: Origin Press, 1995), 497.

4. R. B. Ferguson, "Violence and war in prehistory," in D. Martin and D. Frayer (eds.), *Troubled Times: Violence and Warfare in the Past*, 321–55 (Amsterdam: Gordon and Breach, 1997), 323, 340.

5. Lawrence H. Keeley, *War Before Civilization: The Myth of the Peaceful Savage* (Oxford: Oxford University Press, 1996), 39; Marilyn Roper, "A survey of the evidence for intrahuman

killing in the Pleistocene," *Current Anthropology* 10 (1969): 427–59; see also Jonathan Haas, "Warfare and the evolution of culture," in G. Feinman and T. D. Price (eds.), *Archaeology at the Millennium: A Sourcebook*, 329–50 (New York: Kluwer Academic/Plenum, 2001).

6. Keith Otterbein, "The origins of war," *Critical Review* 2 (1997): 251–77, quote from 271; Keeley, *War Before Civilization*, 36–39; Raymond Kelly, *Warless Societies and the Origin of War* (Ann Arbor: University of Michigan Press, 2000), 157.

7. Lewis R. Binford, *Constructing Frames of Reference: An Analytical Method for Archaeological Theory Building Using Hunter-Gatherer and Environmental Data Sets* (Berkeley: University of California Press, 2001); Robert Kelly, *The Foraging Spectrum: Diversity in Hunter-Gatherer Lifeways* (Washington, D.C.: Smithsonian Institution Press, 1995), 302; Bruce Knauft, "Violence and sociality in human evolution," *Current Anthropology* 32 (1991): 391–428, quote from 392; Elman Service, *Primitive Social Organization: An Evolutionary Perspective*, 2nd ed. (New York: Random House, 1971).

8. Knauft, "Violence and sociality," 392; Michael Alvard and L. Kuznar, "Deferred harvests: The transition from hunting to animal husbandry," *American Anthropologist* 103 (2001): 295–311, 295; Donald Henry, "Preagricultural sedentism: The Natufian example," in T. Price and J. Brown (eds.), *Prehistoric Hunter-Gatherers: The Emergence of Cultural Complexity*, 365–84 (New York: Academic Press, 1985).

9. Kelly, *The Foraging Spectrum*, 294; see also Knauft, "Violence and sociality."

10. Alvard and Kuznar, "Deferred Harvests," 295; Henry, "Preagricultural sedentism," 366; Kelly, *The Foraging Spectrum*, 304; Knauft, "Violence and sociality," 392.

11. Henry, "Preagricultural sedentism," 365.

12. Ibid., 365.
13. James Brown and T. D. Price, "Complex hunter-gatherers: Retrospect and prospect," in T. Price and J. Brown (eds.), *Prehistoric Hunter-Gatherers: The Emergence of Cultural Complexity*, 436–42 (New York: Academic Press, 1985), 437.
14. Herbert Maschner, "The evolution of Northwest Coast warfare," in D. Martin and D. Frayer (eds.), *Troubled Times: Violence and Warfare in the Past*, 267–302 (Amsterdam: Gordon and Breach, 1997), 293–94, 270.
15. Marilyn Roper, "Evidence of warfare in the Near East from 10,000–4,300 B.C.," in M. Nettleship, R. Dalegivens, and A. Nettleship (eds.), *War, Its Causes and Correlates*, 299–340 (The Hague: Mouton, 1975), see 300.
16. Ibid.
17. Ibid., 329.
18. Jonathan Haas, "The origins of war and ethnic violence," in J. Carman and A. Harding (eds.), *Ancient Warfare: Archaeological Perspectives*, 11–24 (Gloucestershire, U.K.: Sutton Publishing, 1999), 16.
19. Ibid.
20. Ibid., 21.
21. Kent Flannery and Joyce Marcus, "The origin of war: New ^{14}C dates from ancient Mexico," *Proceedings of the National Academy of Sciences* 100 (2003): 11801–11.
22. Haas, "Warfare and the evolution of culture."
23. Keeley, *War Before Civilization*; see also Christopher Boehm, *Hierarchy in the Forest: The Evolution of Egalitarian Behavior* (Cambridge: Harvard University Press, 1999), 94–95; Ferguson, "Violence and war in prehistory"; R. Brian Ferguson, "Is war in our genes? Evidence vs. speculation on the antiquity and biology of war," Phi Beta Kappa Lecture, Rutgers University, Newark, N. J.,

February 16, 2000; R. Brian Ferguson, "Archaeology, cultural anthropology, and the origins and intensifications of war," in B. Arkush and M. W. Allen (eds.), *The Archaeology of Warfare: Prehistories of Raiding and Conquest*, 469–524 (Gainesville: University Press of Florida, 2006); Leslie Sponsel, "The natural history of peace: A positive view of human nature and its potential," in T. Gregor (ed.), *A Natural History of Peace*, 95–125 (Nashville, Tenn.: Vanderbilt University Press, 1996); Kelly, *Warless Societies*, 1, 2.

24. Jonathan Haas, "War," in D. Levinson and M. Ember (eds.), *Encyclopedia of Cultural Anthropology*, vol. 4, 1357–61 (New York: Henry Holt and Company, 1996), 1360.

25. See Haas, "Warfare and the evolution of culture."

26. Ferguson, "Violence and war in prehistory," 322, 326.

27. Ferguson, "Is war in our genes?" 6.

28. Haas, "The origins of war and ethnic violence," 13. See the additional references in Fry, *The Human Potential for Peace*, 275, note 21.

29. Sponsel, "The natural history of peace," 104, emphasis in original.

30. Keeley, *War Before Civilization*, 39.

Chapter 6: War and Social Organization

1. Quincy Wright, *A Study of War* (Chicago: University of Chicago Press, 1942); Worldwide sample: L. Hobhouse, G. Wheeler, and M. Ginsberg, *The Material Culture and Social Institutions of the Simpler Peoples: An Essay in Correlation* (London: Chapman and Hall, 1915).

2. Wright, *A Study of War*, Appendix IX.
3. Ibid., 546.
4. See ibid., Tables 5 and 11.
5. Ibid., 546.
6. Kirk Endicott, "The effects of slave raiding on the Aborigines of the Malay Peninsula," in A. Reid (ed.), *Slavery, Bondage and Dependency in Southeast Asia*, 216–45 (New York: St. Martin's Press, 1983); Robert Dentan, "Cautious, alert, polite, and elusive: Semai of Central Peninsular Malaysia," in G. Kemp and D. Fry (eds.), *Keeping the Peace: Conflict Resolution and Peaceful Societies Around the World*, 167–84 (New York: Routledge, 2004); H. Forbes, "On the Kubus of Sumatra," *Journal of the Anthropological Institute of Great Britain and Ireland* 14 (1885): 121–27; Thomas Gregor and Clayton Robarchek, "Two paths to peace: Semai and Mehinaku nonviolence," in T. Gregor (ed.), *A Natural History of Peace*, 159–88 (Nashville: Vanderbilt University Press, 1996); Paul Schebesta, *Among the Forrest Dwarfs of Malaya* (London: Hutchinson and Company, 1929), 280; Paul Schebesta, *My Pygmy and Negro Hosts* (New York: AMS Press, 1978, orig. pub. 1936), 187. The term *Sakai* is pejorative and nowadays is avoided by anthropologists—see Endicott, "The effects of slave raiding," 218.
7. Fredtjof Nansen, *Eskimo Life*, trans. William Archer (London: Longmans, Green, and Company, 1893), 162.
8. See, for example, Jules Henry, *Jungle People: Kaingáng Tribe of the Highlands of Brazil* (New York: J. J. Augustin, 1941), 55; Thomas Gibson, "Symbolic representations of tranquility and aggression among the Buid," in S. Howell and R. Willis (eds.), *Societies at Peace: Anthropological Perspectives*, 60–78 (London: Routledge, 1989), 71; Cornelia van der Sluys, "Jahai," in R. Lee

and R. Daly (eds.), *The Cambridge Encyclopedia of Hunters and Gatherers*, 307–11 (Cambridge: Cambridge University Press, 1999), 307, 310; and other sources listed in Douglas Fry, *The Human Potential for Peace* (New York: Oxford University Press, 2006), 276 n. 9.

9. Dentan, "Cautious, alert, polite."

10. Wright, *A Study of War*.

11. Elman Service, *Primitive Social Organization: An Evolutionary Perspective*, 2nd ed. (New York: Random House, 1971).

12. Robert Kelly, *The Foraging Spectrum: Diversity in Hunter-Gatherer Lifeways* (Washington, D.C.: Smithsonian Institution Press, 1995), 302; Service, *Primitive Social Organization*; T. Douglas Price and James Brown (eds.), *Prehistoric Hunter-Gatherers: The Emergence of Cultural Complexity* (New York: Academic Press, 1985).

13. Christopher Boehm, *Hierarchy in the Forest: The Evolution of Egalitarian Behavior* (Cambridge: Harvard University Press, 1999), quote from 146; Service, *Primitive Social Organization*, 166–69.

14. S. Reyna, "A mode of domination approach to organized violence," in S. Reyna and R. Downs (eds.), *Studying War: Anthropological Perspectives*, 29–65 (Amsterdam: Gordon and Breach, 1994); Boehm, *Hierarchy in the Forest*.

15. J. van der Dennen, *The Origin of War*, 2 vols. (Groningen: Origin Press, 1995), Chapter 2, quote from 142; Jonathan Haas, "Warfare and the evolution of culture," in G. Feinman and T. Price (eds.), *Archaeology at the Millennium: A Sourcebook*, 329–50 (New York: Kluwer Academic/Plenum, 2001), quote from 343; Reyna, "A mode of domination approach"; Wright, *A Study of War*, 66; see also Fry, *The Human Potential for Peace*, 275 nn. 21, 23.

16. Reyna, "A mode of domination approach."
17. Ibid., 40; Napoleon Chagnon, "Life histories, blood revenge, and warfare in a tribal population," *Science* 239 (1988): 985–92.
18. Peter Buck, *Arts and Crafts of Hawaii*, In the electronic Human Relations Area Files, Hawaii, Doc. 2 (New Haven: HRAF, 2003), 417; Letitia Hickson, "The social context of apology in dispute settlement: A cross-cultural study," *Ethnology* 25 (1986): 283–94, 284; Reyna, "A mode of domination approach," 44; Elman Service, *Profiles in Ethnology*, 3rd ed. (New York: Harper and Row, 1978), 268–72.
19. Margaret Mead, "The Samoans," in M. Mead (ed.), *Cooperation and Competition Among Primitive Peoples*, 282–312 (Boston: Beacon Press, 1961, orig. pub. 1937); Margaret Mead, *Social Organization of Manu'a*, 2nd ed. (Honolulu: Bernice P. Bishop Museum, 1969).
20. Robert Carneiro, "Chiefdom-level warfare as exemplified in Fiji and the Cauca Valley," in J. Haas (ed.), *The Anthropology of War*, 190–211 (Cambridge: Cambridge University Press, 1990), 199, 200, 205, quote from 199.
21. Lewis Binford, *Constructing Frames of Reference: An Analytical Method for Archaeological Theory Building Using Hunter-Gatherer and Environmental Data Sets* (Berkeley: University of California Press, 2001), 219; R. Brian Ferguson, "A reexamination of the causes of Northwest Coast Warfare," in R. B. Ferguson (ed.), *Warfare, Culture, and Environment*, 267–328 (Orlando: Academic Press, 1984), Kelly, *The Foraging Spectrum*, 302; Service, *Primitive Social Organization*, 143–45; Elman Service, *Profiles in Ethnology*, rev. ed. (New York: Harper and Row, 1971), quote from 207–8.
22. Ferguson, "A reexamination," 272.
23. Reyna, "A mode of domination approach."

24. Michael Renner, *Critical Juncture: The Future of Peacekeeping*, Worldwatch Paper number 114, 1993, Worldwatch Institute, Washington, D.C., 50, www.globalissues.org/geopolitics/armstrade/spending.asp.

25. Chagnon, "Life histories," 987.

26. Reyna, "A mode of domination approach," 49.

27. Kelly, *The Foraging Spectrum*, 293, italics added.

28. Ibid., italics added; see also Binford, *Constructing Frames of Reference*, 432.

29. For example, Azar Gat, "The human motivational complex: Evolutionary theory and the causes of hunter-gatherer fighting. Part I. Primary somatic and reproductive causes," *Anthropological Quarterly* 73 (2000): 20–34; Azar Gat, "The human motivational complex: Evolutionary theory and the causes of hunter-gatherer fighting. Part II. Proximate, Subordinate, and Derivative Causes," *Anthropological Quarterly* 73 (2000): 74–88; Joshua Goldstein, *War and Gender: How Gender Shapes the War System and Vice Versa* (Cambridge: Cambridge University Press, 2001), 24.

30. Kelly, *The Foraging Spectrum*; George Murdock and Douglas White, "Standard Cross-Cultural Sample," *Ethnology* 8 (1969): 329–69; Douglas White, "Focused ethnographic bibliography: Standard cross-cultural sample," *Behavior Science Research* 23 (1989): 1–145; George Murdock, "Ethnographic Atlas: A Summary," *Ethnology* 6 (1967): 109–236; George Murdock, *Atlas of World Cultures* (Pittsburgh: University of Pittsburgh Press, 1981).

31. Murdock, "Ethnographic Atlas: A Summary"; Murdock, *Atlas of World Cultures*.

32. Roy Prosterman, *Surviving to 3000: An Introduction to the Study of Lethal Conflict* (Belmont, Calif.: Duxbury-Wadsworth, 1972). For further details, see Fry, *The Human Potential for Peace*, Chapter

8, especially Table 8.2. Several cases involving simple nomadic hunter-gatherers (specifically the Aweikoma, Botocudo, and Gilyak) that were coded as "warring" merit special mention, because the type of fighting may actually have constituted only self-redress or feuding. If this is true, "nonwarring" actually would be the appropriate classification. Unfortunately, the descriptions are not clear-cut enough to determine with certainty the presence of war, feuding, self-redress, or some combination of the above, so, conservatively—that is, against my predictions—these simple nomadic societies were rated as "warring" even though the actual evidence for war is sketchy or ambiguous.

33. If the five equestrian hunter-gatherer societies are dropped from the analysis, the results of a Fisher's exact for warring/ nonwarring by simple foragers/complex foragers is also statistically significant (p = .0017, one-tailed).

34. Eleanor Leacock, "Women's status in egalitarian society: Implications for social evolution," *Current Anthropology* 19 (1978): 247–75, 249.

35. Henry, *Jungle People*, 55.

36. Lev Shternberg, *Semya I Rod U Narodov Severo-Vostochnoi Azii*, English translation in the Human Relations Area Files, ID no. RX2 (New Haven: Human Relations Area Files, 1933), 247.

37. Murdock, *Our Primitive Contemporaries* (New York: Macmillan, 1934), 241; M. M. Martin, "Klamath," in D. Levinson (gen. ed.), *Encyclopedia of World Cultures*, vol. 1: *North America*, 190–92 (Boston: G. K. Hall, 1991), 192; E. A. Hoebel, *The Law of Primitive Man* (Cambridge: Harvard University Press, 1967); Ernest Wallace and E. A. Hoebel, *The Comanches* (Norman: University of Oklahoma Press, 1952).

Chapter 7: Seeking Justice

1. Douglas Fry, "Conflict management in cross-cultural perspective," in F. Aureli and F. de Waal (eds.), *Natural Conflict Resolution*, 334–51 (Berkeley: University of California Press, 2000); Douglas Fry, "Reciprocity: The foundation stone of morality," in M. Killen and J. Smetana (eds.), *Handbook of Moral Development*, 399–422 (Mahwah, N.J.: Lawrence Erlbaum, 2006); Douglas Fry, *The Human Potential for Peace* (New York: Oxford University Press, 2006); www.peacefulsocieties.org.
2. Klaus-Friedrich Koch, S. Altorki, A. Arno, and L. Hickson, "Ritual reconciliation and the obviation of grievances: A comparative study in the ethnography of law," *Ethnology* 16 (1977): 270–83; Michael Harner, *The Jívaro: People of the Sacred Waterfall* (Garden City, N.Y.: Anchor Books/Doubleday, 1972).
3. Donald Black, *The Social Structure of Right and Wrong* (San Diego: Academic Press, 1993); see also Klaus-Friedrich Koch, *War and Peace in Jalémó: The Management of Conflict in Highland New Guinea* (Cambridge: Harvard University Press, 1974); Fry, "Conflict management in cross-cultural perspective"; Fry, *The Human Potential for Peace*, Chapter 3.
4. Black, *The Social Structure of Right and Wrong*; Robin Fox, *The Search for Society: Quest for a Biosocial Science and Morality* (New Brunswick, N.J.: Rutgers University Press, 1989), 161.
5. Douglas Fry, "'Respect for the rights of others is peace': Learning aggression versus non-aggression among the Zapotec," *American Anthropologist* 94 (1992): 621–39; Douglas Fry, "Multiple paths to peace: The 'La Paz' Zapotec of Mexico," in G. Kemp and D. Fry (eds.), *Keeping the Peace: Conflict Resolution and Peaceful Societies around the World*, 73–87 (New York: Routledge, 2004); Fry, *The Human Potential for Peace*, Chapter 4.

6. Mervyn Meggitt, *Blood Is Their Argument: Warfare Among the Mae Enga Tribesmen of the New Guinea Highlands* (Mountain View, Calif.: Mayfield, 1977); see also Black, *The Social Structure of Right and Wrong;* Fry, *The Human Potential for Peace,* Chapter 3.

7. Black, *The Social Structure of Right and Wrong;* Fry, "Conflict management in cross-cultural perspective"; Fry, *The Human Potential for Peace;* Koch, *War and Peace in Jalémó.*

8. Robert Dentan, *The Semai: A Nonviolent People of Malaya* (New York: Holt, Rinehart, and Winston, 1968); Robert Dentan, "Cautious, alert, polite, and elusive: Semai of Central Peninsular Malaysia," in G. Kemp and D. Fry (eds.), *Keeping the Peace: Conflict Resolution and Peaceful Societies Around the World,* 167–84 (New York: Routledge, 2004); Clayton Robarchek, "Conflict, emotion, and abreaction: Resolution of conflict among the Semai Senoi," *Ethos* 7 (1979): 104–23; Clayton Robarchek, "A community of interests: Semai conflict resolution," in D. Fry and K. Björkqvist (eds.), *Cultural Variation in Conflict Resolution: Alternatives to Violence,* 51–58 (Mahwah, N.J.: Lawrence Erlbaum, 1997).

9. Robarchek, "Conflict, emotion, and abreaction"; Robarchek, "A community of interests"; quote is from ibid., 55.

10. Christopher Boehm, *Blood Revenge: The Enactment and Management of Conflict in Montenegro and Other Tribal Societies* (Philadelphia: University of Pennsylvania Press, 1987); the quotation is by Vuk Vrcevic, ibid., 127–28.

11. Max Gluckman, "The judicial process among the Barotse," in P. Bohannan (ed.), *Law and Warfare: Studies in the Anthropology of Conflict,* 59–91 (Austin: University of Texas Press, 1967), 77–78.

12. Wendell Bennett and Robert Zingg, *The Tarahumara: An Indian Tribe of Northern Mexico* (Glorieta, N.M.: Rio Grande Press, 1976, orig. pub. 1935), 332; see also Fry, *The Human Potential for Peace,*

36; Laura Nader, *Harmony Ideology: Justice and Control in a Zapotec Mountain Village* (Stanford: Stanford University Press, 1990).

13. Waldemar Jochelson, *The Yukaghir and the Yukaghirized Tungus*, The Jesup North Pacific Expedition Memoir of the American Museum of Natural History, vol. IX (New York: G. E. Stechert, 1926), 132, 383; Black, *The Social Structure of Right and Wrong*.

14. Raymond Firth, *We, The Tikopia: A Sociological Study of Kinship in Primitive Polynesia*, 2nd ed. (London: George Allen and Unwin, 1957), 396–97; R. Brian Ferguson, "A reexamination of the causes of Northwest Coast Warfare," in R. B. Ferguson (ed.), *Warfare, Culture, and Environment*, 267–328 (Orlando: Academic Press, 1984), 289.

15. Fry, "Reciprocity: The foundation stone of morality."

16. Jan Brögger, "Conflict resolution and the role of the bandit in peasant society," *Anthropological Quarterly* 41 (1968): 228–40, 231.

17. Boehm, *Blood Revenge*, 159.

18. L. Hobhouse, G. Wheeler, and M. Ginsberg, *The Material Culture and Social Institutions of the Simpler Peoples: An Essay in Correlation* (London: Chapman and Hall, 1915), 71, 254.

19. E. A. Hoebel, *The Law of Primitive Man: A Study in Comparative Legal Dynamics* (Cambridge: Harvard University Press, 1967), 327.

20. Karen Ericksen and Heather Horton, "'Blood feuds': Cross-cultural variations in kin group vengeance," *Behavior Science Research* 26 (1992): 57–85, 73–74.

21. Napoleon Chagnon, "Life histories, blood revenge, and warfare in a tribal population," *Science* 239 (1988): 985–92, 990.

22. See Bruce Knauft, "Violence and sociality in human evolution," *Current Anthropology* 32 (1991): 391–428, 405.

23. See Raymond Kelly, *Warless Societies and the Origin of War* (Ann Arbor: University of Michigan Press, 2000), quote from 47.

24. Ibid.
25. For example, Martin Gusinde, *The Yahgan: The Life and Thought of the Water Nomads of Cape Horn*, trans. Frieda Schütze, in the electronic Human Relations Area Files, Yahgan, Doc. 1 (New Haven: HRAF, 2003, orig. pub. 1937), 898–905; Joel Janetski, "Ute," in D. Levinson (gen. ed.), *Encyclopedia of World Cultures*, vol. I: *North America*, 360–63 (Boston: G. K. Hall, 1991), 362; Kelly, *Warless Societies*.
26. Richard Lee, *The !Kung San: Men, Women, and Work in a Foraging Community* (Cambridge: Cambridge University Press, 1979), 382–96, esp. 389.
27. Fry, "Reciprocity: The foundation stone of morality."
28. For example, Black, *The Social Structure of Right and Wrong*; Boehm, *Blood Revenge*; Ericksen and Horton, "'Blood feuds'"; Hobhouse, Wheeler, and Ginsberg, *The Material Culture and Social Institutions of the Simpler Peoples*; Hoebel, *The Law of Primitive Man*; Bronislaw Malinowski, "An anthropological analysis of war," *American Journal of Sociology* 46 (1941): 521–50; S. Reyna, "A mode of domination approach to organized violence," in S. Reyna and R. Downs (eds.), *Studying War: Anthropological Perspectives*, 29–65 (Amsterdam: Gordon and Breach, 1994).
29. Brögger, "Conflict resolution"; J. Rubin, D. Pruitt, and S. H. Kim, *Social Conflict: Escalation, Stalemate, and Settlement*, 2nd ed. (New York: McGraw-Hill, 1994); Fry, "Conflict management in cross-cultural perspective"; Fry, *The Human Potential for Peace*.
30. E. A. Hoebel, "Law-ways of the Comanche Indians," in P. Bohannan (ed.), *Law and Warfare: Studies in the Anthropology of Conflict*, 183–203 (Austin: University of Texas Press, 1967), 193.
31. Chagnon, "Life histories."
32. Reyna, "A mode of domination approach."

Chapter 8: Man the Warrior

1. Junius Bird, "The Alacaluf," in J. Steward (ed.), *Handbook of South American Indians*, vol. 1: *The Marginal Tribes*, 55–80 plus plates (Washington, D.C.: United States Printing Office, 1946), 71.
2. Jane C. Goodale, *Tiwi Wives: A Study of the Women of Melville Island, North Australia* (Seattle: University of Washington Press, 1974), 133–34.
3. C. Hart and Arnold Pilling, *The Tiwi of North Australia*, fieldwork ed. (New York: Holt, Rinehart, and Winston, 1979), 81–82; Victoria Burbank, "Sex, gender, and difference: Dimensions of aggression in an Australian Aboriginal community," *Human Nature* 3 (1992): 251–78, 266; Victoria Burbank, *Fighting Women: Anger and Aggression in Aboriginal Australia* (Berkeley: University of California Press, 1994), 35.
4. Burbank, "Sex, gender, and difference," 266.
5. For example, see John Cooper, "The Ona," in J. H. Steward (ed.), *Handbook of South American Indians*, vol. 1: *The Marginal Tribes*, 107–25 (Washington, D.C.: United States Printing Office, 1946), 117–18; Viktor Lebzelter, *Eingeborenenkulturen in Südwest-und Südafrika* [Native cultures in Southwest and South Africa], trans. Richard Neuse, in the Human Relations Area Files, ID no. FX10, doc. no. 3 (New Haven: Human Relations Area Files, 1934), 30; Baldwin Spencer and Francis Gillen, *The Arunta: A Study of a Stone Age People* (London: Macmillan, 1927); W. L. Warner, *A Black Civilization: A Social Study of an Australian Tribe* (Gloucester, Mass.: Peter Smith, 1969, orig. pub. 1937); see also William Bright, "Karok," in W. Sturtevant (gen. ed.), *Handbook of North American Indians*, vol. 8: *California*, 180–89 (Washington, D.C.: Smithsonian Institution, 1978), 185.

6. Elman Service, *The Hunters* (Englewood Cliffs, N.J.: Prentice-Hall, 1966), 60.

7. Richard Alexander, *Darwinism and Human Affairs* (Seattle: University of Washington Press, 1979), 222–30; Richard Alexander, *The Biology of Moral Systems* (New York: Aldine de Gruyter, 1987), 78–79, 107–10.

8. Alexander, *Darwinism and Human Affairs*, 222, 223; see also Alexander, *The Biology of Moral Systems*, 107.

9. For example, Alexander, *The Biology of Moral Systems*, 78–79, 104, 107–8, 110.

10. R. P. Shaw and Yuwa Wong, *Genetic Seeds of Warfare: Evolution, Nationalism, and Patriotism* (Boston: Unwin Hyman, 1989), 17, see also 3–9, 14–15.

11. Ibid., 14.

12. Ibid., 50, 54.

13. Bobbi Low, "An evolutionary perspective on war," in W. Zimmerman and H. Jacobson (eds.), *Behavior, Culture, and Conflict in World Politics*, 13–55 (Ann Arbor: University of Michigan Press, 1993), 19, 20, 36, 43.

14. Richard Wrangham and Dale Peterson, *Demonic Males: Apes and the Origin of Human Violence* (Boston: Houghton Mifflin, 1996), 25.

15. Michael Ghiglieri, *The Dark Side of Man: Tracing The Origins of Male Violence* (Reading, Mass.: Perseus, 1999), quotes from 161, 163 (italics in original), and 162.

16. Ibid., 160–61, italics in original.

17. Ibid., see 165, 197; quote from 197, italics in original.

18. Ibid., 196.

19. For theoretical background, see John Tooby and Leda Cosmides, "The past explains the present: Emotional adaptations and the structure of ancestral environments," *Ethology and Sociobiology*

11 (1990): 375–424; George C. Williams, *Adaptation and Natural Selection: A Critique of Some Current Evolutionary Thought* (Princeton: Princeton University Press, 1966).

20. In addition to the works discussed, see Gerald Borgia, "Human aggression as a biological adaptation," in J. Lockard (ed.), *The Evolution of Human Social Behavior*, 165–91 (New York: Elsevier, 1980), 183–85; Azar Gat, "The human motivational complex: Evolutionary theory and the causes of hunter-gatherer fighting. Part I. Primary somatic and reproductive causes," *Anthropological Quarterly* 73 (2000): 20–34, esp. 24–25.

21. Christopher Boehm, *Hierarchy in the Forest: The Evolution of Egalitarian Behavior* (Cambridge: Harvard University Press, 1999), 13; Frank Marlowe, "Why the Hadza are still hunter-gatherers," in S. Kent (ed.), *Ethnicity, Hunter-Gatherers, and the "Other,"* 247–75 (Washington, D.C.: Smithsonian Institution Press, 2002), 271; Frank Marlowe, "Hunter-gatherers and human evolution," *Evolutionary Anthropology* 14 (2005): 54–67.

22. Eric Wolf, "Cycles of violence: The anthropology of war and peace," in D. Barash (ed.), *Understanding Violence*, 192–99 (Boston: Allyn and Bacon, 2001), 197; James Woodburn, "African hunter-gatherer social organization: Is it best understood as a product of encapsulation?" in T. Ingold, D. Riches, and J. Woodburn (eds.), *Hunters and Gatherers*, vol. 1: *History, Evolution and Social Change*, 31–64 (Oxford: Berg, 1988); Susan Kent, "Interethnic encounters of the first kind: An introduction," in S. Kent (ed.), *Ethnicity, Hunter-Gatherers, and the "Other,"* 1–27 (Washington, D.C.: Smithsonian Institution Press, 2002), 1; Marlowe, "Hunter-gatherers and human evolution."

23. See Boehm, *Hierarchy in the Forest*; Raymond Kelly, *Warless Societies and the Origin of War* (Ann Arbor: University of

Michigan Press, 2000); Bruce Knauft, "Violence and sociality in human evolution," *Current Anthropology* 32 (1991): 391–428, 405; George Murdock, "The current status of the world's hunting and gathering peoples," in R. Lee and I. DeVore (eds.), *Man the Hunter*, 13–20 (Chicago: Aldine, 1968). The Spanish introduced the horse into the Americas some 500 years ago. Some of the North American cultures that adopted the horse for hunting some 300 years ago were sedentary agriculturalists prior to contact. Following Murdock and Knauft, among others, I think it is critically important *not* to lump horse-riding hunters or complex sedentary, socially hierarchical fisherfolk together with simple nomadic hunter-gatherers. Especially for the purposes of reconstructing past lifeways, we should draw analogies from simple foragers, rather than more complex and relatively recent cultural forms. See Marlowe, "Hunter-gatherers and human evolution," 55–56.

24. Boehm, *Hierarchy in the Forest*, 13, 95, 221; Knauft, "Violence and sociality," 392; Marlowe, "Why the Hadza are still hunter-gatherers," 248, 271; Leslie Sponsel, "The natural history of peace: A positive view of human nature and its potential," in T. Gregor (ed.), *A Natural History of Peace*, 95–125 (Nashville, Tenn.: Vanderbilt University Press, 1996), 104.

Chapter 9: Insights from the Outback

1. Elman Service, *The Hunters* (Englewood Cliffs, N.J.: Prentice-Hall, 1966), 103; Robert Tonkinson, *The Mardudjara Aborigines: Living the Dream in Australia's Desert* (New York: Holt, Rinehart, and Winston, 1978), 1–6; Michael Walsh, "Languages and Their Status in Aboriginal Australia," in M. Walsh and

C. Yallop (eds.), *Language and Culture in Aboriginal Australia*, 1–13 (Canberra: Aboriginal Studies Press, 1993), 1; John White and Derek Mulvaney, "How many people?" in D. Mulvaney and J. White (eds.), *Australians to 1788*, 115–17 (Sydney: Fairfax, Syme, and Weldon Associates, 1987), 115–17.

2. Joseph Birdsell, "Australia: Ecology, spacing mechanisms and adaptive behaviour in aboriginal land tenure," in R. Crocombe (ed.), *Land Tenure in the Pacific*, 334–61 (New York: Oxford University Press, 1971), 337–39, 345; Tonkinson, *The Mardudjara Aborigines*, 3; Service, *The Hunters*, 104.

3. Tonkinson, *The Mardudjara Aborigines*, 6.

4. Ronald Berndt, "Law and order in Aboriginal Australia," in R. Berndt and C. Berndt (eds.), *Aboriginal Man in Australia: Essays in Honour of Emeritus Professor A. P. Elkin*, 167–206 (London: Angus and Robertson, 1965), 174; Tonkinson, *The Mardudjara Aborigines*, 140.

5. Ronald Berndt and Catherine Berndt, *The World of the First Australians*, 5th ed. (Canberra: Aboriginal Studies Press, 1996), chapter 10.

6. Victoria Burbank, *Fighting Women: Anger and Aggression in Aboriginal Australia* (Berkeley: University of California Press, 1994); W. L. Warner, *A Black Civilization: A Social Study of an Australian Tribe* (Gloucester, Mass.: Peter Smith, 1969, orig. pub. 1937).

7. Edward Westermarck, "Prefatory note," in G. Wheeler, *The Tribe, and Intertribal Relations in Australia* (London: John Murray, 1910), vi.

8. David Horton, "Warfare," in D. Horton (ed.), *The Encyclopedia of Aboriginal Australia: Aboriginal and Torres Strait Islanders History, Society, and Culture*, vol. 2, 1152–4 (Canberra: Aboriginal Studies Press, 1994), 1153; Maurice Davie, *The Evolution of War* (New

Haven: Yale University Press, 1929), 52 (the quote within Davie's quote is by William Sumner). See also the following references pertaining to specific nonwarring societies (the Arunta, Walmadjeri, Gugadja, and Mardu): Baldwin Spencer and Francis Gillen, *The Arunta: A Study of a Stone Age People* (London: Macmillan, 1927), 27–28; George Murdock, *Our Primitive Contemporaries* (New York: Macmillan, 1934), 45; Elman Service, *Profiles in Ethnology*, rev. ed. (New York: Harper and Row, 1971), 18; Ronald Berndt, "The Walmadjeri and Gugadja," in M. Bicchieri (ed.), *Hunters and Gatherers Today*, 177–216 (Prospect Heights, Ill.: Waveland, 1972), 203; Tonkinson, *The Mardudjara Aborigines*, 118, 127; Robert Tonkinson, "Resolving conflict within the law: The Mardu Aborigines of Australia," in G. Kemp and D. Fry (eds.), *Keeping the Peace: Conflict Resolution and Peaceful Societies Around the World*, 89–104 (New York: Routledge, 2004).

9. Nancy Williams, *Two Laws: Managing Disputes in a Contemporary Aboriginal Community* (Canberra: Australian Institute of Aboriginal Studies, 1987), 31, 39; see also 99, 152–53.

10. See Azar Gat, "The human motivational complex: Evolutionary theory and the causes of hunter-gatherer fighting. Part I. Primary somatic and reproductive causes," *Anthropological Quarterly* 73 (2000): 20–34, 27 for a recent reiteration of Warner's interchangeable use of *war* and *feud* for the Murngin; see also Jane C. Goodale, *Tiwi Wives: A Study of the Women of Melville Island, North Australia* (Seattle: University of Washington Press, 1974), 133–34; and C. Hart and Arnold Pilling, *The Tiwi of North Australia*, fieldwork ed. (New York, Holt, Rinehart, and Winston, 1979) on the Tiwi; see also Spencer and Gillen, *The Arunta*, 447. Warner, *A Black Civilization*, 144–79, quote from 155.

11. Berndt and Berndt, *The World of the First Australians*, 358; Williams, *Two Laws;* Warner, *A Black Civilization*, 148, 155–56.

12. Warner, *A Black Civilization*, 162, see also 161–63; see also Berndt and Berndt, *The World of the First Australians*, 358.

13. Mervyn Meggitt, *Desert People: A Study of the Walbiri Aborigines of Central Australia* (Chicago: University of Chicago Press, 1965), 245–46; Birdsell, "Australia," 341.

14. Meggitt, *Desert People*, 245–46.

15. Gerald Wheeler, *The Tribe, and Intertribal Relations in Australia* (London: John Murray, 1910), 149; Service, *The Hunters*, 103.

16. Berndt and Berndt, *The World of the First Australians*, 362; E. A. Hoebel, *The Law of Primitive Man: A Study in Comparative Legal Dynamics* (Cambridge: Harvard University Press, 1967), 306; see also Catherine Berndt, "In Aboriginal Australia," in A. Montagu (ed.), *Learning Non-Aggression: The Experience of Non-Literate Societies*, 144–60 (Oxford: Oxford University Press, 1978), 159; Berndt, "Law and order," 202.

17. Birdsell, "Australia," 341.

18. See ibid., 340–41; Berndt and Berndt, *The World of the First Australians*. When Gat, in "The human motivational complex," emphasizes Australian Aborigine warfare, he does not weigh the totality of the evidence. Instead, he cites exceptions as if they represent a typical pattern for Australia. Additionally, he does not clearly distinguish between war and other forms of violence such as homicide and revenge killings. This is why Gat's perspective on Australian Aborigine warfare is at odds with what others who have examined this issue in depth have concluded, for example, Berndt, "In Aboriginal Australia"; Berndt, "Law and order"; Birdsell, "Australia"; Davie, *The Evolution of War;* Hoebel, *The Law of Primitive Man;* Service, *The*

Hunters; Westermarck, "Prefatory note"; and Wheeler, *The Tribe.* Gat, "The human motivational complex," 23–24, refers to the atypical Walbiri waterhole "war of conquest" from Meggitt's 1965 book *Desert People* (which was written after the disruption of the native population by Europeans) in such a way that implies that such events were common in Aboriginal Australia. Additionally, Gat, in "The human motivational complex," 27, overlooks the personal, homicidal nature of most of the so-called Murngin warfare—granted, something that might be easy to do given Warner's inconsistent and contradictory use of terminology in *A Black Civilization,* as pointed out in the chapter.

19. Berndt, "Law and order," 174, 167; Tonkinson, *The Mardudjara Aborigines;* Berndt and Berndt, *The World of the First Australians;* Hoebel, *The Law of Primitive Man,* 302–3.

20. Berndt, "Law and order," 176; Phyllis Kaberry, *Aboriginal Woman: Sacred and Profane* (New York: Gordon Press, 1973), 179.

21. For example, Berndt, "Law and order," 176, 185; Berndt and Berndt, *The World of the First Australians,* Chapter 10; Tonkinson, "Resolving conflict within the law," 102–4.

22. A. P. Elkin, "The kopara: The settlement of grievances," *Oceania* 2 (1931): 191–98; Berndt, "Law and order," 185; Berndt and Berndt, *The World of the First Australians,* 346.

23. Berndt, "Law and order," 181, 194–97; Berndt and Berndt, *The World of the First Australians,* 350–53; Goodale, *Tiwi Wives,* 133–34; Hart and Pilling, *The Tiwi of North Australia,* 80–87; Kaberry, *Aboriginal Woman,* 143–53; Wheeler, *The Tribe,* 134–35, 140–47.

24. Berndt, "Law and order," 177; Kaberry, *Aboriginal Woman,* 150–51.

25. Berndt and Berndt, *The World of the First Australians*, 347; Hart and Pilling, *The Tiwi of North Australia*, 79–83; Spencer and Gillen, *The Arunta*, 446; Tonkinson, *The Mardudjara Aborigines*, 118, 124; Tonkinson, "Resolving conflict within the law", 98; Wheeler, *The Tribe*, 135–38.

26. Berndt, "Law and order," 187–90; Ronald Berndt and Catherine Berndt, "A preliminary report on field work in the Ooldea region, Western South Australia," *Oceania* 15 (1945): 239–66, 262–66; Berndt and Berndt, *The World of the First Australians*, 349–50; Warner, *A Black Civilization*, 163–65.

27. Elkin, "The kopara."

28. Ibid., 197.

29. Hart and Pilling, *The Tiwi of North Australia*, 83–87; Wheeler, *The Tribe*, 140–47, 148; see also Berndt and Berndt, *The World of the First Australians*, Chapter 10.

30. Hart and Pilling, *The Tiwi of North Australia*, 84.

31. Ibid., 84–85.

32. Ibid., 85. Is the use of language by Hart and Pilling poetic or just pain confusing? Otterbein (Keith Otterbein, "Internal war: A cross-cultural study," *American Anthropologist* 70 [1968]: 277–89) coded the Tiwi as having infrequent external war and frequent internal war (see Chapter 2). A careful reading of the Tiwi material, as just quoted at length, suggests that Otterbein (or his student coders) actually misinterpreted juridical fighting —that is, conflict resolution—as internal war. Otterbein defines internal war as armed conflict between political communities within the same culture. Hart and Pilling, however, conclude that the Tiwi did not and could wage war, band versus band as political communities. It is understandable that such a misunderstanding could happen in light of Hart and Pilling's

poetic and apparent contradictory use of language (see *The Tiwi of North Australia*, 83–87). For example, as we have just seen, they sometimes put the words *war* and *battle* in quotes and at other times do not, they sometimes refer to "so-called battles" and other times simply "battles," and finally, under the chapter subheading "Warfare," they arrive at the paradoxical conclusion that warfare did not occur. However, when read carefully in its entirety, Hart and Pilling's portrayal corresponds with Wheeler's conclusion that such events are juridical in nature. Hart and Pilling themselves, by the way, use legal terminology in their description (for example, "the rules of Tiwi procedure," 84) and categorized the whole topic (including the section subheaded as "Warfare") under the label "Legal Affairs" (p. 79). Otterbein's recent comments on the Tiwi, however, sidestep this central point (Keith Otterbein, "A history of research on warfare in anthropology," *American Anthropologist* 101 [1999]: 794–805; Keith Otterbein, *How War Began* [College Station, Tex.: Texas A&M University Press, 2004], 83, 202, 256 n. 8). The fact that the Tiwi used sneak attacks during blood feuds, for example, seems fairly clear and is not the issue here (Arnold Pilling, "Discussions, part III, 17.g: Predation and warfare," in R. Lee and I. DeVore [eds.], *Man the Hunter*, 157–58 [Chicago: Aldine, 1968], 158; C. Hart, Arnold Pilling, and Jane Goodale, *The Tiwi of North Australia*, 3rd ed. [New York: Holt, Rinehart, and Winston, 1988], 93–95). As noted earlier in this chapter, Warner's description of Murngin revenge seeking and juridical processes in *A Black Civilization* also uses the same type of confusing terminology in a chapter dubiously titled "Warfare"—see his Chapter VI; see also Spencer and Gillen, *The Arunta*, 447.

33. Berndt and Berndt, "A preliminary report," 262–66.

34. Ibid., 262.

35. Ibid., 265.

36. Berndt, "Law and order," 174; Hart and Pilling, *The Tiwi of North Australia*; Meggitt, *Desert People*, 245; Warner, *A Black Civilization*, 163; Wheeler, *The Tribe*, 116.

37. Berndt and Berndt, *The World of the First Australians*, 340–41; Meggitt, *Desert People*, 246; Service, *The Hunters*, 105.

38. Berndt, "Law and order," 170, 172, 203; Berndt, "In Aboriginal Australia," 159; Birdsell, "Australia," 349, 353, 357; Elkin, "The kopara," for instance, see 197–98; Hart and Pilling, *The Tiwi of North Australia*, 85–86; Fred Myers, "Always ask: Resource use and land ownership among Pintupi Aborigines of the Australian Western Desert," in N. Williams and E. Hunn (eds.), *Resource Managers: North American and Australian Hunter-Gatherers*, 173–95 (Boulder, Colo.: Westview, 1982), 181; Service, *The Hunters*, 104; Tonkinson, *The Mardudjara Aborigines*, 6; Tonkinson, "Resolving conflict within the law"; Warner, *A Black Civilization*, for example, see 145–46; Wheeler, *The Tribe*, 160 and Chapter V.

39. Berndt and Berndt, *The World of the First Australians*, for example, see 145–46; Birdsell, "Australia," 351–52, 357; Hart and Pilling, *The Tiwi of North Australia*, 84–85; Meggitt, *Desert People*, 242, 246; Tonkinson, *The Mardudjara Aborigines*, 118; Tonkinson, "Resolving conflict within the law."

40. Berndt, "In Aboriginal Australia," 159; Berndt and Berndt, *The World of the First Australians*, 140; Birdsell, "Australia"; Kaberry, *Aboriginal Woman*, 179; Meggitt, *Desert People*, 42, 241; Wheeler, *The Tribe*, 65, 86.

41. Birdsell, "Australia," 339–50; Myers, "Always ask," for example, 184; Wheeler, *The Tribe*, 66–69.

42. Berndt, "Law and order," 174, 185–90, 202, 204–5; Berndt, "The Walmadjeri and Gugadja," 203; Berndt and Berndt, "A preliminary report," 260–66; Berndt and Berndt, *The World of the First Australians*, Chapter 10; Elkin, "The kopara"; Kaberry, *Aboriginal Woman*, for example, 143–53; Meggitt, *Desert People*, 251–63; Spencer and Gillen, *The Arunta*, Chapter 18; Tonkinson, *The Mardudjara Aborigines*, Chapter 6; Tonkinson, "Resolving conflict within the law"; Warner, *A Black Civilization*, for example, 156–57, 163–65; Wheeler, *The Tribe*, 130–47; Williams, *Two Laws*.

43. Berndt, "Law and order," 176; Berndt, "The Walmadjeri and Gugadja," 199, 203; Elkin, "The kopara," 194; Goodale, *Tiwi Wives*, 132–33; Kaberry, *Aboriginal Woman*, 179; Meggitt, *Desert People*, 242, 245–46; Spencer and Gillen, *The Arunta*, Chapter 18; Warner, *A Black Civilization*, 148.

44. Berndt, "In Aboriginal Australia," 158; Berndt, "Law and order," 173, 178, 190–91; Berndt and Berndt, *The World of the First Australians*, Chapter 10; Birdsell, "Australia," 347, 351; Elkin, "The kopara," 197; Spencer and Gillen, *The Arunta*, Chapter 18; Warner, *A Black Civilization*, 166–79; Wheeler, *The Tribe*, 130, 148–65.

Chapter 10: Void if Detached . . . from Reality

1. W. L. Warner, *A Black Civilization: A Social Study of an Australian Tribe* (Gloucester, Mass.: Peter Smith, 1969, orig. pub. 1937), 163, 164; see also Ronald Berndt, "Law and order in Aboriginal Australia," in R. Berndt and C. Berndt (eds.), *Aboriginal Man in Australia: Essays in Honour of Emeritus Professor A. P. Elkin*, 167–206 (London: Angus and Robertson, 1965).

2. P. Tacon and C. Chippindale, "Australia's ancient warriors: Changing depictions of fighting in the rock art of Arnhem Land, N.T." *Cambridge Archaeological Journal* 4 (1994): 211–48, 214.

3. Ibid., 218 (Fig. 3), 220. A few scenes do show more than one victim. See also Bruce Knauft, "Comment" [on "Australia's ancient warriors" by Paul Tacon and Christopher Chippindale], *Cambridge Archaeological Journal* 4 (1994): 229–31; Warner, *A Black Civilization*, 165; Robert Tonkinson, *The Mardudjara Aborigines: Living the Dream in Australia's Desert* (New York: Holt, Rinehart, and Winston, 1978); Robert Tonkinson, "Resolving conflict within the law: The Mardu Aborigines of Australia," in G. Kemp and D. Fry (eds.), *Keeping the Peace: Conflict Resolution and Peaceful Societies Around the World*, 89–104 (New York: Routledge, 2004).

4. See Knauft, "Comment."

5. Tacon and Chippindale, "Australia's ancient warriors," 220.

6. See Berndt, "Law and order"; Ronald Berndt and Catherine Berndt, *The World of the First Australians*, 5th ed. (Canberra: Aboriginal Studies Press, 1996); Jane C. Goodale, *Tiwi Wives: A Study of the Women of Melville Island, North Australia* (Seattle: University of Washington Press, 1974); C. Hart and Arnold Pilling, *The Tiwi of North Australia*, fieldwork ed. (New York: Holt, Rinehart, and Winston, 1979); Phyllis Kaberry, *Aboriginal Woman: Sacred and Profane* (New York: Gordon Press, 1973); Baldwin Spencer and Francis Gillen, *The Arunta: A Study of a Stone Age People* (London: Macmillan, 1927); Tonkinson, "Resolving conflict within the law"; Warner, *A Black Civilization*; Gerald Wheeler, *The Tribe, and Intertribal Relations in Australia* (London: John Murray, 1910).

7. Tacon and Chippindale, "Australia's ancient warriors," 225.

8. Napoleon Chagnon, *Yanomamö: The Fierce People*, 3rd ed. (New York: Holt, Rinehart and Winston, 1983), 214; David Buss, *Evolutionary Psychology: The New Science of the Mind* (Boston: Allyn and Bacon, 1999), 300; Michael Ghiglieri, *The Dark Side of Man: Tracing the Origins of Male Violence* (Reading, Mass.: Perseus, 1999), 193–94.

9. Napoleon Chagnon, "Life histories, blood revenge, and warfare in a tribal population," *Science* 239 (1988): 985–92; Napoleon Chagnon, "On Yanomamö violence: Reply to Albert," *Current Anthropology* 31 (1990): 49–53, 51; Napoleon Chagnon, *Yanomamö*, 4th ed. (Fort Worth: Harcourt Brace Jovanovich College Publishers, 1992); Richard Alexander, *Darwinism and Human Affairs* (Seattle: University of Washington Press, 1979); R. P. Shaw and Yuwa Wong, *Genetic Seeds of Warfare: Evolution, Nationalism, and Patriotism* (Boston: Unwin Hyman, 1989); Bobbi Low, "An evolutionary perspective on war," in W. Zimmerman and H. Jacobson (eds.), *Behavior, Culture, and Conflict in World Politics*, 13–55 (Ann Arbor: University of Michigan Press, 1993), 21, 26, 31; Richard Wrangham and Dale Peterson, *Demonic Males: Apes and the Origin of Human Violence* (Boston: Houghton Mifflin, 1996), 64–74; Ghiglieri, *The Dark Side of Man*, 144, 192–94; Buss, *Evolutionary Psychology*, 300.

10. Chagnon, "Life histories."

11. Ibid., 987.

12. Napoleon Chagnon, "Reproductive and somatic conflicts of interest in the genesis of violence and warfare among tribesmen," in J. Haas (ed.), *The Anthropology of War*, 77–104 (Cambridge: Cambridge University Press, 1990), 95; Chagnon, *Yanomamö*, 205; Napoleon Chagnon, *Yanomamö: The Last Days of Eden* (San Diego: Harcourt Brace & Company,

1992), 239–40. In "Reproductive and somatic conflicts of interest," Chagnon claims only "over twice" as many wives for the *unokais*. In *Yanomamö*, Chagnon explains that *"unokais* (men who have killed) are more successful at obtaining wives and, as a consequence, have more offspring than *men their own age* who are not *unokais"* (italics added). He specifies that *"unokais* had, on the average, more than two-and-a-half times as many wives as non-*unokais* and over three times as many children."

13. Chagnon, "Life histories"; quotes are from William Allman, "A laboratory of human conflict," *U.S. News and World Report*, April 11, 1988: 57–58, 57.

14. As examples, see David Barash, *Understanding Violence* (Boston: Allyn and Bacon, 2001), 165–74; William Booth, "Warfare over Yanomamö Indians," *Science* 243 (1989): 1138–40; Terry Burnham and Jay Phelan, *Mean Genes: From Sex to Money to Food* (New York: Penguin, 2000), 88; Buss, *Evolutionary Psychology*, 304–5; David Buss, *The Murderer Next Door: Why the Mind Is Designed to Kill* (New York: Penguin Press, 2005), 210; Anne Campbell, "Staying alive: Evolution, culture and women's intra-sexual aggression," with commentaries, *Behavioral and Brain Sciences* 22 (1999): 203–52, 212; Lee Cronk, *That Complex Whole: Culture and the Evolution of Human Behavior* (Boulder, Colo.: Westview, 1999), 80; Martin Daly and Margo Wilson, "Evolutionary psychology of male violence," in J. Archer (ed.), *Male Violence*, 253–88 (London: Routledge, 1994), 274; Azar Gat, "The human motivational complex: Evolutionary theory and the causes of hunter-gatherer fighting. Part I. Primary somatic and reproductive causes," *Anthropological Quarterly* 73 (2000): 20–34, 21; Azar Gat, "The human motivational complex: Evolutionary theory and the causes of hunter-gatherer fighting. Part II. Proximate,

subordinate, and derivative causes," *Anthropological Quarterly* 73 (2000): 74–88, 75, 76, 87 n. 4; David Geary, *Male, Female: The Evolution of Human Sex Differences* (Washington, D.C.: American Psychological Association, 1998), 317–18; David Geary, "Evolution of parental investment," in D. Buss (ed.), *The Handbook of Evolutionary Psychology*, 483–505 (Hoboken, N.J.: John Wiley and Sons, 2005), 496; Ghiglieri, *The Dark Side of Man*, 144, 193–94; Judith Harris, *The Nurture Assumption: Why Children Turn Out the Way They Do* (New York: Simon and Schuster, 1999); Melvin Konner, "Human nature, ethnic violence, and war," in M. Fitzduff and C. Stout (eds.), *The Psychology of Resolving Global Conflicts: From War to Peace*, vol. 1: *Nature vs. Nurture*, 1–39 (Westport, Conn.: Praeger Security International, 2006), 5; Low, "An evolutionary perspective on war," 21, 26, 31; Joseph Manson and Richard Wrangham, "Intergroup aggression in chimpanzees and humans," *Current Anthropology* 32 (1991): 369–90, 369, 374; Barry McCarthy, "Warrior values: A socio-historical survey," in J. Archer (ed.), *Male Violence*, 105–20 (London: Routledge, 1994), 107; Steven Pinker, *How the Mind Works* (New York: W. W. Norton, 1997), 510; Steven Pinker, *The Blank Slate: The Modern Denial of Human Nature* (New York: Penguin Books, 2003), 116; Lawrence Sugiyama, "Physical attractiveness in adaptionist perspective," in D. Buss (ed.), *The Handbook of Evolutionary Psychology*, 292–343 (Hoboken, N.J.: John Wiley and Sons, 2005), 319; Donald Symons, "Adaptiveness and adaptation," *Ethology and Sociobiology* 11 (1990): 427–44, 436–37; Wrangham and Peterson, *Demonic Males*, 64–74.

15. Barash, *Understanding Violence*; Buss, *Evolutionary Psychology*, 304–5; Geary, "Evolution of parental investment," 496; Harris, *The Nurture*

Assumption, 185; Pinker, *How the Mind Works*, 510; Sugiyama, "Physical attractiveness," 319.

16. Pinker, *The Blank Slate*, 116.

17. R. B. Ferguson, "Do Yanomamö killers have more kids?" *American Ethnologist* 16 (1989): 564–65, 564; R. B. Ferguson, *Yanomami Warfare: A Political History* (Santa Fe, N.M.: School of American Research Press, 1995), 359–60; Douglas Fry, *The Human Potential for Peace* (New York: Oxford University Press, 2006), 188–99, 290–305.

18. Fry, *The Human Potential for Peace*, 190, Figure 15.1.

19. Ibid., Chapter 15.

20. In reanalyzing the data, I noted that *unokais* and non-*unokais* are members of the same Yanomamö population for which demographic and reproductive data already had been published by Chagnon in a series of publications. Data on age and reproduction available in other articles by Chagnon (that are not repeated in Chagnon's 1988 article) provided a way to address some critically important questions about *unokais* versus non-*unokais*. See Fry, *The Human Potential for Peace*, Chapter 15, and associated notes for a full discussion and detailed mathematical reanalysis.

21. George Williams, *Adaptation and Natural Selection: A Critique of Some Current Evolutionary Thought* (Princeton: Princeton University Press, 1966), 4, 8, 9.

22. Donald Symons, *Play and Aggression: A Study of Rhesus Monkeys* (New York: Columbia University Press, 1978), 4.

23. For example, Richard Alexander, *The Biology of Moral Systems* (New York: Aldine de Gruyter, 1987), 107–10, 232; David Buss, *Evolutionary Psychology: The New Science of the Mind* (Boston: Allyn and Bacon, 1999), 300, 301, 306; Ghiglieri, *The Dark Side*

of Man, 165, 197; Pinker, How the Mind Works, 509–17; Richard Wrangham, "Is military incompetence adaptive?" Evolution and Human Behavior 20 (1999): 3–17, 5–6, 14; Richard Wrangham, "Evolution of coalitionary killing," Yearbook of Physical Anthropology 42 (1999): 1–30, 19.

24. Wrangham, "Evolution of coalitionary killing," 19, 22; Wrangham, "Is military incompetence adaptive?" 14; Buss, Evolutionary Psychology, 300, 301, 306.

25. Alexander, The Biology of Moral Systems, for example, 79; Buss, Evolutionary Psychology, 298, 302; Ghiglieri, The Dark Side of Man, for example, see 163, 164, 170, 196; Pinker, How the Mind Works, 509–10; Wrangham, "Evolution of coalitionary killing," 18, 19; Wrangham and Peterson, Demonic Males: Apes and the Origin of Human Violence, for example, 24, 81.

26. Ghiglieri, The Dark Side of Man, 165–77; Michael Wilson and Richard Wrangham, "Intergroup relations in chimpanzees," Annual Review of Anthropology 32 (2003): 363–92; Wrangham, "Is military incompetence adaptive?"; Wrangham, "Evolution of coalitionary killing," for example, 20; Wrangham and Peterson, Demonic Males, 22, 71.

27. Robert Carneiro, "War and peace: Alternating realities in human history," in S. Reyna and R. Downs (eds.), Studying War: Anthropological Perspectives, 3–27 (Amsterdam: Gordon and Breach, 1994); R. B. Ferguson, "Is war in our genes? Evidence vs. speculation on the antiquity and biology of war," Phi Beta Kappa Lecture, Rutgers University, Newark, N. J., February 16, 2000; Robert Sussman, "The myth of man the hunter/man the killer and the evolution of human morality," in R. Sussman (ed.), The Biological Basis of Human Behavior: A Critical Review, 2nd ed., 121–29 (Upper Saddle River, N.J.: Prentice Hall, 1999).

28. See Sussman, The *Biological Basis of Human Behavior*, 126.

29. Donna Hart and Robert Sussman, *Man the Hunted: Primates, Predators, and Human Evolution* (New York: Westview Press, 2005), 207–11; Sussman, *The Biological Basis of Human Behavior*, 126–27; Wilson and Wrangham, "Intergroup relations in chimpanzees," 372–75, see Table 1.

30. Wilson and Wrangham, "Intergroup relations in chimpanzees," 374.

31. Ibid., 265; Frans de Waal, *Our Inner Ape* (New York: Riverhead Books, 2005), 4, 30, see also 13–15; see also Katherine C. MacKinnon and Agustin Fuentes, "Reassessing male aggression and dominance: The evidence from primatology," in S. McKinnon and S. Silverman (eds.), *Complexities: Beyond Nature and Nurture*, 83–105 (Chicago: University of Chicago Press, 2005).

32. Wrangham, "Evolution of coalitionary killing," 23, 22.

33. See, for example, Hart and Pilling, *The Tiwi of North Australia*, 85–86; Allan Holmberg, *Nomads of the Long Bow: The Siriono of Eastern Bolivia* (New York: American Museum of Natural History, 1969, orig. pub. 1950), 158; Knauft, "Violence and sociality," 402; Mervyn Meggitt, *Desert People: A Study of the Walbiri Aborigines of Central Australia* (Chicago: University of Chicago Press, 1965), 24; Julian Steward, "Causal factors and processes in the evolution of pre-farming societies," in R. Lee and I. DeVore (eds.), *Man the Hunter*, 321–34 (Chicago: Aldine, 1968), 333–34, 334.

34. Wrangham, "Evolution of coalitionary killing," 23.

35. Buss, *Evolutionary Psychology*, 305, 306; Pinker, *How the Mind Works*, 509–17; Wrangham and Peterson, *Demonic Males*, 68.

36. Donald Symons, *The Evolution of Human Sexuality* (New York: Oxford University Press, 1979); Donald Symons, "Adaptiveness

and adaptation," *Ethology and Sociobiology* 11 (1990): 427–44; Donald Symons, "On the use and misuse of Darwinism in the study of human behavior," in J. Barkow, L. Cosmides, and J. Tooby (eds.), *The Adapted Mind: Evolutionary Psychology and the Generation of Culture*, 137–59 (New York: Oxford University Press, 1992); John Tooby and Leda Cosmides, "The past explains the present: Emotional adaptations and the structure of ancestral environments," *Ethology and Sociobiology* 11 (1990): 375–424.

37. See Symons, "Adaptiveness and adaptation," 436–38; Tooby and Cosmides, "The past explains the present," 420.

38. For example, Buss, *Evolutionary Psychology*; R. P. Shaw and Yuwa Wong, *Genetic Seeds of Warfare: Evolution, Nationalism, and Patriotism* (Boston: Unwin Hyman, 1989), 14.

39. Williams, *Adaptation and Natural Selection*.

Chapter 11: Returning to the Evidence

1. Frank Speck, *Naskapi: The Savage Hunters of the Labrador Peninsula* (Norman: University of Oklahoma Press, 1935), 13–16.

2. Eleanor Leacock, "Seventeenth-century Montagnais social relations and values," in W. Sturtevant (gen. ed.), *Handbook of North American Indians*, vol. 6: *Subarctic*, 190–95 (Washington, D.C.: Smithsonian Institution, 1981), 191.

3. For example, Eleanor Leacock, "Women's status in egalitarian society: Implications for social evolution," *Current Anthropology* 19 (1978): 247–75, 249.

4. Julian Lips, *Naskapi Law* (Philadelphia: American Philosophical Society, 1947), 470.

5. Lips, *Naskapi Law*, 470.

6. Lips, *Naskapi Law*, 469, 470; Gerald Reid, "Montagnais-Naskapi," in D. Levinson (gen. ed.), *Encyclopedia of World Cultures*, vol. 1: *North America*, 243–46 (Boston: G. K. Hall, 1991), 245.

7. Leacock, "Seventeenth-century Montagnais social relations," 193; Lips, *Naskapi Law*, 469, 471–72, quote from 402; Leacock, "Women's status in egalitarian society," 249.

8. Reid, "Montagnais-Naskapi," 245; Speck, *Naskapi*, 44; Lips, *Naskapi Law*, quote from 469.

9. Lips, *Naskapi Law*, 398.

10. Lips, *Naskapi Law*, 399; see also Speck, *Naskapi*, 31.

11. Lips, *Naskapi Law*, 399; Leacock, "Women's status in egalitarian society," quote from 249–50.

12. Eleanor Leacock, *The Montagnais "Hunting Territory" and the Fur Trade*, Memoirs of the American Anthropological Association no. 78, *American Anthropologist* 56, 2, part 2 (1954): 43; Leacock, "Women's status in egalitarian society," 250, 253; Reid, "Montagnais-Naskapi," 245.

13. Asen Balikci, *The Netsilik Eskimo* (Garden City, N.Y.: Natural History Press, 1970), xx; Timothy O'Leary and David Levinson, "Netsilik Inuit," in D. Levinson (gen. ed.), *Encyclopedia of World Cultures*, vol. I: *North America*, 254 (Boston: G. K. Hall, 1991), 254.

14. Balikci, *The Netsilik Eskimo*, 176, 178.

15. Knud Rasmussen quoted in Penelope Eckert and Russell Newmark, "Central Eskimo song duels: A contextual analysis of ritual ambiguity," *Ethnology* 19 (1980): 191–211, 209–10.

16. Balikci, *The Netsilik Eskimo*, 179; quote from C. Irwin, "The Inuit and the evolution of limited group conflict," in J. van der Dennen and V. Falger (eds.), *Sociobiology and Conflict:*

Evolutionary Perspectives on Competition, Cooperation, Violence and Warfare, 189–240 (London: Chapman and Hall, 1990), 201.

17. Balikci, *The Netsilik Eskimo*, 156, 157; see also Irwin, "The Inuit and the evolution of limited group conflict," 200–2.

18. Balikci, *The Netsilik Eskimo*, 179, 180.

19. Ibid., 180–81.

20. Irwin, "The Inuit and the evolution of limited group conflict," 196–97; on supernatural revenge, see Balikci, *The Netsilik Eskimo*, 179, 181.

21. Irwin, "The Inuit and the evolution of limited group conflict," 194–99, quote from 199; Balikci, *The Netsilik Eskimo*, 182–84.

22. Balikci, *The Netsilik Eskimo*, 185–86.

23. Ibid.; quotes from 186.

24. See Hoebel, *The Law of Primitive Man*, 88–90; on decisions, see Balikci, *The Netsilik Eskimo*, 192; on preventing revenge, see Hoebel, *The Law of Primitive Man*, 89.

25. Knud Rasmussen quoted in Balikci, *The Netsilik Eskimo*, 190–91.

26. Balikci, *The Netsilik Eskimo*, 193.

27. Richard Lee, *The Dobe Ju/'hoansi*, 2nd ed. (Fort Worth: Harcourt Brace College Publishers, 1993), ix.

28. Patricia Draper, "The learning environment for aggression and anti-social behavior among the !Kung (Kalahari Desert, Botswana, Africa)," in A. Montagu (ed.), *Learning Non-Aggression: The Experience of Non-Literate Societies*, 31–53 (Oxford: Oxford University Press, 1978), 35; Lee, *The Dobe Ju/'hoansi*, 10. Lee (p. 9) provides a historical context: "As White settlement expanded north in the eighteenth century, bitter conflicts arose with the native peoples, conflicts that escalated into genocidal warfare against the San [of which the Ju/'hoansi are but one group]. By the late nineteenth century the San had

been virtually exterminated within the boundaries of the present-day Republic of South Africa, and most writers of the day spoke of them as a dying race. As exploration pushed father north, however, the grim obituary of the San proved, happily, to be premature. In the security of the Kalahari Desert, thousands of San continue to live as hunter-gatherers in relatively peaceful proximity to a variety of neighboring Black herders and farmers."

29. Richard Lee, *The !Kung San: Men, Women, and Work in a Foraging Community* (Cambridge: Cambridge University Press, 1979), 338, 370, quote from 335, italics in original; Lee, *The Dobe Ju/'hoansi*, 93.

30. Patricia Draper, "!Kung women: Contrasts in sexual egalitarianism in foraging and sedentary contexts," in R. Reiter (ed.), *Toward an Anthropology of Women*, 77–109 (New York: Monthly Review Press, 1975), 86; Melvin Konner, *The Tangled Wing: Biological Constraints on the Human Spirit* (New York: Henry Holt, 1982); Lee, *The !Kung San*, 398; Lorna Marshall, *The !Kung of Nyae Nyae* (Cambridge: Harvard University Press, 1976), 53; see also Elizabeth Thomas, *The Harmless People* (New York: Vintage, 1959), 21–24; quote from Lee, *The Dobe Ju/'hoansi*, 35–36.

31. Polly Wiessner, "Risk, reciprocity and social influences on !Kung San economics," in E. Leacock and R. Lee (eds.), *Politics and History in Band Society*, 61–84 (Cambridge: Cambridge University Press, 1982); Lee, *The !Kung San*, 456; Elizabeth Cashdan, "Egalitarianism among hunters and gatherers," *American Anthropologist* 82 (1980): 116.

32. See Konner, *The Tangled Wing*, 204; Douglas Fry, "Conclusion: Learning from peaceful societies," in G. Kemp and D. Fry

(eds.), *Keeping the Peace: Conflict Resolution and Peaceful Societies Around the World*, 185–204 (New York: Routledge, 2004).

33. See Christopher Boehm, *Hierarchy in the Forest: The Evolution of Egalitarian Behavior* (Cambridge: Harvard University Press, 1999); Leacock, "Women's status in egalitarian society"; James Woodburn, "Egalitarian societies," *Man* 17 (1982): 431–51.

34. Marjorie Shostak, *Nisa: The Life and Words of a !Kung Woman* (New York: Vintage, 1983), 287–88.

35. Draper, "!Kung women"; Draper, "The learning environment," 33; Susan Kent, "And justice for all: The development of political centralization among newly sedentary foragers," *American Anthropologist* 91 (1989): 703–12, 704; Konner, *The Tangled Wing*, 204; Lee, *The Dobe Ju/'hoansi*, 93; Lorna Marshall, "Sharing, talking, and giving: Relief of social tensions among !Kung Bushmen," *Africa* 31 (1961): 231–49; Marshall, *The !Kung of Nyae Nyae*; Elizabeth Thomas, "Management of violence among the Ju/wasi of Nyae Nyae: The old way and a new way," in S. P. Reyna and R. E. Downs (eds.), *Studying War: Anthropological Perspectives* (Amsterdam: Gordon and Breach, 1994), 71, 75; Irenäus Eibl-Eibesfeldt, "The myth of the aggression-free hunter and gatherer society," in R. Holloway (ed.), *Primate Aggression, Territoriality, and Xenophobia: A Comparative Perspective*, 425–57 (New York: Academic Press, 1974); Irenäus Eibl-Eibesfeldt, *The Biology of Peace and War: Men, Animals, and Aggression*, trans. E. Mosbacher (New York: Viking, 1979); see also Steven LeBlanc (with K. Register), *Constant Battles: Why We Fight* (New York: St. Martin's Griffin, 2003). On p. 115 LeBlanc concedes that the Ju/'hoansi do not make war, but immediately adopts an approach paralleling Eibl-Eibesfeldt's of citing information from *different* southern African San populations

across *different* time periods to imply that the Ju/'hoansi were not so friendly in the past. This is a time and place shifting fallacy—see Fry, "Conclusion: Learning from peaceful societies," 193.

36. Lee, *The Dobe Ju/'hoansi*, 93, italics added; Draper, "The learning environment," 33; see also Kent, 2002; Fry, "Conclusion: Learning from peaceful societies"; Konner, *The Tangled Wing*, 204; Thomas, *The Harmless People*, 24, 186.

37. Lee, *The !Kung San*, chapter 13; Lee, *The Dobe Ju/'hoansi*, 97–102; Marshall, "Sharing, talking, and giving," 235.

38. Lee, *The !Kung San*, 377.

39. Shostak, *Nisa*, 258, 259, 261.

40. See Draper, "The learning environment," 33, 43–44; Lee, *The !Kung San*, 376, 380; Lee, *The Dobe Ju/'hoansi*, 98–99; Thomas, *The Harmless People*, 186; Thomas, 1994, 76.

41. Lee, *The !Kung San*; Lee, *The Dobe Ju/'hoansi*.

42. Lee, *The !Kung San*, 382, 397, on poison arrows and executions, see 388; see also Draper, "The learning environment," 40; Thomas, 1994, 78.

43. Lee, *The !Kung San*, 383 and Table 13.2, Table 13.3, codes K2, K6, K17, and K19.

44. Ibid., 393, case number 6.

45. Draper, "The learning environment," 40; see also Thomas, 1994, 75; Lee, *The Dobe Ju/'hoansi*, 81, italics in original.

46. Boehm, *Hierarchy in the Forest*, 80; see also Draper, "The learning environment," 40.

47. Lee, *The !Kung San*, 390, 394.

48. Draper, "The learning environment"; Lee, *The !Kung San*, chapter 13; Lee, *The Dobe Ju/'hoansi*, chapter 7; Kent, "And justice for all"; Marshall, "Sharing, talking, and giving"; Thomas, 1994.

Chapter 12: Darwin Got It Right

1. Charles Darwin, *The Origin of Species: By Means of Natural Selection of the Preservation of Favoured Races in the Struggle for Life* (New York: New American Library, 1958 [1859]), 90, 91; Donald Symons, "Adaptiveness and adaptation," *Ethology and Sociobiology* 11 (1990): 427–44, 427–28.

2. George Williams, *Adaptation and Natural Selection: A Critique of Some Current Evolutionary Thought* (Princeton: Princeton University Press, 1966), 82–83.

3. Charles Darwin, *The Descent of Man* (New York: Prometheus Books, 1998, orig. pub. 1871), quote from 229.

4. Robert Trivers, "Parental investment and sexual selection," in B. Campbell (ed.), *Sexual Selection and the Descent of Man, 1871–1971*, 136–79 (Chicago: Aldine, 1972); Darwin, *The Descent of Man*, quote from 214–15; Trivers, "Parental investment and sexual selection," quote from 139.

5. Darwin, *The Descent of Man*, quote from 583; Donald Symons, *The Evolution of Human Sexuality* (New York: Oxford University Press, 1979), quote from 142, emphasis in original, see also 153, 163; David Buss, "Mate preference mechanisms: Consequences for partner choice and intrasexual competition," in J. Barkow, L. Cosmides, and J. Tooby (eds.), *The Adapted Mind: Evolutionary Psychology and the Generation of Culture*, 249–66 (New York: Oxford University Press, 1992); Martin Daly and Margo Wilson, *Homicide* (New York: Aldine de Gruyter, 1988).

6. See Douglas P. Fry, "The evolution of aggression and the level of selection controversy," *Aggressive Behavior* 6 (1980): 69–89; John Maynard Smith, "The objects of selection," *Proceedings of the National Academy of Science* 94 (1997): 2091–4; Susan

Riechert, "Game theory and animal contests," in L. Dugatkin and H. Reeve (eds.), *Game Theory and Animal Behavior*, 64–93 (New York: Oxford University Press, 1998), 65; Williams, *Adaptation and Natural Selection*.

7. Donald Brown, *Human Universals* (New York: McGraw-Hill, 1991), 137; Douglas Fry, "Anthropological perspectives on aggression: Sex differences and cultural variation," *Aggressive Behavior* 24 (1998): 81–95; quote from Daly and Wilson, *Homicide*, 161.

8. For example, Victoria Burbank, "Female aggression in cross-cultural perspective," *Behavior Science Research* 21 (1987): 70–100; Victoria Burbank, *Fighting Women: Anger and Aggression in Aboriginal Australia* (Berkeley: University of California Press, 1994); Daly and Wilson, *Homicide*; Fry, "Anthropological perspectives on aggression"; Nicole Hines and Douglas Fry, "Indirect modes of aggression among women of Buenos Aires, Argentina," *Sex Roles* 30 (1994): 213–36, Eleanor Maccoby and C. Jacklin, *The Psychology of Sex Differences* (Stanford: Stanford University Press, 1974).

9. Burbank, "Female aggression in cross-cultural perspective," 71; Burbank, *Fighting Women*, 202; Darwin, *The Descent of Man*.

10. To return for a moment to the tribal Yanomamö (who, of course, are not nomadic foragers): Despite the huge amount of ink that has been devoted to discussing killing and other violence within this society as a predominant feature, if we consider all the men age twenty and older in Chagnon's study population, only 14 percent (54 of 380) of the men have participated in more than one killing and 22 percent (83 of 380) have participated in only one killing, whereas the majority, 64 percent (243 of 380), have not participated in any killings at all (see Napoleon Chagnon, "Life histories, blood

revenge, and warfare in a tribal population," *Science* 239 [1988]: 985–92, Figure 1 and Table 2). These percentages suggest, first, that only a minority of men are involved in the bulk of the killings and, second, that the vast majority of men are not raiders or murderers. It is also relevant to keep in mind that the phrase "participated in a killing" often reflects a shared event with several or numerous other men. This can produce multiple "participants in a killing" per single victim. Ethnographic descriptions of nomadic forager societies, such as those considered in Chapters 3, 9, and 11, suggest that even lower levels of killing typify band society.

11. Quote from Richard Wrangham and Dale Peterson, *Demonic Males: Apes and the Origin of Human Violence* (Boston: Houghton Mifflin, 1996), 84; see Douglas Fry, *The Human Potential for Peace* (New York: Oxford University Press, 2006), Chapters 5, 6, and 7 for examples of peaceful societies; see also www.peacefulsocieties.org.

12. For example, see Douglas Fry, "Play aggression among Zapotec children: Implications for the practice hypothesis," *Aggressive Behavior* 16 (1990): 321–40; Douglas Fry, "Rough-and-tumble social play in children," in A. Pellegrini and P. K. Smith (eds.), *The Nature of Play: Great Apes and Humans*, 54–85 (New York: Guilford, 2005).

13. Pertaining to animal aggression, see Felicity Huntingford and Angela Turner, *Animal Conflict* (London: Chapman and Hall, 1987), 79. For examples of variable behavioral responses from the discipline of human behavioral ecology, see R. Dyson-Hudson and Eric Alden Smith, "Human territoriality: An ecological reassessment," *American Anthropologist* 80 (1978): 21–41; Bruce Winterhalder and Eric Alden Smith, "Analyzing

adaptive strategies: Human behavioral ecology at twenty-five," *Evolutionary Anthropology* 9 (2000): 51–72.

14. Fry, *The Human Potential for Peace*, Chapters 5, 6, and 7; Signe Howell and Roy Willis (eds.), *Societies at Peace: Anthropological Perspectives* (London: Routledge, 1989); Leslie Sponsel and Thomas Gregor (eds.), *The Anthropology of Peace and Nonviolence* (Boulder, Colo.: Lynne Rienner, 1994); Graham Kemp and Douglas Fry (eds.), *Keeping the Peace: Conflict Resolution and Peaceful Societies Around the World* (New York: Routledge, 2004).

15. Dyson-Hudson and Smith, "Human territoriality"; Winterhalder and Smith, "Analyzing adaptive strategies"; Williams, *Adaptation and Natural Selection;* see also Agustin Fuentes, "It's not all sex and violence: Integrated anthropology and the role of cooperation and social complexity in human evolution," *American Anthropologist* 106 (2004): 710–18; Katherine C. MacKinnon and Agustin Fuentes, "Reassessing male aggression and dominance: The evidence from primatology," in S. McKinnon and S. Silverman (eds.), *Complexities: Beyond Nature and Nurture*, 83–105 (Chicago: University of Chicago Press, 2005).

Chapter 13: A New Evolutionary Perspective

1. John Archer and Felicity Huntingford, "Game theory models and escalation of animal fighting," in M. Potegal and J. Knutson (eds.), *The Dynamics of Aggression: Biological and Social Processes in Dyads and Groups*, 3–31 (Hillsdale, N.J.: Lawrence Erlbaum, 1994), for example 10; Christopher Boehm, *Hierarchy in the Forest: The Evolution of Egalitarian Behavior* (Cambridge: Harvard

University Press, 1999); Susan Riechert, "Game theory and animal contests," in L. Dugatkin and H. Reeve (eds.), *Game Theory and Animal Behavior*, 64–93 (New York: Oxford University Press, 1998), 82.

2. John Archer, *The Behavioural Biology of Aggression* (Cambridge: Cambridge University Press, 1988); Frans de Waal, "The first kiss: Foundations of conflict resolution research in animals," in F. Aureli and F. de Waal (eds.), *Natural Conflict Resolution*, 15–33 (Berkeley: University of California Press, 2000); Caroline Blanchard and Robert Blanchard, "Experimental animal models of aggression: What do they say about human behaviour?" in J. Archer and K. Browne (eds.), *Human Aggression: Naturalistic Approaches*, 94–121 (London: Routledge, 1989), 104–5; Felicity Huntingford and Angela Turner, *Animal Conflict* (London: Chapman and Hall, 1987); Riechert, "Game theory and animal contests," 82.

3. George Schaller, *The Serengeti Lion* (Chicago: University of Chicago Press, 1972); Edward Wilson, "Book review," *Science* 179 (1973): 466–67; Edward Wilson, *Sociobiology: The New Synthesis* (Cambridge: Harvard University Press, 1975), 246; Robert Hinde, *Biological Bases of Human Social Behaviour* (New York: McGraw-Hill, 1974); Blanchard and Blanchard, "Experimental animal models of aggression," 104.

4. Archer, *The Behavioural Biology of Aggression*; Wilson, *Sociobiology*, 242–43; Frans de Waal, *Peacemaking Among Primates* (Cambridge: Harvard University Press, 1989).

5. Given the typicality of sexual affairs in many band societies (as reflected in the Siriono, Paliyan, and Ju/'hoansi case studies, for example), obviously the overwhelming majority of sexual affairs do not lead to homicides.

6. For example, Ronald Berndt, "Law and order in Aboriginal Australia," in R. Berndt and C. Berndt (eds.), *Aboriginal Man in Australia: Essays in Honour of Emeritus Professor A. P. Elkin*, 167–206 (London: Angus and Robertson, 1965); Boehm, *Hierarchy in the Forest*, 7, 80–81; and the other references in Fry, *The Human Potential for Peace*, 311, note 15. Based on Lee's data in *The !Kung San: Men, Women, and Work in a Foraging Community* (Cambridge: Cambridge University Press, 1979), a fair number of Ju/'hoansi homicides seem to be crimes of passion. It seems likely that some attacks would not otherwise have resulted in lethal injuries if the readily available poisoned arrows had not been used to inflict wounds.

7. Asen Balikci, *The Netsilik Eskimo* (Garden City, N.Y.: Natural History Press, 1970), 181; Lee, *The !Kung San*.

8. Douglas Fry, "Reciprocity: The foundation stone of morality," in M. Killen and J. Smetana (eds.), *Handbook of Moral Development*, 399–422 (Mahwah, N.J.: Lawrence Erlbaum, 2006); see also Martin Gusinde, *The Yahgan: The Life and Thought of the Water Nomads of Cape Horn*, trans. Frieda Schütze, in the electronic Human Relations Area Files, Yahgan, Doc. 1 (New Haven: HRAF, 2003, orig. pub. 1937), 887, 898–905; Raymond Kelly, *Warless Societies and the Origin of War* (Ann Arbor: University of Michigan Press, 2000); Lee, *The !Kung San*, 383, 389.

9. Karen Ericksen and Heather Horton, "'Blood feuds': Cross-cultural variations in kin group vengeance," *Behavior Science Research* 26 (1992): 57–85. See also their Table 2, for the codings for seventeen nomadic band societies for which information was available, SCCS numbers 2, 13, 77, 79, 90, 91, 119, 122, 124, 125, 126, 127, 128, 129, 137, 180, 186.

10. Balikci, *The Netsilik Eskimo*, 180; also see references in Fry, *The Human Potential for Peace*, 312, note 25; quote from Lee, *The !Kung San*, 390.

11. Balikci, *The Netsilik Eskimo*, 182; see also Gusinde, *The Yahgan*, 899–900.

12. William Hamilton, "The genetical evolution of social behaviour, II," *Journal of Theoretical Biology* 7 (1964): 17–52.

13. Tim Asch and Napoleon Chagnon, *The Ax Fight*, 16mm film (Somerville, Mass.: Documentary Educational Resources, 1975); Napoleon Chagnon and Paul Bugos Jr., "Kin selection and conflict: An analysis of a Yanomamö ax fight," in N. Chagnon and W. Irons (eds.), *Evolutionary Biology and Human Social Behavior: An Anthropological Perspective*, 213–38 (North Scituate, Mass.: Duxbury Press, 1979); Michael Ghiglieri, *The Dark Side of Man: Tracing The Origins of Male Violence* (Reading, Mass.: Perseus, 1999).

14. Junius Bird, "The Alacaluf," in J. Steward (ed.), *Handbook of South American Indians*, vol. 1: *The Marginal Tribes*, 55–80 plus plates (Washington, D.C.: United States Printing Office, 1946); see also Gusinde, *The Yahgan*, 886, 987.

15. Martin Daly and Margo Wilson, *Homicide* (New York: Aldine de Gruyter, 1988); John Maynard Smith, "The theory of games and the evolution of animal conflicts," *Journal of Theoretical Biology* 47 (1974): 209–21.

16. Lee, *The !Kung San*, 391. A wife and husband are unlikely to be more closely related to each other than as first cousins.

17. John Maynard Smith and G. Price, "The logic of animal conflict," *Nature* 246 (1973): 15–18, quote from 15; Maynard Smith, "The theory of games." See also Riechert, "Game theory and animal contests"; Archer and Huntingford, "Game theory models."

18. Archer, *The Behavioural Biology of Aggression;* Archer and Huntingford, "Game theory models"; Douglas P. Fry, "The evolution of aggression and the level of selection controversy," *Aggressive Behavior* 6 (1980): 69–89, 73; Riechert, "Game theory and animal contests."

19. Robert Axelrod, *The Evolution of Cooperation* (New York: Basic Books, 1984), quote from 54.

20. For example, Boehm, *Hierarchy in the Forest;* David Damas, "The Copper Eskimo," in M. Bicchieri (ed.), *Hunters and Gatherers Today,* 3–49 (Prospect Heights, Ill.: Waveland, 1972), 24–25; Elman Service, *The Hunters* (Englewood Cliffs, N.J.: Prentice-Hall, 1966); Cornelia van der Sluys, "Gifts from the immortal ancestors," in P. Schweitzer, M. Biesele, and R. Hitchcock (eds.), *Hunters and Gatherers in the Modern World: Conflict, Resistance, and Self-Determination,* 427–54 (New York: Berghahn, 2000); and the additional references in Fry, *The Human Potential for Peace,* 311 n. 2.

21. For example, Damas, "The Copper Eskimo," 33; A. Irving Hallowell, "Aggression in Saulteaux society," in A. I. Hallowell (ed.), *Culture and Experience,* 277–90 (Philadelphia: University of Pennsylvania Press, 1974), 279; E. Adamson Hoebel, *The Law of Primitive Man: A Study in Comparative Legal Dynamics* (Cambridge: Harvard University Press, 1967), 88–89; Service, *The Hunters,* 50; and the additional references in Douglas Fry, *The Human Potential for Peace,* 311 n. 4; quote from David Damas, "Copper Eskimo," in D. Levinson (gen. ed.), *Encyclopedia of World Cultures,* vol. I: *North America,* 76–79 (Boston: G. K. Hall, 1991), 78.

22. Hoebel, *The Law of Primitive Man,* 88.

23. Boehm, *Hierarchy in the Forest,* 82; Napoleon Chagnon, "Life histories, blood revenge, and warfare in a tribal population," *Science* 239 (1988): 985–92.

24. For example, Gusinde, *The Yahgan*, 633–34, 635, 908, 911, 1031; Hallowell, *Culture and Experience*; Sluys, "Gifts from the immortal ancestors"; and the additional references in Fry, *The Human Potential for Peace*, 311 n. 9.

25. For example, see Gusinde, *The Yahgan*, 635, 886.

26. For example, Damas, "Copper Eskimo," 78; Gusinde, *The Yahgan*, 888, 984; Lee, *The !Kung San*, 367; Berndt, "Law and order"; and the other references in Fry, *The Human Potential for Peace*, 311 n. 11.

27. Archer and Huntingford, "Game theory models"; Irenäus Eibl-Eibesfeldt, "The fighting behavior of animals," *Scientific American* 205 (1961): 112–22; Irenäus Eibl-Eibesfeldt, *The Biology of Peace and War: Men, Animals, and Aggression*, trans. E. Mosbacher (New York: Viking, 1979), 37–40; Maynard Smith and Price, "The logic of animal conflict"; Riechert, "Game theory and animal contests," 65; Schaller, *The Serengeti Lion*, 55.

28. On rattlesnakes: Eibl-Eibesfeldt, "The fighting behavior of animals"; Wilson, *Sociobiology*, 243; quote from Maynard Smith and Price, "The logic of animal conflict," 15. On nonlethal, restrained competition: Archer and Huntingford, "Game theory models"; Hinde, *Biological Bases of Human Social Behaviour*, 269; Riechert, "Game theory and animal contests," 65. On ritualized competition: Archer and Huntingford, "Game theory models", 3–4; Maynard Smith and Price, "The logic of animal conflict"; see also Douglas Fry, "Rough-and-tumble social play in children," in A. Pellegrini and P. K. Smith (eds.), *The Nature of Play: Great Apes and Humans*, 54–85 (New York: Guilford, 2005). On submission and appeasement signals: Filippo Aureli and Frans de Waal (eds.), *Natural Conflict Resolution* (Berkeley: University of California Press, 2000); Hinde, *Biological Bases of Human Social Behaviour*, 270. On restrained

aggression: See Fry, "The evolution of aggression"; Hinde, *Biological Bases of Human Social Behaviour*, 272; Maynard Smith and Price, "The logic of animal conflict."

29. Gusinde, *The Yahgan*, 887.

30. Balikci, *The Netsilik Eskimo*, 192.

31. Lorna Marshall, "Sharing, talking, and giving: Relief of social tensions among ǃKung Bushmen," *Africa* 31 (1961): 231–49; Lee, *The ǃKung San*; Richard Lee, *The Dobe Ju/'hoansi*, 2nd ed. (Fort Worth: Harcourt Brace College Publishers, 1993).

32. For example, Damas, "The Copper Eskimo," 33; Fry, "Rough-and-tumble social play"; Hoebel, *The Law of Primitive Man*, 92; Colin Turnbull, *Wayward Servants: The Two Worlds of the African Pygmies* (Garden City, N.Y.: Natural History Press, 1965), 188–89.

33. Balikci, *The Netsilik Eskimo*, 181; Gusinde, *The Yahgan*, 890; Fry, "Reciprocity: The foundation stone of morality."

34. Chagnon, "Life histories"; Chagnon, "On Yanomamö violence: Reply to Albert," *Current Anthropology* 31 (1990): 49–53; Napoleon Chagnon, *Yanomamö*, 4th ed. (Fort Worth: Harcourt Brace Jovanovich College Publishers, 1992); Napoleon Chagnon, "Chronic problems in understanding tribal violence and warfare," in G. Bock and J. Goode (eds.), *Genetics of Criminal and Antisocial Behaviour*, plus discussion, 202–36 (Chichester: John Wiley and Sons, 1996); Asch and Chagnon, *The Ax Fight*.

35. Archer and Huntingford, "Game theory models."

36. See Frans de Waal, *Good Natured: The Origin of Right and Wrong in Humans and Other Animals* (Cambridge: Harvard University Press, 1996); de Waal, "The first kiss."

37. See Edward Westermarck, *The Origin and Development of the Moral Ideas*, 2 vols., 2nd ed. (London: Macmillan, 1924), 479.

38. Fry, "Reciprocity: The foundation stone of morality."

Chapter 14: Setting the Record Straight

1. Richard Alexander, *Darwinism and Human Affairs* (Seattle: University of Washington Press, 1979); Richard Alexander, *The Biology of Moral Systems* (New York: Aldine de Gruyter, 1987).

2. Julian Steward, "Causal factors and processes in the evolution of pre-farming societies," in R. Lee and I. DeVore (eds.), *Man the Hunter*, 321–34 (Chicago: Aldine, 1968), 333–34; Bruce Knauft, "Violence and sociality in human evolution," *Current Anthropology* 32 (1991): 391–428, 402; John Gowdy, "Hunter-gatherers and the mythology of the market," in R. Lee and R. Daly (eds.), *The Cambridge Encyclopedia of Hunters and Gatherers*, 391–98 (Cambridge: Cambridge University Press, 1999), 397; see also Colin Turnbull, "Discussions, part VII, 35.b: Primate behavior and the evolution of aggression," in R. Lee and I. DeVore (eds.), *Man the Hunter*, 339–44 (Chicago: Aldine, 1968), 341.

3. Jane Goodale, *Tiwi Wives: A Study of the Women of Melville Island, North Australia* (Seattle: University of Washington Press, 1974), 133–34.

4. For example, see Alexander, *Darwinism and Human Affairs*, 222–30; Joshua Goldstein, *War and Gender: How Gender Shapes the War System and Vice Versa* (Cambridge: Cambridge University Press, 2001), 24; Michael Ghiglieri, *The Dark Side of Man: Tracing The Origins of Male Violence* (Reading, Mass.: Perseus, 1999), 164; Lawrence Keeley, *War Before Civilization: The Myth of the Peaceful Savage* (Oxford: Oxford University Press, 1996), 31; Richard Wrangham and Dale Peterson, *Demonic Males: Apes and the Origin of Human Violence* (Boston: Houghton Mifflin, 1996), 75.

5. Carol Ember, "Myths about hunter-gatherers," *Ethnology* 17 (1978): 439–48, both quotes from 443.

6. Goldstein, *War and Gender*, 24, italics in original.

7. This point is noted by Leslie Sponsel, "The natural history of peace: A positive view of human nature and its potential," in T. Gregor (ed.), *A Natural History of Peace*, 95–125 (Nashville, Tenn.: Vanderbilt University Press, 1996), 110.

8. Ember, "Myths about hunter-gatherers," refers readers to another article for her definition of war. Of the five sources listed in note 4 above, all of which cite Ember's article, only Goldstein, *War and Gender*, also cites the earlier article that contains the definition of war (Melvin Ember and Carol Ember, "The conditions favoring matrilocal versus patrilocal residence," *American Anthropologist* 73 [1971]: 571–94, see 578). Presumably most readers don't go reference-hopping back to find out more precisely how so-called war is being defined. I suspect that a common implicit assumption by readers is that we all know what war is.

9. For a more detailed discussion of these points, see Douglas Fry, *The Human Potential for Peace* (New York: Oxford University Press, 2006), Chapter 14.

10. Ibid., Chapters 13 and 14.

11. Joseph Birdsell, "Australia: Ecology, spacing mechanisms and adaptive behaviour in aboriginal land tenure," in R. Crocombe (ed.), *Land Tenure in the Pacific*, 334–61 (New York: Oxford University Press, 1971), 347; Richard Lee, *The !Kung San: Men, Women, and Work in a Foraging Community* (Cambridge: Cambridge University Press, 1979), 360–61; Frank Marlowe, "Hunter-gatherers and human evolution," *Evolutionary Anthropology* 14 (2005): 54–67.

12. Fry, *The Human Potential for Peace*, 284–85, references in Chapter 13 nn. 36, 37, 38; Marlowe, "Hunter-gatherers and human evolution," 60.

13. Christopher Boehm, *Hierarchy in the Forest: The Evolution of Egalitarian Behavior* (Cambridge: Harvard University Press, 1999), 67; Robert Kelly, *The Foraging Spectrum: Diversity in Hunter-Gatherer Lifeways* (Washington, D.C.: Smithsonian Institution Press, 1995); Eleanor Leacock, "Women's status in egalitarian society: Implications for social evolution," *Current Anthropology* 19 (1978): 247–75, 249; Marlowe, "Hunter-gatherers and human evolution," 60; Elman Service, *The Hunters* (Englewood Cliffs, N.J.: Prentice-Hall, 1966), 51; James Woodburn, "Egalitarian societies," *Man* 17 (1982): 431–51, 444.

14. Birdsell, "Australia"; Boehm, *Hierarchy in the Forest*, 71, 112; Elizabeth Cashdan, "Territoriality among human foragers: Ecological models and an application to four Bushman groups," *Current Anthropology* 24 (1983): 47–66; L. Hiatt, "Ownership and use of land among Australian Aborigines," in R. Lee and I. DeVore (eds.), *Man the Hunter*, 99–102 (Chicago: Aldine, 1968), 101–2; Kelly, *The Foraging Spectrum*, Chapters 5 and 8; Eleanor Leacock, *The Montagnais "Hunting Territory" and the Fur Trade*, memoirs of the American Anthropological Association no. 78, *American Anthropologist* 56, 2, part 2 (1954): 7; Richard Lee, *The Dobe Ju/'hoansi*, 2nd ed. (Fort Worth: Harcourt Brace College Publishers, 1993), 88; Marlowe, "Hunter-gatherers and human evolution," 62–63; Service, *The Hunters*, 51; Robert Tonkinson, "Resolving conflict within the law: The Mardu Aborigines of Australia," in G. Kemp and D. Fry (eds.), *Keeping the Peace: Conflict Resolution and Peaceful Societies Around the World*, 89–104 (New York: Routledge, 2004); Polly Wiessner, "Risk,

reciprocity and social influences on !Kung San economics," in E. Leacock and R. Lee (eds.), *Politics and History in Band Society*, 61–84 (Cambridge: Cambridge University Press, 1982); Woodburn, "Egalitarian societies," 445.

15. Fry, *The Human Potential for Peace*, Chapters 13 and 14.

16. Fry, *The Human Potential for Peace*, especially Chapters, 5, 7, 13 and 14; Peter Gardner, "Symmetric respect and memorate knowledge: The structure and ecology of individualistic culture," *Southwestern Journal of Anthropology* 22 (1966): 389–415, 402–3.

Chapter 15: A Macroscopic Anthropological View

1. E. A. Hoebel, "Law-ways of the Comanche Indians," in P. Bohannan (ed.), *Law and Warfare: Studies in the Anthropology of Conflict*, 183–203 (Austin: University of Texas Press, 1967), 193; Jan Brögger, "Conflict resolution and the role of the bandit in peasant society," *Anthropological Quarterly* 41 (1968): 228–40, 231.

2. Christopher Boehm, *Hierarchy in the Forest: The Evolution of Egalitarian Behavior* (Cambridge: Harvard University Press, 1999). On human flexibility: Agustin Fuentes, "It's not all sex and violence: Integrated anthropology and the role of cooperation and social complexity in human evolution," *American Anthropologist* 106 (2004): 710–18; Katherine C. MacKinnon and Agustin Fuentes, "Reassessing male aggression and dominance: The evidence from primatology," in S. McKinnon and S. Silverman (eds.), *Complexities: Beyond Nature and Nurture*, 83–105 (Chicago: University of Chicago Press, 2005), for example, 99.

3. See R. Brian Ferguson and Neil Whitehead (eds.), *War in the Tribal Zone: Expanding States and Indigenous Warfare* (Santa Fe, N.M.: School of American Research Press, 1992); Eleanor Leacock, "Relations of production in band society," in E. Leacock and R. Lee (eds.), *Politics and History in Band Society*, 159–70 (Cambridge: Cambridge University Press, 1982); W. Newcomb, "A re-examination of the causes of Plains warfare," *American Anthropologist* 52 (1950): 317–30; S. Reyna, "A mode of domination approach to organized violence," in S. Reyna and R. Downs (eds.), *Studying War: Anthropological Perspectives*, 29–65 (Amsterdam: Gordon and Breach, 1994); Quincy Wright, *A Study of War* (Chicago: University of Chicago Press, 1942), 66; see also R. Brian Ferguson, "Archaeology, cultural anthropology, and the origins and intensifications of war," in B. Arkush and M. W. Allen (eds.), *The Archaeology of Warfare: Prehistories of Raiding and Conquest*, 469–524 (Gainesville: University Press of Florida, 2006).

4. Esko Orma, *Huoli Ihmisestä: Uudistuvaa Psykiatriaa* (Helsinki: Therapeia-säätiö, 1986), 14–15.

5. David Adams and Sarah Bosch, "The myth that war is intrinsic to human nature discourages action for peace by young people," in J. M. Ramírez, R. Hinde, and J. Groeble (eds.), *Essays On Violence*, 121–37 (Seville: University of Seville Press, 1987); Douglas Fry and James Welch, "Beliefs about human nature and conflict: Implications for peace education," paper presented at the meetings of the American Anthropological Association, December 1992, San Francisco; Raymond Dart, "The predatory implemental technique of australopithecines," *American Journal of Physical Anthropology* 7 (1949): 1–38; Raymond Dart, "The predatory transition from ape to man," *International Anthropological and Linguistic Review* 1 (1953): 201–18;

Raymond Dart, "The minimal bone-breccia content of Makapansgat and the australopithecine predatory habit," *American Anthropologist* 60 (1958): 923–31; Robert Ardrey, *African Genesis* (New York: Dell, 1961).

6. For example, see Michael Ghiglieri, *The Dark Side of Man: Tracing The Origins of Male Violence* (Reading, Mass.: Perseus, 1999), 178–79.

7. C. Richards, "Comment," in M. Nettleship, R. Dalegivens, and A. Nettleship (eds.), *War, Its Causes and Correlates*, 342–43 (The Hague: Mouton, 1975), 343.

8. Wright, *A Study of War*; Carol Ember, "Myths about hunter-gatherers," *Ethnology* 17 (1978): 439–48, 443.

9. Richard Alexander, *Darwinism and Human Affairs* (Seattle: University of Washington Press, 1979), 222–30; Joshua Goldstein, *War and Gender: How Gender Shapes the War System and Vice Versa* (Cambridge: Cambridge University Press, 2001), 24; Ghiglieri, *The Dark Side of Man*, 164; Lawrence Keeley, *War Before Civilization: The Myth of the Peaceful Savage* (Oxford: Oxford University Press, 1996), 31; Melvin Konner, "Human nature, ethnic violence, and war," in M. Fitzduff and C. Stout (eds.), *The Psychology of Resolving Global Conflicts: From War to Peace*, vol. 1: *Nature vs. Nurture*, 1–39 (Westport, Conn.: Praeger Security International, 2006), 5; Richard Wrangham and Dale Peterson, *Demonic Males: Apes and the Origin of Human Violence* (Boston: Houghton Mifflin, 1996), 75.

10. Keeley, *War Before Civilization*, 36–39; see also Steven LeBlanc (with K. Register), *Constant Battles: Why We Fight* (New York: St. Martin's Griffin, 2003), 59–60; P. Tacon and C. Chippindale, "Australia's ancient warriors: Changing depictions of fighting in the rock art of Arnhem Land, N.T," *Cambridge Archaeological Journal* 4 (1994): 211–48.

11. William Ury, *Getting to Peace: Transforming Conflict at Home, at Work, and in the World* (New York: Viking, 1999), 199; see also Robert Hinde, "Why is war acceptable?" in M. Martinez (ed.), *Prevention and Control of Aggression and the Impact on Its Victims*, 323–30 (New York: Kluwer Academic/Plenum, 2001).

Chapter 16: Enhancing Peace

1. Ilsa Glazer, "Beyond the competition of tears: Black-Jewish conflict containment in a New York neighborhood," in D. Fry and K. Björkqvist (eds.), *Cultural Variation in Conflict Resolution: Alternatives to Violence*, 137–44 (Mahwah, N.J.: Lawrence Erlbaum, 1997); Kenneth Smail, "The giving of hostages," *Politics and the Life Sciences* 16 (1997): 77–85, 82.

2. Margaret Mead, "Alternatives to war," in M. Fried, M. Harris, and R. Murphy (eds.), *War: The Anthropology of Armed Conflict and Aggression*, 215–28 (Garden City, N.Y.: Natural History Press, 1967), 224; see also Klaus-Friedrich Koch, *War and Peace in Jalémó: The Management of Conflict in Highland New Guinea* (Cambridge: Harvard University Press, 1974), for example, 168; Johan van der Dennen, *The Origin of War*, 2 vols. (Groningen: Origin Press, 1995).

3. Kenneth Smail, "Building bridges via reciprocal 'hostage exchange': A confidence-enhancing alternative to nuclear deterrence," *Bulletin of Peace Proposals* 16 (1985): 167–77; Smail, "The giving of hostages."

4. Robert Tonkinson, "Resolving conflict within the law: The Mardu Aborigines of Australia," in G. Kemp and D. Fry (eds.), *Keeping the Peace: Conflict Resolution and Peaceful Societies Around the World*, 89–104 (New York: Routledge, 2004), 101; for a

theoretical discussion, see Agustin Fuentes, "It's not all sex and violence: Integrated anthropology and the role of cooperation and social complexity in human evolution," *American Anthropologist* 106 (2004): 710–18.

5. E. A. Hoebel, *The Law of Primitive Man: A Study in Comparative Legal Dynamics* (Cambridge: Harvard University Press, 1967), 139; Christopher Boehm, *Blood Revenge: The Enactment and Management of Conflict in Montenegro and Other Tribal Societies*, (Philadelphia: University of Pennsylvania Press, 1987), 119; Thomas Gregor, "Symbols and rituals of peace in Brazil's Upper Xingu," in L. Sponsel and T. Gregor (eds.), *The Anthropology of Peace and Nonviolence*, 241–57 (Boulder, Colo.: Lynne Rienner, 1994).

6. Lester Kurtz and Jennifer Turpin, "Conclusion: Untangling the web of violence," in J. Turpin and L. Kurtz (eds.), *The Web of Violence: From Interpersonal to Global*, 207–32 (Urbana: University of Illinois Press, 1997), 222; Michael Renner, "Assessing the military's war on the environment," in L. Brown et al. (eds.), *The State of the World 1991*, 132–52 (New York: W. W. Norton, 1991).

7. Kurtz and Turpin, *The Web of Violence*, 216; Michael Renner, "Ending violent conflict," in L. Brown et al. (eds.), *The State of the World 1999* (New York: W. W. Norton, 1999), 164; Robert Hinde and Joseph Rotblat, *War No More: Eliminating Conflict in the Nuclear Age* (London: Pluto Press, 2003), 166–71.

8. Boehm, *Blood Revenge*; Dennen, *The Origin of War*; Gregor, "Symbols and rituals of peace"; Tonkinson, "Resolving conflict within the law."

9. Renner, 1999, 167.

10. For example, Douglas Fry, "'Respect for the rights of others is peace': Learning aggression versus non-aggression among the Zapotec," *American Anthropologist* 94 (1992): 621–39; Robert

Dentan, *The Semai: A Nonviolent People of Malaya* (New York: Holt, Rinehart, and Winston, 1968); Peter Gardner, "Respect for all: The Paliyans of South India," in G. Kemp and D. Fry (eds.), *Keeping the Peace: Conflict Resolution and Peaceful Societies Around the World*, 53–71 (New York: Routledge, 2004); Gregor, "Symbols and rituals of peace"; Clayton Robarchek and Carole Robarchek, "Waging peace: The psychological and sociocultural dynamics of positive peace," in A. Wolfe and H. Yang (eds.), *Anthropological Contributions to Conflict Resolution*, 64–80 (Athens: University of Georgia Press, 1996); Clayton Robarchek and Carole Robarchek, "The Acuas, the cannibals, and the missionaries: From warfare to peacefulness among the Waorani," in T. Gregor (ed.), *A Natural History of Peace*, 189–212 (Nashville, Tenn.: Vanderbilt University Press, 1996).

11. Douglas Fry and C. B. Fry, "Culture and conflict resolution models: Exploring alternatives to violence," in D. Fry and K. Björkqvist (eds.), *Cultural Variation in Conflict Resolution: Alternatives to Violence*, 9–23 (Mahwah, N.J.: Lawrence Erlbaum, 1997); Robert Hinde, "Why is war acceptable?" in M. Martinez (ed.), *Prevention and Control of Aggression and the Impact on Its Victims*, 323–30 (New York: Kluwer Academic/Plenum, 2001); Robert Hinde and J. Groebel, "The problem of aggression," in J. Groebel and R. Hinde (eds.), *Aggression and War: Their Biological and Social Bases*, 3–9 (Cambridge: Cambridge University Press, 1989); Hinde and Rotblat, *War No More*, Chapter 10.

12. David Adams and Sarah Bosch, "The myth that war is intrinsic to human nature discourages action for peace by young people," in J. M. Ramírez, R. Hinde, and J. Groeble (eds.), *Essays on Violence*, 121–37 (Seville: University of Seville Press, 1987).

13. Albert Einstein quoted in David Krieger, "Ending the scourge of war," in R. Elias and J. Turpin (eds.), *Rethinking Peace*, 318–25 (Boulder, Colo.: Lynne Rienner, 1994), 319.

14. Krieger, "Ending the scourge of war," 319.

15. Hilary French, "Strengthening global environmental governance," in L. Brown et al. (eds.), *The State of the World 1992*, 155–73 (New York: W. W. Norton, 1992); Hilary French, *Vanishing Borders: Protecting the Planet in the Age of Globalization* (New York: W. W. Norton, 2000); Douglas Fry, "Utilizing human capacities for survival in the nuclear age," *Bulletin of Peace Proposals* 16 (1985): 159–66; Fry and Fry, "Culture and conflict resolution models"; Judith Hand, *A Future Without War: The Strategy of a Warfare Transition* (San Diego: Questpath, 2006); Robert Johansen, "Toward an alternative security system," in. B. Weston (ed.), *Toward Nuclear Disarmament and Global Security*, 569–603 (Boulder, Colo.: Westview, 1984); William Ury, Jeanne Brett, and Stephen Goldberg, *Getting Disputes Resolved: Designing Systems to Cut the Costs of Conflict* (San Francisco: Jossey-Bass, 1988).

16. Elie Wiesel and Douglas Fry, "On respecting others and preventing hate: A conversation with Elie Wiesel," in D. Fry and K. Björkqvist (eds.), *Cultural Variation in Conflict Resolution: Alternatives to Violence*, 235–41 (Mahwah, N.J.: Lawrence Erlbaum, 1997), 239–40, emphasis in original.

17. Robarchek and Robarchek, "Waging peace"; Napoleon Chagnon, "Life histories, blood revenge, and warfare in a tribal population," *Science* 239 (1988): 985–92.

18. Donald Black, *The Social Structure of Right and Wrong* (San Diego: Academic Press, 1993); Dennen, *The Origin of War*, 519; Hinde and Rotblat, *War No More*, 178–79.

19. See Christopher Boehm, *Hierarchy in the Forest: The Evolution of Egalitarian Behavior* (Cambridge: Harvard University Press, 1999).

20. Jan-Willem Bertens, "The European movement: Dreams and realities," paper presented at the seminar "The EC After 1992: The United States of Europe?" Maastricht, the Netherlands, January 2, 1994.

21. Neil Whitehead, "The snake warriors—sons of the tiger's teeth: A descriptive analysis of Carib warfare ca. 1500–1820," in J. Haas (ed.), *The Anthropology of War*, 146–70 (Cambridge: Cambridge University Press, 1990), 155.

22. See Douglas Fry, "Conflict management in cross-cultural perspective," in F. Aureli and F. de Waal (eds.), *Natural Conflict Resolution*, 334–51 (Berkeley: University of California Press, 2000); Douglas Fry, *The Human Potential for Peace* (New York: Oxford University Press, 2006), Chapter 3; William Ury, *Getting to Peace: Transforming Conflict at Home, at Work, and in the World* (New York: Viking, 1999).

23. Ury, Brett, and Goldberg, *Getting Disputes Resolved*, 172.

24. Robarchek and Robarchek, "The Acuas, the cannibals, and the missionaries," 72–73.

25. Michael Renner, *Critical Juncture: The Future of Peacekeeping*, Worldwatch Paper no. 114 (Washington, D.C.: Worldwatch Institute, 1993); Hinde and Rotblat, *War No More*, Chapter 15.

26. Fry, "Conflict management in cross-cultural perspective"; Robarchek and Robarchek, "Waging peace"; Robarchek and Robarchek, "The Acuas, the cannibals, and the missionaries"; Ury, Brett, and Goldberg, *Getting Disputes Resolved*; Ury, *Getting to Peace*.

27. R. Brian Ferguson, "Introduction: Studying war," in R. B. Ferguson (ed.), *Warfare, Culture, and Environment*, 1–81 (Orlando: Academic Press, 1984), 12.

28. Douglas Fry, "The relationship of environmental attitudes and knowledge to environmental behavior," paper presented at the

meeting of the American Anthropological Association, Washington, D.C., November 1993, 17–21.

29. Charles Darwin, *The Descent of Man* (New York: Prometheus Books, 1998, orig. pub. 1871), 120.

30. Boehm, *Hierarchy in the Forest;* Donald Brown, *Human Universals* (New York: McGraw-Hill, 1991), 138; E. A. Hoebel, *The Law of Primitive Man: A Study in Comparative Legal Dynamics* (Cambridge: Harvard University Press, 1967).

31. Darwin, *The Descent of Man*, 126–27.

Appendix 2: Nonwarring Societies

1. G. Huntingford, "The political organization of the Dorobo," *Anthropos* 49 (1954): 123–48, 132–36.

2. Roy Willis, "The 'peace puzzle' in Ufipa," in S. Howell and R. Willis (eds.), *Societies at Peace: Anthropological Perspectives*, 133–45 (London: Routledge, 1989).

3. J. van der Dennen, *The Origin of War*, 2 vols. (Groningen: Origin Press, 1995), 638.

4. George Silberbauer, "The G/wi Bushmen," in M. Bicchieri (ed.), *Hunters and Gatherers Today*, 271–326 (Prospect Heights, Ill.: Waveland, 1972).

5. James Woodburn, "Discussions, part III, 17.g: Predation and warfare," in R. Lee and I. DeVore (eds.), *Man the Hunter*, 157–58 (Chicago: Aldine, 1968), 157–58; van der Dennen, *The Origin of War*, 638–39.

6. Richard Lee, *The !Kung San: Men, Women, and Work in a Foraging Community* (Cambridge: Cambridge University Press, 1979), Chapter 13; Patricia Draper, "!Kung women: Contrasts in

sexual egalitarianism in foraging and sedentary contexts," in R. Reiter (ed.), *Toward An Anthropology of Women*, 77–109 (New York: Monthly Review Press, 1975), 86.

7. E. Drower, *The Mandaeans of Iraq and Iran: Their Cults, Customs, Magic Legends, and Folklore* (Leiden: E. J. Brill, 1962), 1, 14, 15, 48.

8. Colin Turnbull, *Wayward Servants: The Two Worlds of the African Pygmies* (Garden City, N.Y.: Natural History Press, 1965), 218–23.

9. Robert Fernea, "Putting a stone in the middle: The Nubians of Northern Africa," in G. Kemp and D. Fry (eds.), *Keeping the Peace: Conflict Resolution and Peaceful Societies Around the World*, 105–21 (New York: Routledge, 2004), 120.

10. J. Loudon, "Teasing and socialization on Tristan da Cunha," in Philip Mayer (ed.), *Socialization: The Approach from Social Anthropology*, 293–332 (London: Tavistock, 1970); Peter A. Munch, "Anarchy and *anomie* in an atomistic community," *Man* (n.s.) 9 (1974): 243–61.

11. Alfred Radcliffe-Brown, *The Andaman Islanders* (Cambridge: Cambridge University Press, 1922), 49–50, 84–87.

12. Paul Hockings, "Badaga," in D. Levinson (gen. ed.), *Encyclopedia of World Cultures*, vol. III: *South Asia*, 14–18 (Boston: G. K. Hall, 1992), 15, 17.

13. Ashley Montagu, *The Nature of Human Aggression* (Oxford: Oxford University Press, 1976), 268–69.

14. Charles Warren, "Batak," in F. LeBar (ed. and comp.), *Ethnic Groups of Insular Southeast Asia*, vol. 2: *Philippines and Formosa*, 68–70 (New Haven, Conn.: Human Relations Area Files Press, 1975).

15. Kirk Endicott, "The effects of slave raiding on the Aborigines of the Malay Peninsula," in A. Reid (ed.), *Slavery, Bondage and*

Dependency in Southeast Asia, 216–45 (New York: St. Martin's Press, 1983), 224, 238.

16. D. Sinha, "The Birhors," in M. Bicchieri (ed.), *Hunters and Gatherers Today*, 371–403 (Prospect Heights, Ill.: Waveland, 1972), 390, 392–93.

17. Thomas Gibson, 1990, "Raiding, trading, and tribal autonomy in insular Southeast Asia," in J. Haas (ed.), *The Anthropology of War*, 125–45 (Cambridge: Cambridge University Press, 130–33.

18. Herbert Phillips, *Thai Peasant Personality: The Patterning of Interpersonal Behavior in the Village of Band Chan* (Berkeley: University of California Press, 1974).

19. Signe Howell, "From child to human: Chewong concepts of self," in G. Jahoda and I. Lewis (eds.), *Acquiring Culture: Cross Cultural Studies in Child Development*, 147–68 (London: Croom Helm, 1988), 150.

20. Harold Conklin, "The Relation of Hanunóo Culture to the Plant World," doctoral dissertation, Anthropology Department, Yale University, 1954, 48–49.

21. Kamil Zvelebil, *The Irulas of the Blue Mountains* (Syracuse, N.Y.: Syracuse University, Maxwell School of Citizenship and Public Affairs, 1988).

22. Cornelia van der Sluys, "Jahai," in R. Lee and R. Daly (eds.), *The Cambridge Encyclopedia of Hunters and Gatherers*, 307–11 (Cambridge: Cambridge University Press, 1999), 307, 310.

23. Peter Gardner, "Symmetric respect and memorate knowledge: The structure and ecology of individualistic culture," *Southwestern Journal of Anthropology*, 22 (1966): 389–415, 402.

24. Richart Wolf, "Kota," in D. Levinson (gen. ed.), *Encyclopedia of World Cultures*, vol. III: *South Asia*, 134–38 (Boston: G. K. Hall, 1992), 137.

25. H. Forbes, "On the Kubus of Sumatra," *Journal of the Anthropological Institute of Great Britain and Ireland*, 14 (1885): 121–27.

26. Sara Dick, "Kurumbas," in D. Levinson (gen. ed.), *Encyclopedia of World Cultures*, vol. III: *South Asia*, 142–43 (Boston: G. K. Hall, 1992), 143.

27. R. Mann, *The Ladakhi: A Study in Ethnography and Change* (Calcutta: Anthropological Survey of India, Indian Government, 1986).

28. Geoffrey Gorer, *Himalayan Village: An Account of the Lepchas of Sikkim*, 2nd ed. (New York: Basic Books, 1967, orig. pub. 1938).

29. Brian Morris, "Tappers, trappers and the Hill Pandaram (South India)," *Anthropos* 72 (1977): 225–41, 230, 237–38.

30. Van der Dennen, *The Origin of War*, 651.

31. Charles Warren, "Palawan," in F. LeBar (ed. and comp.), *Ethnic Groups of Insular Southeast Asia*, vol. 2: *Philippines and Formosa* (New Haven, Conn.: Human Relations Area Files Press, 1975), 64.

32. Peter Gardner, *Bicultural Versatility as a Frontier Adaptation Among Paliyan Foragers of South India* (Lewiston, N.Y.: Edwin Mellen Press, 2000).

33. C. Hose, "The natives of Borneo," *Journal of the Anthropological Institute of Great Britain and Ireland* 23 (1894): 156–72, 157–58.

34. Clifford Sather, "Bajau Laut," in F. LeBar (ed. and comp.), *Ethnic Groups of Insular Southeast Asia*, vol. 2: *Philippines and Formosa*, 9–12 (New Haven, Conn.: Human Relations Area Files Press, 1975); Clifford Sather, "Keeping the peace in an island world: The Sama Dilaut of Southeast Asia," in G. Kemp and D. Fry (eds.), *Keeping the Peace: Conflict Resolution and Peaceful Societies Around the World*, 123–47 (New York: Routledge, 2004).

35. Robert Dentan, *The Semai: A Nonviolent People of Malaya* (New York: Holt, Rinehart, and Winston, 1968); Thomas Gregor

and Clayton Robarchek, "Two paths to peace: Semai and Mehinaku nonviolence," in T. Gregor (ed.), *A Natural History of Peace*, 159–88 (Nashville: Vanderbilt University Press, 1996), 161.

36. Frank LeBar, Gerald Hickey, and John Musgrave, "Semang," in F. LeBar, G. Hickey, and J. Musgrave (eds.), *Ethnic Groups of Mainland Southeast Asia*, 181–86 (New Haven, Conn.: Human Relations Area Files Press, 1964), 185.

37. Robert Paul, "Sherpa," in D. Levinson (gen. ed.), *Encyclopedia of World Cultures*, vol. III: *South Asia*, 257–60 (Boston: G. K. Hall, 1992), 259.

38. Charles Frake, "The Eastern Subanun of Mindanao," in G. Murdock (ed.), *Social Structure in Southeast Asia*, 51–64 (New York: Wenner-Gren Viking Fund Publications in Anthropology, 1960), 53.

39. W. Rivers, *The Todas* (Jaipur, India: Rawat, 1986, orig. pub. 1906).

40. C. Seligmann and Brenda Seligmann, *The Veddas* (Oosterhout, The Netherlands: Anthropological Publications, 1969, orig. pub. 1911), 34.

41. V. Raghaviah, *The Yanadis* (New Delhi: Bharatiya Adimjati Sevak Sangh, 1962).

42. Myrdene Anderson and Hugh Beach, "Saami," in D. Levinson (gen. ed.), *Encyclopedia of World Cultures*, vol. IV: *Europe (Central, Western, and Southeastern Europe)*, 220–23 (Boston: G. K. Hall, 1992), 222.

43. Franz Boas, *The Central Eskimo* (Lincoln: University of Nebraska Press, 1964, orig. pub. 1888), 57.

44. Joseph Jorgensen, *Western Indians: Comparative Environments, Languages, and Cultures of 172, Western American Indian Tribes* (San Francisco: W. H. Freeman, 1980), 503–7, 509–15, 613–14, see also 316.

45. David Damas, "The Copper Eskimo," in M. Bicchieri (ed.), *Hunters and Gatherers Today*, 3–49 (Prospect Heights, Ill.: Waveland, 1972).

46. Fredtjof Nansen, *Eskimo Life*, trans. William Archer (London: Longmans, Green, 1893), 162.

47. Maurice Zigmond, "Kawaiisu," in W. Sturtevant (gen. ed.), *Handbook of North American Indians*, vol. 11: *Great Basin*, 398–411 (Washington, D.C.: Smithsonian Institution Press, 1986), 399.

48. Isabel Kelly and Catherine Fowler, "Southern Paiute," in W. Sturtevant (gen. ed.), *Handbook of North American Indians*, vol. 11: *Great Basin*, 368–97 (Washington, D.C.: Smithsonian Institution Press, 1986), 368–70, 381–82.

49. William Bright, "Karok," in D. Levinson (gen. ed.), *Encyclopedia of World Cultures*, vol. I: *North America*, 175–78 (Boston: G. K. Hall, 1991), 177.

50. Alexander Lesser, "War and the state," in M. Fried, M. Harris, and R. Murphy (eds.), *War: The Anthropology of Armed Conflict and Aggression*, 92–96 (Garden City, N.Y.: Natural History Press, 1967), 94.

51. L. Hobhouse, G. Wheeler, and M. Ginsberg, *The Material Culture and Social Institutions of the Simpler Peoples: An Essay in Correlation* (London: Chapman and Hall, 1915), 229.

52. George Murdock, *Our Primitive Contemporaries* (New York: Macmillan, 1934), 210–11.

53. Verne Ray, *The Sanpoil and Nespelem: Salishan Peoples of Northeastern Washington* (New York: AMS Press, 1980), 114–15.

54. A. I. Hallowell, "Aggression in Saulteaux society," in A. I. Hallowell (ed.), *Culture and Experience*, 277–90 (Philadelphia: University of Pennsylvania Press, 1974), 278.

55. Specifically the Panamint, Battle Mountain, Hukundika, and Gosiute Shoshone groups: Jorgensen, *Western Indians*, 503–7, 509–15, 613–14; see also 316.

56. Raymond Kelly, *Warless Societies and the Origin of War* (Ann Arbor: University of Michigan Press, 2000), 53.

57. Jorgensen, *Western Indians*, 505–7, 509–15, 613–14; see also 316.

58. Baldwin Spencer and Francis Gillen, *The Arunta: A Study of a Stone Age People* (London: Macmillan, 1927), 27–28.

59. See Chapter 9 and associated references in the endnotes.

60. Edwin Burrows, "From value to ethos on Ifaluk Atoll," *Southwestern Journal of Anthropology* 8 (1952): 13–35, 23.

61. Robert Tonkinson, "Resolving conflict within the law: The Mardu Aborigines of Australia," in G. Kemp and D. Fry (eds.), *Keeping the Peace: Conflict Resolution and Peaceful Societies Around the World*, 89–104 (New York: Routledge, 2004), 93.

62. Raymond Firth, *We, the Tikopia: A Sociological Study of Kinship in Primitive Polynesia*, 2nd ed. (London: George Allen and Unwin, 1957); Raymond Firth, *Tikopia Ritual and Belief* (London: George Allen and Unwin, 1967).

63. C. Hart and Arnold Pilling, *The Tiwi of North Australia*, fieldwork ed. (New York: Holt, Rinehart, and Winston, 1979), 85, 79–87; see also the discussion in Chapter 9.

64. S. Barrett, *The Cayapa Indians of Ecuador*, Indian Notes and Monographs, vol. 40 (New York: Museum of the American Indian, Heyes Foundation, 1925); John Murra, "The Cayapa and Colorado," in J. Steward (ed.), *Handbook of South American Indians*, vol. 4: *The Circum-Caribbean Tribes*, 277–91 (Washington, D.C.: United States Printing Office, 1948), 282.

65. Hobhouse, Wheeler, and Ginsberg, *The Material Culture and Social Institutions* (London: Chapman, 1915), 229.

66. Allen Johnson, "Machiguenga gardens," in R. Hames and W. Vickers (eds.), *Adaptive Responses of Native Amazonians*, 29–63 (New York: Academic Press, 1983), 62–63.

67. Paul Henley, *The Panare: Tradition and Change on the Amazonian Frontier* (New Haven: Yale University Press, 1982).

68. Hobhouse, Wheeler, and Ginsberg, *The Material Culture and Social Institutions*, 229 and references therein.

69. David Thomas, *Order Without Government: The Society of the Pemon Indians of Venezuela* (Urbana: University of Illinois Press, 1982), 272–73.

70. Joanna Overing, "Styles of manhood: An Amazonian contrast in tranquility and violence," in S. Howell and R. Willis (eds.), *Societies at Peace: Anthropological Perspectives*, 79–99 (London: Routledge, 1989).

71. Allan Holmberg, *Nomads of the Long Bow: The Siriono of Eastern Bolivia* (New York: American Museum of Natural History, 1969, orig. pub. 1950).

72. Catherine Howard, "Wáiwai," in D. Levinson (gen. ed.), *Encyclopedia of World Cultures*, vol. VII: *South America*, 345–48 (Boston: G. K. Hall, 1994), 347–48.

73. H. D. Heinen, "Warao," in D. Levinson (gen. ed.), *Encyclopedia of World Cultures*, vol. VII: *South America*, 356–59 (Boston: G. K. Hall, 1994), 359.

74. Martin Gusinde, *The Yahgan: The Life and Thought of the Water Nomads of Cape Horn*, trans. by Frieda Schütze, in the electronic Human Relations Area Files, Yahgan, Doc. 1 (New Haven, Conn.: HRAF, 2003, orig. pub. 1937), 885, 893.

Suggested Reading

Boehm, Christopher. *Hierarchy in the Forest: The Evolution of Egalitarian Behavior*. Cambridge: Harvard University Press, 1999.

Borofsky, Robert. *Yanomami: The Fierce Controversy and What We Can Learn from It*. Berkeley: University of California Press, 2005.

De Waal, Frans. *Our Inner Ape: A Leading Primatologist Explains Why We Are Who We Are*. New York: Riverhead Books, 2005.

Hart, Donna, and Robert Sussman. *Man the Hunted: Primates, Predators, and Human Evolution*. New York: Westview Press, 2005.

Hinde, Robert, and Joseph Rotblat. *War No More: Eliminating Conflict in the Nuclear Age*. London: Pluto Press, 2003.

Kemp, Graham, and Douglas Fry (eds.). *Keeping the Peace: Conflict Resolution and Peaceful Societies Around the World*. New York: Routledge, 2004.

O'Connell, Robert. *Ride of the Second Horseman: The Birth and Death of War*. New York: Oxford University Press, 1995.

Renner, Michael, Hillary French, Erik Assadourian, et al. *State of the World 2005: Redefining Global Security*. New York: W. W. Norton, 1995.

Ury, William. *Getting to Peace: Transforming Conflict at Home, at Work, and in the World*. New York: Viking, 1999.

Index